Kinds of Blue

Kinds of Blue

THE JAZZ AESTHETIC IN AFRICAN AMERICAN NARRATIVE

Jürgen E. Grandt

THE OHIO STATE UNIVERSITY PRESS
Columbus

Library of Congress Cataloging-in-Publication Data
Grandt, Jürgen E., 1968–
Kinds of blue : the jazz aesthetic in African American narrative / Jürgen E. Grandt.
p. cm.
Includes bibliographical references and index.
ISBN 0-8142-0980-7 (cloth : alk. paper) — ISBN 0-8142-5132-3 (pbk. : alk. paper) —
ISBN 0-8142-9065-5 (cd-rom)
1. American prose literature—African American authors—History and criticism. 2. African Americans—Intellectual life-20th century. 3. Music and literature—History—20th century. 4. Autobiography—African American authors. 5. African Americans in literature. 6. Jazz—History and criticism. 7. African American aesthetics. 8. Narration (Rhetoric) 9. Jazz in literature. I. Title.
PS374.N4G727 2005
818'.50809357-dc22
2004029047

An earlier version of chapter 4 appeared in the Summer 2004 issue of *African American Review* as "Kinds of Blue: Toni Morrison, Hans Jancowitz, and the Jazz Aesthetic."

Cover and text design by James Baumann. Text design by Jennifer Forsythe.
Type set in Adobe Palatino.
Printed by Thomson-Shore, Inc.

The paper used in this publication meets the minimum requirements of the American National Standard for Information Sciences—Permanence of Paper for Printed Library Materials. ANSI Z39.48–1992.

9 8 7 6 5 4 3 2 1

For Yvonne and Werner—

so good a rhythm section, I've never felt the need for a piano

Contents

Acknowledgments

Every now and then, someone asks me which jazz legend I would have liked to see in concert, or even joined on the bandstand. My answers usually involve the likes of Dexter Gordon, or John Coltrane, or Sidney Bechet. Of course, my contribution to such an imaginary jam session would not be particularly impressive at all. In actuality, however, I could not wish for a better group than the people who comprise the roster of my personal All-Star Big Band, and any jarring dissonances emanating from the following pages are most certainly not for their lack of chops, but solely a reflection of my own shortcomings:

DoVeanna Fulton, Michael Hendrick, Nicholyn Hutchinson, La Vinia Jennings, Hubert McAlexander, Iyabo Osiapem, and especially R. Baxter Miller, Edward Pavliç, Jed Rasula, and Lorenzo Thomas, generously offered advice and support at various stages of the manuscript, and their input has been invaluable. The students in my Fall 2001 AFAM 4880 class at the University of Georgia helped immeasurably in clarifying my critical argument with their challenging questions and trenchant insights. At The Ohio State University Press, I want to thank Malcolm Litchfield as well as Heather Lee Miller, who knew that this was going to be a book before I did. Simone and Daniel Althaus, Jennifer Griffith, Sandra and Martin Kindlimann, Sibylle and Thomas Menzi, Friederike Pohlenz and Stephan Brunner, and Aliya Tugelbayeva have been keeping me (relatively) sane for all these years; I am thankful for and proud of their friendship. Karen and Richard Lyle have most graciously and generously provided me with a veritable home away from home away from home—they are truly the best America has to offer. And all the musicians, famous and unknown, who have been bringing so much passion, joy, and dedication to their art, have made this project fun, not work.

Finally, and most importantly, I must thank my parents, Yvonne and Werner, who have always, without wavering or hesitation, supported and encouraged me in all of my various adventures, no matter how dubious they might have appeared to them at the time—without them, none of this would have been possible.

Athens, Georgia, November 2004

PRELUDE

So What?

> But jazz to me is one of the inherent expressions of Negro life in America; the eternal tom-tom beating in the Negro soul—the tom-tom of revolt against weariness in a white world, a world of subway trains, and work, work, work; the tom-tom of joy and laughter, and pain swallowed in a smile.
>
> POET LANGSTON HUGHES in "The Negro Artist and the Racial Mountain," 1926

> And it's going to take a long time before Charlie Parker and Dizzy Gillespie disappear. The strains of that are going to be around for a long time. And they should be. It's part of life.
>
> BASSIST RAY BROWN to critic Ira Gitler, 2000

When he was interviewed in 1995, veteran trumpeter and flugelhornist Joe Wilder was asked what made him such a compelling ballad player. In response, Wilder, whose résumé included gigs with Lionel Hampton, Dizzy Gillespie, Count Basie, and Lucky Millinder, recalled going to jam sessions in his native Philadelphia as an up-and-coming young jazz musician where "[t]hey used to say, 'Tell a story.' . . . And that's basically what I try to do. That's the way I try to think" (122). Wilder's succinct summary of the art of jazz improvisation is neither singular nor extraordinary: musicians, critics, and musicologists all resort consistently and recurrently to language metaphors when they discuss the art of jazz. Solos 'tell a story,' performances are 'musical conversations,' and youngsters are admonished to 'say something' with their instruments instead of just playing flurries of notes. In fact, the two most in-depth studies to date of jazz improvisation, Paul Berliner's *Thinking in Jazz* and Ingrid Monson's appropriately titled *Saying Something,* are organized around the two major tropes of storytelling and language acquisition:

> Ultimately . . . youngsters must also learn various skills associated with the overriding aesthetic principles that guide the activities of advanced artists. These involve mastery over expressivity, over the shaping and pacing of ideas, and over any referential meanings that musical patterns have acquired in the jazz tradition. Improvisers illuminate these principles with perhaps the richest of their language metaphors, storytelling, whose multilayered meanings have been passed from generation to generation within the jazz community since its earliest days. (Berliner 200–201)

Virtually every single jazz instrumentalist at one point or another has likened the art of improvisation to the art of storytelling. Even a drummer like Roy Haynes, for instance, will say, "I like . . . to tell a musical story according to how I feel" (qtd. in Monson, *Saying* 86).[1]

Thus, it appears that jazz can offer heretofore untapped opportunities for the critical analysis of African American literature. But while there is a substantial body of jazz criticism of poetry, African American prose narrative has not drawn nearly as much critical attention, despite renewed interest over the past few years.[2] In fact, literary critic Lloyd W. Brown even proclaims that "[a]s a European import, the novel can never compete with jazz or the blues as a peculiarly American medium rooted in the history and ethnic experiences of America," while Brown's colleague Alan Munton intones categorically that "[j]azz and fiction should be kept separate" (L. W. Brown 60; Munton 251). And to some extent, Brown and Munton are right: Hughes, Ellison, Baldwin, and Baraka notwithstanding, there has been a consistent trend in African American literary criticism and theory to privilege the blues, rather than jazz, as a defining "matrix" of black American literary production (Baker 3). Critics like Henry Louis Gates, Jr., Houston Baker, and others have proffered critiques that draw on the vernacular folk culture of the rural black South. Perhaps this is so because a blues critique can lend itself much more easily to a mythology of 'pure' and 'undiluted' origin, to a discourse of authentic blackness. Furthermore, the vast majority of blues are sung, and their lyrics therefore provide unmediated access for textual analysis, whereas jazz is primarily an instrumental music. Finally, the jazz critic is always confronted, too, with the music's inherent hybridity—after all, jazz is paradoxically both, at once a distinct black American art form and 'world music.' Pianist McCoy Tyner inadvertently highlights this paradox when he says that "[t]his music, *even though it's universal,* moves only as far as black people move in this country" (qtd. in McFarlane 41; emphasis added). The dialectic tension between specificity and universality, between racial identity and cultural production, between tradition and appropriation, is comparatively heightened in jazz. For jazz, bebop veteran Dexter Gordon averred, is also "the great octopus; it'll do anything, it'll use anything" (qtd. in Gerard 37). Thus, a critical jazz aesthetic of African American literature poses certain challenges that a blues critique can eschew—and one may be tempted to ask, with Miles Davis, so what?

Even so, the question is a compelling one: what do we stand to gain if we read African American narrative to the tune of jazz? What new perspectives on literary meaning and textual analysis can a literary-critical jazz aesthetic provide? When Gates argues that texts in the African American literary tradition "speak" to each other, surely prose texts can speak to music, too—or vice versa—especially if it is a music which, though mostly instrumental, relies so much on the tropes of language acquisition and storytelling (*Figures* 236–52; *Signifying* 239–40, 256).[3] In fact, when trombonist and musicologist George Lewis points out that one crucial aspect of jazz "is the notion of the importance of personal narrative, of 'telling your own story,'" he is describing, unintentionally, the African American literary tradition, too (117). Therefore, the present study seeks to illuminate not how African American authors write *about* jazz, but how African American narratives *are* jazz—in other words, how they attempt to wrest beautiful art from the terrors of American history, to improvise a meaningful narrative of freedom over the dissonant sound clusters of the American experience.

Such an interdisciplinary approach does indeed pose certain challenges, perhaps most formidably among them: what is jazz? I shall refrain from exploring the thorny issue of what constitutes jazz—not least because jazz is jazz precisely because it eludes empirical definition to some degree. The literature on the subject is immense, and there are almost as many views on what is and is not jazz as there are books.[4] It cannot be my aim here to rewrite or even reinterpret jazz music and jazz history, as my focus is primarily on *literary* jazz. However, for the purposes of the present study, jazz can be loosely defined as an art form pioneered and developed by African Americans that seeks to integrate freedom with structure, spontaneity with forethought, individual expression with collective interplay, West African musical residuals with certain European concepts and instruments. What Lawrence Kramer says of music in general is, I think, particularly relevant for jazz, because jazz must be

> understood as communicative action and therefore as embedded in a continuous texture of psychological, social, and cultural relations.

> Music—and in this *it is no different from more explicitly semantic modes such as narration* and visual depiction—means not primarily by what it says but by the way it models the symbolization of experience. . . . Musical meaning is understood, both in practice and in analytical reflection, not by translating music as a virtual utterance or depiction, but by grasping the dynamic relations between musical experience and its contexts. (7; emphasis added)

More crucial than a detailed definition of jazz music, if such a thing were possible at all, is therefore the realization that any literary-critical practice aspiring to be useful must always also heed the history of the music. Critiques of literary jazz must avail themselves not only of the structural characteristics of the music, but also of the history of the (predominantly) African American musicians who invented, shaped, and innovated it.

Secondly, I use the term *aesthetic* not in the sense of a pat template or theory of literary jazz; this would be, as I hope to demonstrate in the following chapters, itself antithetical to the jazz aesthetic. For the most part, jazz has always been an unruly art form, much too fluid, much too subversive to fit neatly into determinate grids or fixed categories. "They tried to fool you / Now I got to school you / About jazz, about jazz," as Sun Ra warned us so memorably of any normative critiques—and Sun Ra's recordings are definitely a better source to learn more about this music called jazz than this present study (qtd. in Lock 25). By *aesthetic* I simply mean the various and sometimes even antithetical ways in which black American narratives avail themselves of certain characteristics and aspects of jazz music. And while Albert Murray would perhaps cringe at being quoted in the same chorus, as it were, as Sun Ra, my critical practice nevertheless takes to heart what *Stomping the Blues* has to say about (literary) critical theory and African American music:

> For art is always a matter of idiomatic stylization, it transcends both time and place. Thus criticism, the most elementary obligation of which is to increase the accessibility of aesthetic presentation, is primarily a matter of coming to terms with such special peculiarities as may be involved in a given process of stylization. What counts in a work of art, which after all must achieve such universality as it can through the particulars of the experience most native to it, is not the degree to which it conforms to theories, formulas, and rules that are best regarded as being, like Aristotle's *Poetics*, generalizations after the fact, but how adequately it fulfills the requirements of the circumstances for which it was

> created. . . . [T]he most fundamental prerequisite for mediating between the work of art and the audience, spectators, or readers, as the case may be, is not reverence for the so-called classics but rather an understanding of what is being stylized plus an accurate insight into how it is being stylized. (196)

The present study attempts to be such a mediation, intending to make more accessible how African American novels, short stories, and autobiographies avail themselves of a *literary* jazz aesthetic.

For similar reasons, the tricky differentiation between jazz and blues—between the jazz text and the blues text—is one that I suspect detracts from our understanding of the interface between black literature and music, rather than contributing to it. The two idioms are different, to be sure, but at the same time the blues is also the main tributary to jazz, making it almost impossible to draw clearly delineated, separate categories. To Murray, jazz is mostly an "extension, elaboration, and refinement of blues-break riffing and improvisation," and I therefore agree with Gayl Jones's literary distinction (A. Murray 63):

> [T]he jazz text is generally more complex and sophisticated than blues text in its harmonies, rhythms, and surface structure. . . . Jazz text is stronger in its accents; its vocabulary and syntax are often more convoluted and ambiguous than blues. It is often more difficult to read than a blues text, tending to abstractions over concreteness of detail. It shares with a blues text a sense of extemporaneity in its fluid rhythmical design and syncopated understructure, its sound and meaning systems, its rejection of duality. Jazz tends to have a faster pace and tempo than a blues text. (200)

Overall, blues *tends* to be a guitar-based vocal music over certain chordal patterns, whereas jazz *tends* to be a horn-based instrumental music extending and amending the harmonic and rhythmic language of the blues. Thus, a *literary* jazz aesthetic is not necessarily completely different from a blues aesthetic; rather, the jazz aesthetic can offer a complementary way of interpreting African American narrative.

"Tell a story," Joe Wilder was admonished as a youngster. Given the prominence of the trope of storytelling in jazz discourse, it seems appropriate to begin an examination of the jazz aesthetic in African American narrative with the story of a jazz musician; and given the pertinence of the trope of language acquisition, it seems also appropriate to start with the story of a pioneer of early jazz. Sidney Bechet's autobiography, *Treat It Gentle,* delineates a (literary) jazz aesthetic that furnishes some of the key patterns and concepts for the interpretation of African American prose fiction. Analyzing the text and contexts especially of Bechet's fictional account of his grandfather as well as his famous recording of "Summertime," I argue that Bechet the storyteller in the book uses the same improvisational strategies that Bechet the musician uses on stage. Rather than presenting an 'inauthentic' self, the book's very refusal to separate clearly fact from fiction, written text from spoken word, story from music, history from myth, author from editor, creates a persona of Bechet that is the dynamic, unstable self of his (its) own story rather than the static, stable self of somebody else's history. The text's many hybridizations converge to turn the self from a narrated object of history into the narrating subject of story. The (literary) jazz aesthetic thus affords its practitioners a figurative space of temporary freedom that plays on and against the social, cultural, and racial binaries of the American landscape.

However, it should come as no surprise that the autobiography of a jazz musician is informed by a narrative jazz aesthetic. Thus, the question of what we stand to gain by reading African American narrative to the tune of jazz must necessarily be extended to prose fiction and to a work in which jazz music does not figure prominently at all. Ann Petry's novel *The Street* is such a work, for its protagonist's foray into the jazz world is quite accidental and seemingly ancillary. However, Lutie Johnson's arresting rendition of the sentimental torch song "Darlin'" is located precisely in the middle of the narrative. Moreover, the scene's strategic placement is crucial structurally because it accelerates the inevitability of Lutie's eventual tragic downfall. The compelling central positioning of Lutie as a jazz artist suggests that jazz—after all, like narrative, another form of configuring time—plays a pivotal role as a structural device in *The Street.* My literary-critical analysis of Petry's novel draws on that most unique element of jazz time, namely swing. Accompanied by an analysis of the book's gender politics, I discuss how the element of swing informs not only Lutie's renditions of the Mills Brothers' 1934 "Swing It, Sister" and Lucky Millinder's 1944 hit "Darlin,'" but the novel's narrative structure as a whole.

Key passages in both *The Street* and *Treat It Gentle* point to another salient motif in African American jazz narrative, namely the linkage between jazz, power, and violence. First, I investigate the implications of this nexus in Langston Hughes's short story "Bop." Drawing on the oral histories of bebop pioneers Dizzy Gillespie, Dexter Gordon, and Budd

Johnson, as well as Jacques Attali's theory of music and violence, my reading of "Bop" focuses on its seemingly nonsensical and blatantly fraudulent etymology of the term *bop* and the equally fictional explanation of the difference between rebop and bebop. The story's imaginative and improvisational storytelling makes sense out of nonsense and in the process unmasks the power structure's politics of implementing and maintaining what purports to be a sensible order—an order based on the systematic oppression of African Americans—for what it is: utterly unreasonable, brutally irrational. While the violence is only figurative in "Bop," it erupts dramatically in Ralph Ellison's "Cadillac Flambé." Extending the discussion of sense and nonsense to the binary pair of noise and harmony, I show how the protagonist's violent improvisation of noise, his ritual sacrifice, directly opposes and challenges the existing syntax of harmony orchestrated by a political system which condones the continued subjugation of Americans of African descent. Hughes's and Ellison's protagonists both lay claim to the right to make ostensibly meaningless noise, and in doing so, unmask the laws of 'harmony' according to which society is arranged as truly arbitrary themselves. The jazz aesthetic's revision of the past that occurs, to varying degrees, in "Bop" and "Cadillac Flambé" is accompanied not only by the possibility of violence and revolution; it also contains a utopian impulse in its struggle towards that metaphorical place of freedom to which *Treat It Gentle* aspires. The futuristic premise of Amiri Baraka's "Answers in Progress," where blue space aliens in search of Art Blakey records land in New Jersey amidst the chaos and carnage of a nationwide black uprising, draws explicitly on the free jazz of Sun Ra and Albert Ayler. This, the last, selection in *Tales* departs deliberately from the conventions of storytelling—just as free jazz deliberately departed from the conventions of diatonic music. With the search for a more viable public and private self in the earlier stories now aborted, "Answers in Progress" consequently depicts a brutal, violent revolt against the (white) political system in a style that revolts against conventional prose, too. The bloody uprising is juxtaposed with the utopian vision of a harmonious future after the emergence of a new race, a new *black* race.

Finally, in the last chapter I discuss some of the ramifications of the previous chapters for critical practice and return to the jazz aesthetic's negotiation of authenticity and hybridity. A comparison of two novels, both of which bear the title *Jazz,* clarifies some of the challenges and opportunities in reading African American narrative to the tune of jazz. The first one, published in 1994, is Toni Morrison's *Jazz,* set during the Harlem Renaissance. The second one was originally published in 1927, a year after Morrison's Violet Trace mutilates the face of a dead girl at a Harlem funeral. Also entitled *Jazz,* that novel's plot is set in London and Paris and was written by Hans Janowitz, a German-speaking Jew born in Czechoslovakia. Despite the obvious and enormous differences between Morrison and Janowitz and their books, and despite the fact that each has a different understanding of jazz, both employ virtually identical narrative strategies to describe a world that has become jazz, as Janowitz put it. In theme, cast of characters, and setting, the two novels diverge dramatically, and yet, in their attempt to forge an aesthetic of literary jazz, they employ identical structural and stylistic devices. This, then, underscores the need for a critical practice that is not predicated primarily on either style and structure or history and sociology as most existing jazz critiques are. If the full potential of jazz aesthetics for the study of African American narrative is to be tapped, its critical analysis must incorporate not only a firm knowledge of the music's technical aspects, but also an equally firm sense of the history of both the music and the people who have been creating it. Connecting Morrison's novel to the jazz ritual of the cutting contest, specifically the legendary battles between Dexter Gordon and Wardell Gray, shows that Morrison's and Janowitz's texts differ after all as each enacts a different aesthetic gesture in its attempt to merge words and music.

The conclusion elaborates on some of the issues raised by my comparative reading of Morrison and Janowitz. The jazz aesthetic is inextricably grounded in the black experience in America—and yet, at the same time, its inherent hybridity challenges the received binary pairs of white and black, the New World and the Old (both Europe and Africa, even Asia), oppression and freedom, authenticity and imitation, the individual and the collective, jazz and 'non-jazz.' A brief look at the interface between jazz and modernism and at some of the ways in which literary critics have (mis)appropriated the music of John Coltrane raises some pertinent points about literary-critical practice. It suggests that the 'blackness' of black culture, of both the music and the literature, in fact thrives on hybridity, harnessing the energies inherent in the tension-filled process of cultural production as well as simultaneously affirming the African American (literary) tradition. The jazz aesthetic appears to me a very viable way to describe and interrogate this ostensible paradox.

Lastly, a word on the musical examples analyzed and referenced herein. Roland Barthes once observed that "[i]f one examines the current practice of music criticism . . . one sees that the work (or its execution) is always translated into the poorest linguistic category: the adjective" (236). This, I believe, is the case in jazz even more so than in other musics. "The variety of structures, moods, notational frameworks, and musical textures at work in the jazz archive defies the capacity of the linguistic terms we rely on to make sense of things," notes Jim Merod, and my own experience, unfortunately, bears him out (7). This is a difficulty that I can mediate only to an extent. However, the musical selections discussed here were chosen because, I believe, they do illuminate an aspect of the *literature,* and I have tried to render these discussions accessible to readers without any prior knowledge of musical theory or jazz history. Jazz aficionados are notoriously combative, and surely some will find fault with, say, my omission of Cecil Taylor or my interpretation of "Summertime." But again, the present study aims not to rewrite or summarize jazz history. It is first and foremost a literary-critical study, one that also probes the interplay between jazz music and literary narrative. I hope that the following chapters not only provide a few fresh insights into the interface between jazz and narrative—ideally, they also will encourage us to *listen.*

CHAPTER 1

The Remembering Song

TOWARD AN AESTHETIC OF LITERARY JAZZ IN SIDNEY BECHET'S *TREAT IT GENTLE*

> . . . people send messages in what they play, calling somebody, or making facts and emotions known. Painting a picture, or having a story to go with what you were going to play, was of vital importance in those days. The audience didn't know anything about it, but the cats in the band did.
>
> DUKE ELLINGTON, *Music Is My Mistress*

Stretching along North Rampart Street lies New Orleans's Louis Armstrong Park. The tourists who flock to the park every day will, of course, immediately notice the larger-than-life statue of Satchmo beaming from a tall pillar. Fewer will notice a circle paved with cobblestones in the southwestern corner of the Park. This is Congo Square, the mythical cradle of jazz. Still fewer will descry a bust standing near the eastern edge of Congo Square, almost hidden behind the foliage of the trees surrounding it. It is the bust of New Orleans native Sidney Bechet, clarinet and soprano sax virtuoso and the first international envoy of jazz.[1]

The interested observer can learn from the accompanying plaque that the bust is in fact an exact replica of the statue erected in 1960 in the southern French town of Juan-les-Pins, site of some of Bechet's most glorious triumphs during his European exile. The original is believed to be the world's first statue honoring a jazz musician (Chilton 290; Persica A-15). The copy on Congo Square was unveiled on May 6, 1997, a full eight days prior to Bechet's actual birthday on May 14, as the grand finale of the Sidney Bechet Centennial Celebration.[2] On a day with "weather just this side of heaven," as the *Times-Picayune* boasted on its front page, a brass band parade featuring a giant papier-mâché head of Bechet was winding its way through the French Quarter from Jackson Street to

Congo Square. Once the procession had reached its destination, the ambassador of France to the United States, François Bujon de l'Estang—who as a boy had heard Bechet perform many times in Paris and had studied classical guitar in his youth—unveiled the bust in front of a massive crowd of musicians, dignitaries, fans, and tourists ("Made" A-1; Mullener B-1–B-2).

The replica of Bechet's bust on Congo Square encapsulates the (ostensible) paradoxes and contradictions that shaped Sidney Bechet the man as well as his music. Straddling the fault line between authenticity and imitation, the past and the present, jazz and classical, black and white, the New World and the Old, the statue occupies a symbolic territory fraught with ironic tension.[3] It is precisely this tension which also shapes Bechet's autobiography, *Treat It Gentle.* The statue, the music, and, as we shall see, the book all play on and against the historical, social, cultural, and racial binaries that constitute the American landscape. Bechet's poetics of place delineate a (literary) jazz aesthetic which affords its practitioners a figurative or mythical space of at least temporary freedom. Or, in Bechet's own words:

> I want to tell you about this music before I go. A man don't have all the time in the world, and there's things he has to do before he can go happy. . . . It's like a man being born in a little place, just a bend in the road somewhere. After a while he begins to travel the road. He travels all the road there is and then he comes back. He knows the road goes away and he knows the road comes back. He knows that road comes back just the same way it goes away. . . . But the music itself, the road itself—there's no stopping that. It goes on all the time. It's the thing that brings you to everything else. You have to trust that. There's no one ever came back who can't tell you that. And when you get back, there's the river by the road. You're back where you started from and you're looking across the river, and you're getting yourself ready to go. I'm feeling I almost got myself happy enough inside now. I'm feeling I'm almost ready. (4–5)

I. Improvising Facts: Sidney Bechet's Poetics of Figurative Space

Born in New Orleans in 1897 into a musical Creole family, soprano saxophonist and clarinetist Sidney Bechet was, along with Louis Armstrong, the most gifted exponent of early jazz. A tireless ambassador of Crescent City "ragtime," as he insisted on calling his music, he left his hometown in 1917 and played gigs throughout the South and Midwest before eventually choosing Chicago as his base of operations (3).[4] In 1919 he joined Will Marion Cook's Southern Syncopated Orchestra for a highly successful overseas tour—Swiss classical composer Ernst-Alexandre Ansermet's glowing review of the Orchestra's London stint is today considered to be the first serious discussion of jazz, and features Bechet prominently—and throughout the 1920s he shuttled back and forth between New York City and Europe (Ansermet 117–18). His fortunes waned during the Depression years, and even the Dixieland revival of the 1940s could not secure him steady work. He returned to Europe in 1949 and two years later settled permanently in France, where his popularity approached rock-star status. *Treat It Gentle,* published in 1960, a year after his death, chronicles the birth and triumph of jazz and the journeys of one of its most spectacular performers.

Significantly, Bechet begins the account of his life by conflating jazz and storytelling:

> You know there's people, they got the wrong idea of Jazz. They think it's all that red-light business. But that's not so. And the real story I've got to tell, it's right here. It's Jazz. *What* it is—how it come to be what it is. People come up to me and they ask me, "Are you going to play *Tin Roof Blues?*" They ask me, "What's be-bop?" or what do I think of some record Louis Armstrong put out. But if I was to answer that, I'd have to go back a long way. That's why I have to tell a lot more than people would expect. (1)

Here, Bechet links not only music and storytelling, but also history and memory, the past and the present. How important this linkage is to Bechet and his story is underlined again towards the close of the brief expository chapter, where he reiterates this same point: "My story goes a long way back. It goes further back than anything I had to do with. My music is like that . . . I got it from something inherited, just like the stories my father gave down to me. And those stories are all I know about some of the things bringing me to where I am" (4). Thus, identity, story, and history all merge in jazz.

Accordingly, in order to explain jazz in general and his life in particular, Bechet in the next chapter narrates the story of his grandfather, Omar (probably the Anglicized variant of the French *Homère*), which was passed on to him by his father. Omar "was a free slave long before

Emancipation. And he had his music and he could play it whenever he wanted" (7). Hence, from the very beginning, the degree of freedom Omar enjoys is evidenced in and by the music he plays. Furthermore, the curious paradox of "a free slave" here already foreshadows the jazz aesthetic's interrogation of received binary pairs. His grandfather, Bechet explains, was the property of a very lenient master who let him work, hunt, or play music at his own discretion. Omar would spend his Sundays on New Orleans's Congo Square to dance and play the drums. Sunday on Congo Square was so-called "free day," when slaves were allowed to gather for a temporary respite from their chores (Baraka, *Blues* 19, 70–73; Floyd, *Power* 35–37). Congo Square is, of course, the mythical birthplace of jazz, too, and so this is where Bechet's account of Omar fittingly begins[5]:

> But Sunday mornings it was different [for the slave]. He'd wake up and start to be a slave and then maybe someone would tell him: "Hell, no. Today's Sunday, man. It ain't Monday and it ain't Tuesday. Today's free day." And then he'd hear drums from the square. First one drum, then another one answering it. Then a lot of drums. Then a voice, one voice. And then a refrain, a lot of voices joining in and coming into each other. And all of it having to be heard. The music being born right inside itself, not knowing how it was getting to be the music, one thing being responsible for another. Improvisation . . . that's what it was. It was primitive and it was crude, but down at the bottom of it—inside it, where it starts and gets into itself—down there it had the same thing there is at the bottom of ragtime. It was already born and making the music they played at Congo Square. And that square, in a way of speaking, was my grandfather's square. He never had to hear it from a distance, because he was always ahead of the music there. It was there in his mind even before he got to the square and began performing it. It was *his* drum, *his* voice, *his* dancing. And people had to come, they couldn't move away from it. It was *all* the people, the masters too. . . . Everybody was mixing, just mixing as much as there could be. Some was dancing, if there was a feeling in them that way. Others, they were just hollering. But everybody, *everybody* was tapping their feet. (8–9)

In addition to identifying some of the most crucial characteristics of jazz—improvisation, call and response, and swing—Bechet's description is remarkable in that it performs a shift from the realm of the literal to the realm of the figurative. First, the passage begins in literal time: Sunday, a day with a clearly definable linear time frame, has been designated free day by the white slaveholding society of New Orleans. But the music—significantly it is drum-based music—translates linear, historical time into figurative, cyclical time, "where [the music] starts and gets into itself." With this translation, this shift, the musicians, dancers, and singers avail themselves of a certain amount of power: not even the masters can resist the infectious rhythms as "everybody, *everybody* was tapping their feet," and the resulting interaction between black and white collapses and even inverts temporarily the prevailing hierarchy of power. When Omar takes the lead in the musical performance and figuratively takes possession of Congo Square, he is no longer property but owner. At the same time, the slaves' figurative ownership of property effected by music relegates the masters, unable to resist the groove, to become the property of the music, as "they couldn't move away from it." This powerful music is at once collective and highly individual: in "*his* drum, *his* voice, *his* dancing" Omar can tell his own story in his own words; the assertion of his human individuality thus liberates him from his legally prescribed status as chattel, at least for the duration of the performance. Bechet reiterates this same point in the autobiography's conclusion by locating freedom in metaphorical space and coupling it with the imaginative production of music: "My people, all they want is a place where they can be people, a place where they can stand up and be a part of that place, just being natural to the place without worrying how someone may be coming along to take that place away from them. There's a pride in it, too. The man singing it, the man playing it, he makes a place. For as long as the song is being played, *that's* the place he's been looking for" (203). Here again, staking a claim is a precarious undertaking for African Americans in an America still fraught with the legacies of chattel slavery. Since the prospect of one day owning forty acres and a mule is questionable at best, Bechet's narrative seizes forty acres and a horn, as it were. "You see," Bechet confirms, "you want something of your own, and it's a pretty tough proposition to get something of your own in America" (186). Thus, while freedom is attainable, it is more often than not a temporary and tenuous freedom—if it is attained at all—precisely because it is situated in an alternative figurative space rather than in sociopolitical space.

In interrogating the juncture between slavery and freedom, black and white, the individual and the collective, property and ownership by translating the literal into the figurative, the passage is indicative of another narrative strategy that propels Bechet's entire autobiography.

The narrative's jazz aesthetic probes and challenges the received binary pairs of the dominant culture, collapsing the absolute homogeneity of all concepts, categories, and frameworks (including, as we shall see, its own). One of the recurring binary pairs deconstructed is that of the past and the present, cultural memory and experiential fact, of history and the future even. For instance, Bechet prefaces his description of free day on Congo Square by limning the connection between the vague memories of the Old World—in this case, of course, Africa—and the brutal experience in the New World: "Sometimes, if they [the slaves] dreamed, things would come to them out of Africa, things they'd heard about or had seen. And in all that recollecting, somehow there wasn't any of it that didn't have part of a music-form in it," and so, Bechet continues, in the slave's existence "[p]art of him was always there, standing still with his head turned to hear it, listening to someone from a distance, hearing something that was kind of a promise, even then" (7). Once again, linear, historical time transforms into cyclical, cultural time and collapses historical as well as geographical distances when memory, "that recollecting," occasions a music that draws the past promise of freedom—the betrayed promise of the Emancipation Proclamation—from a perhaps utopian future back into the present.

However, in seeking to collapse the distance between binaries, the jazz aesthetic simultaneously recognizes that complete erasure of these conceptual lines of division and their subsequent transcendence is ultimately impossible—after all, every Sunday is followed by another Monday. As Omar is soon to find out, his mastery of the music does not only have beneficiary results, but also disastrous consequences. As Bechet tells it, his grandfather discovers just how temporary is the assertion of his human individuality, his tenuous freedom, when one Sunday he sees a young, beautiful girl dance on Congo Square and falls in love with her. Unfortunately, the girl's master is also taken with her and seeks to foil the blossoming relationship between Omar and Marie. What follows is an at once lyrical and gripping tale of love and lust, betrayal and loyalty, murder and magic, mistaken identities, incest by proxy, and tragic intrigue. The two lovers eventually manage to escape from the jealous eye of Marie's master and make love in the bayou. They are caught in the act, however, by the master, who shoots Omar in the arm during the ensuing struggle. Nonetheless, Omar eludes capture for the time being and manages to reunite with Marie one last time, siring Bechet's father, before he meets his fate when he is murdered by a slave hoping to collect the reward for the fugitive Omar.

This, then, is the story Bechet tells us in order to explain what jazz is and where it came from, a story that deals with music only marginally. However, checking the story of Omar against historical fact reveals that it is a complete fabrication: Sidney Bechet's real grandfather was a free Creole named Jean Bechet, a prosperous carpenter who was listed in the 1860 Louisiana census as the owner of property worth in excess of 2,500 dollars and of personal funds totaling 800 dollars (Chilton 1). Moreover, Omar bears a striking resemblance to one Bras Coupé, hero of many a Louisiana folk tale—and of a George Washington Cable short story based on it, which eventually became a part of Cable's novel *The Grandissimes*—who reigned supreme over Congo Square, escaped from his master to live as a brigand in the swamps with other runaways, and was shot and suffered the amputation of an arm (Saxon et al. 253–54; Cable, "Story" 20–46, *Grandissimes* 219–52). Obviously, Omar's story is of little if any historical value, and jazz scholars have long chastised Bechet for this and other deceptions. For instance, Bechet claimed in a 1939 interview to be a native of Senegal, and in another he explained that the word *jass*—an early spelling variant of *jazz*—was really an acronym he had coined from an expression often overheard at New Orleans funerals, "Jesus Almighty Save our Souls" (Mouly 104; Chilton 291). As one historian complained in exasperation, "He had a way of brushing off interviewers by telling them lies so transparent as to be obvious: 'I made my first soprano sax myself in 1906, but it got stolen by Attapakas Indians when I was nine. Years later I saw it in Uncle Jake's Pawn Shop'" (qtd. in Ogren, "'Jazz'"122). Although *Treat It Gentle* was generally well-received, Bechet's friends felt compelled to defend him for years afterwards; even John Chilton, his biographer, stresses that Omar's tale was not the product of "a congenital liar" or of Bechet's alleged senility (291). Curiously, many eminent jazz historians continued to proliferate Bechet's fraudulent account of his ancestry; others sought to downplay its importance.[6]

Strangely enough, no critic has pointed to the simple fact that Bechet the storyteller avails himself of exactly the same strategies in *Treat It Gentle* as Bechet the improvising jazz musician does on stage. For example, Bechet ingeniously begins the chapter following his epic story of Omar with a prolepsis:

> One night I was in Paris—I was playing at the Vieux Colombier—and I got to thinking that story inside me, about my grandfather Omar, and I got to talking it like almost I was playing the music, going back into it as it came. I got to talking it and looking at the room. . . . [Afterwards] I got to talking and there was some friends there. I was just talking like I was inside the music, just letting it

> come out of itself, and remembering like that, all about my grandfather . . . you know, it's almost like I'm him. (45)

Not surprisingly, the verb *to talk* is here synonymous with the act of jazz improvisation. It is therefore the *story* of Omar, that "awful early beginning" of the music, rather than the figure of Omar itself, that serves as the catalyst for Bechet's playing (44). Bechet continues: "And at the same time, I was asking myself, 'Why am I here?' Well, just as soon as I asked the question I knew why. France, it's closer to Africa. I've wanted to be as close to it as I could. It's a mood, you'd call it, an atmosphere I wanted to put myself into. My grandfather, he was Africa. It was like getting back, and I wanted to get back as far as I could. It's all true, all that I said about my grandfather. And it's all so mixed up with the music" (45). On the one hand, this is another prevarication on Bechet's part: by the late 1940s, the early jazz revival was being taken over by the increasingly commercialized bop-craze, making it more difficult even for a legend like Bechet to secure gigs. The promise of steady work and the public's boundless adulation he encountered during a visit to France in the spring of 1949 caused him to settle there permanently two years later (Chilton 214–15). That his actual motivations were much more prosaic than the romantic, Africanist "mood" he cites in *Treat It Gentle,* Bechet made clear to a reporter from *Esquire:* "I live in France because that's where I can make a living. If I could make out with money back home, I'd be back in New York tomorrow" (qtd. in Ehrlich 95). He was also very aware of his adopted country's policies in the colonies and commented in the same article, "The French have no call to crow over Americans. I've told them so. I've told them I've been in Dakar and I've seen what they do to Negroes there, and Frenchmen are no better than anyone else" (qtd. in Ehrlich 95).[7]

And yet, the strategic framing of Omar's story, as well as Bechet's numerous references to it subsequently, not only serves to constitute jazz as an *African* American art form; the story of Omar lends thematic and narrative cohesion to the autobiography and highlights that for Bechet, storytelling and jazz improvisation are one and the same thing. Consequently, the fraudulent story of Omar tells us more about the jazz aesthetic than the factual story of Jean Bechet ever could: as a jazz musician, Sidney Bechet improvises over the fixed melody and chord progression of a song; that is, he superimposes a new melody (fiction) on an already existing melody (fact). However, he must also be sure that the new melodies he invents are related to and fit the underlying harmonic framework. As a storyteller, Bechet improvises the fictitious tale of Omar over the historical fact of chattel slavery in America; that is, he superimposes a new story (fiction) over the already existing historical context (fact).[8] But again, in doing so, he must be sure here, too, that the new story he invents is related to and fits the underlying context, the story of jazz and the black experience in America. Therefore, it is not so much *what* Bechet says about his life or his music, but *how* he narrates it that makes *Treat It Gentle* a virtuoso jazz performance.

The dramatic love story of Omar and Marie also links Bechet's autobiography to the African American blues tradition and, more indirectly, to the slave narrative. The blues are, of course, the single most important and consistent influence upon jazz. More than with any other topic, blues lyrics are frequently concerned with love lost, betrayed, unrequited, warped, craved, or denied. Several blues critics have observed that the ubiquity of the theme of love, more often than not sexual love, is actually a reconfiguration of a longing for freedom (A. Davis 473–75; Oliver 85). After all, not only is freedom defined by the ability to tell your own story in your own words, but also by the ability to love who you want (Morrison, *Beloved* 162). As Angela Davis points out, "[i]n the vast disappointment that followed the emancipation—when economic and political liberation must have seemed more unattainable than ever—blues created a discourse [which] registered sexuality as a tangible expression of freedom" (473). The true story of the free Creole Jean Bechet would probably not have allowed his grandson Sidney to tap the blues reservoir, certainly not in such dramatic fashion. The story of Omar, on the other hand, not only extends the blues tradition, but also echoes the tradition of the African American slave narrative. William Andrews, in his definitive study of the genre, sees in the slave narrative a "mediative" and often "revisionistic instrument" whose goal is the *telling* of a free story rather than telling a story *about* freedom: "the slave narrative implied that the writing of autobiography was itself to be understood as an act of self-liberation, part of the continuum of events narrated in the text" (18, 14, 103–4).[9] Unlike Omar's story, which ends in death, Bechet's story not only resurrects Omar at the Vieux Colombier, but eventually ends with freedom: "And somehow when the music is played right it does an explaining of all those things" (218). Telling his own story in his own words, playing his own music in his own inimitable style, his autobiography is indeed a tale striving towards freedom where, finally, "the music has a home" (219). It is, ultimately, in music—and by extension storytelling—where his freedom resides, and so the elderly Bechet, in the twilight of his career, can conclude that "[a]s long as I got a heart to be filled by it, the music has a place that's natural to it.

I could sit there and listen, and I'd smile. And when I've got to go I could go that way. I could remember all the richness there is, and I could go smiling" (219). In other words, the imaginative, improvisational act of reconfiguration transforms the historical reality of chattel slavery in America into the free richness of art.

II. Waking Up the Dead: Renarrating "Summertime"

It should therefore come as no surprise that the music of Sidney Bechet is particularly rich in this intricate and vital interweaving of storytelling and jazz improvisation. Descriptions of his art evoke the trope of storytelling so consistently that they inadvertently elucidate the narrative strategies in *Treat It Gentle* as well. Bob Wilber, for instance, who started taking lessons with Bechet in the 1940s and went on to become an accomplished musician in his own right, remembers that his teacher would use the trope of storytelling as a pedagogical tool:

> He showed me how to start out by starting the melody and bringing out its beauty. Using that as a foundation, the next step was to start the variations, but always initially relating them closely to the melody. As they progressed the variations gradually moved further away from the melody—in fact became new melodies based on the harmony—before the piece concluded with a return to the melody and, often, a coda. It was Sidney's way of telling a story. To tell a story, to grab the listener's attention, to carry him away on a continuously rising curve of excitement to the inevitable triumphant conclusion, this was Bechet's musical credo; it was a principle he firmly believed in and practiced every time he lifted his horn to play. (25)

That Bechet's storytelling—both musical and narrative—was not random by any means is also crucial; as Wilber continues, "he wanted discipline in his music, and never went for complete freedom of expression without regard to how each part fitted with the others" (27). British trombonist Bernard Tipping, with whom Bechet worked occasionally in London in 1920, seconds this observation: "Some of his ideas used to strike one as being a little far-fetched, but as crazy as his tricks might at first appear, when one analysed them one found that they always fitted properly and were always musically correct" (qtd. in Chilton 49). By analogy, the story of Omar might not be historically accurate, but it is certainly "musically correct" as the jazz aesthetic in *Treat It Gentle* turns the "far-fetched" tale of Omar from ostensible history into poetic fact.

No wonder, then, that musicologists have termed Bechet's approach to improvisation "vocalistic" (Porter and Ullman 139). Of course, any jazz solo is, in a way, a 're-telling' of the original melody and underlying chord structure. However, arguably one of Bechet's most moving musical narrations is his famous 1939 recording of the Gershwin standard "Summertime." Originally, in Du Bose Heyward and Ira Gershwin's libretto to the folk opera *Porgy and Bess*, "Summertime" is a tender lullaby Clara sings to her baby in the opening scene (and that Bess repeats in Act II, Scene iv) (15–17). Of the hundreds of different renditions of the song, just recall the sweet fragility of Miles Davis's muted trumpet over Gil Evans's softly swinging orchestral arrangement, the whimsical interaction between Ella Fitzgerald and Louis Armstrong that quickly moves from subdued melancholy to tender playfulness—or, in a drastic shift to the opposite end of the emotional spectrum, John Coltrane's blistering rendition that is not likely to put even the most somnolent listener to sleep. In the hands of Sidney Bechet and his cohorts, "Summertime" became something different still that summer day in 1939. Alfred Lion, co-founder of the new, fledgling Blue Note label, hand-picked the group of musicians assembling in his New York studio on June 8. As was house policy at Blue Note, Lion gave the musicians completely free reign over repertoire and arrangements. Guitarist Teddy Bunn would later remember the Blue Note dates as "just informal jam sessions, drinks were provided and except for a time limit the musicians scarcely knew that they were being recorded" (qtd. in Chilton 120). Despite the ideal conditions, a pallor of deep sadness hung over the session. Just four days earlier, Tommy Ladnier, highly regarded New Orleans trumpeter and as close a friend as the difficult Bechet would have in his life, had died at the age of thirty-nine. The passing of Ladnier, who was supposed to participate on the Blue Note date, was "an awful thing" for Bechet and the others, and so it was decided to record a tribute to Ladnier, "a man we'd all liked, a man who really had the feeling" (170). Ironically, "Blues for Tommy" turned out to be less than successful—perhaps because it was the first tune recorded at the session (Chilton 119; Morgenstern 3). On "Summertime," however, Bechet tells a moving story of death and resurrection in five solo choruses.

"Summertime" opens with Teddy Bunn's blues-drenched single-note guitar in a four-bar introduction, accompanied only by drummer Sid Catlett's light brushwork in the background. Bechet then enters, stating but immediately embellishing the theme with an unusually dark tone on the soprano, reminiscent more of his low-register clarinet playing.[10] Bechet's obbligato is replete with glissandi and microtonal pitch bending—note, for example, how he 'sculpts' the long E in bar seven in ways that defy musical notation. Catlett switches to drumsticks for the second chorus and answers a series of menacing growls with which Bechet begins his improvisation that produces a distinct sense of foreboding, danger even, removing "Summertime" entirely from the genre of the lullaby. Bechet enters in the high register on the third chorus, but drops to *pianissimo* initially. Bunn's guitar, no longer playing the chords underneath the soprano, now alludes to the song's theme, weaving single-note lines around Bechet. In measures seven through nine, Bechet resorts to some ominous growling again before switching to double double-time in a sequence of sixteenth-notes straddling the two major chords in measure thirteen—it is as if a ray of sunshine breaks through a brooding cloud cover. On the outgoing turnaround the soprano sustains a repeated A1 before entering the fourth chorus in *forte,* aided and abetted by the forceful on-the-beat playing by Bunn, Catlett, and Johnny Williams's bass. Returning to his idea from the previous turnaround, Bechet plays a sequence of repeated C2s, a third higher, but this time in the two measures preceding the turnaround. Especially Catlett intensifies his accompaniment in the fifth and final chorus by urging Bechet forward with press rolls that evoke the famed New Orleans funeral marches. The performance ends with Bechet's spectacular coda, initially swooping down to D1, then nimbly climbing up with a fast run of notes, ending with an ascending glissando on A2 in *fortissimo.* It is as if everything in this performance, Bechet's sense of dynamics, rhythm, and melodic structure as well as the rhythm section's interactive accompaniment, inexorably leads to this break and the glorious final A.

In these five immaculately constructed choruses, Bechet turns "Summertime" from a lullaby into a story of loss, longing, and, at the end, dramatic redemption. One year before this performance, Bechet had urged his old friend Ladnier to join him in forming "a real New Orleans band" that would "play things the way they really had been played back in New Orleans" (166). Ladnier's premature death precluded the realization of the project, but—as he had, in a way, predicted on "Summertime"—Bechet tried once more "to get together an outfit that would really do the real thing," as he put it (170). However, that effort a few years later never really got off the ground either, as his co-leader, the legendary but ailing Bunk Johnson, expressed a more pronounced interest in alcohol than in music. It proved to be the last time Bechet attempted to form an 'authentic' New Orleans jazz band. In his later years, especially in French exile, Bechet's solos came to include more and more prearranged formulas and phrases he had perfected during practice and previously tested out in concert, and less and less spontaneous improvisation (Porter and Ullman 142–45; Williams 156–57). And so, rather than a lullaby, that one version of "Summertime" also tells us a story about one man's death, another's perseverance, and, above all, the redemption in and by the music.

Thus, "Summertime" and *Treat It Gentle* share the same improvisational strategies of reinterpretation. Bechet's autobiography, too, tells us the story of Omar's death and his resurrection in and by music, and it does so in a manner that is clearly informed by a jazz aesthetic. What tenorist Joshua Redman once remarked about the art of jazz in general is therefore equally valid for "Summertime" and *Treat It Gentle* both: "Each tune establishes an overall theme. After that it is up to us, as improvising musicians, to take these themes and weave them into personalized, inspired, spontaneous narratives" (liner notes).

III. Straight, no Chaser? Authenticity and Hybridity in the Literary Jazz Aesthetic

As the preceding discussion has shown, the musical strategies informing Bechet's revision of "Summertime" are akin to the narrative strategies informing the revision of his family history in *Treat It Gentle.* But, as the above analysis also demonstrates, even the soloist's improvisation is interacting with and responding to the group as a whole and underscores that the improviser's melodic freedom is not so much an individual absolute but the result, to varying degrees, of collective interplay. Even a player of Bechet's overbearing personality will, given the right circumstances, react to and build upon the collective musical context. The same pertains to the larger-than-life Omar: as we have already seen, his virtuoso shift in Congo Square from the literal realm to the figurative occurs within a dynamic that is also communal. Later, when Omar seeks to elude the posse of slave catchers, his individual liberty is embedded even more firmly within a *communal* enactment of freedom. On the run from Marie's master, Omar temporarily finds safety in the Bayou LeFourg with a group of other runaway slaves. As Bechet recounts, the slaves would sing at night:

> The only thing they had that couldn't be taken from them was their music. Their song, it was coming right up from the fields,

> settling itself in their feet and working right up, right up into their stomachs, their spirit, into their fear, into their longing. . . . [I]t was a feeling in them, a memory that came from a long way back. It was like they were trying to work the music back to its beginnings and then start it over again, start it over and build it to a place where it could stop somehow, to a place where the music could put an end to itself and become another music, a new beginning that could begin *them* over again. (30)

Once again, the memory of the Middle Passage and chattel slavery, combined with the longing for freedom, converges in a communal space of renewal, redemption, and self-actualization. Jazz—the music as well as the story of Omar—is that figurative place of freedom. Bechet recognizes, as does his jazz aesthetic, the forces of history, but he simultaneously strives to transform imaginatively the pain and horrors of American history into something else, something new, and to improvise something beautiful and free. Like the title character in Langston Hughes's "Trumpet Player," the slaves in Bechet's tale as well as the storyteller himself are occupying a soundscape where "Trouble / Mellows to a golden note" (lines 43–44).[11] Accordingly, it is Bechet himself who participates in this communal reimagining of history by transforming Omar from an ostensibly historical individual into a collective, mythical figure in the conclusion: "It was Omar started the song. Or maybe he didn't start the song exactly. There was somebody singing and playing the drums and the horns behind Omar, and there was somebody behind that. . . . But if you're a musicianer, if you're any good musicianer, it's Omar's song you're singing" (202). Here, the jazz aesthetic not only blurs the line between history and myth deliberately, it also interrogates the dynamic interaction between individual self-assertion and collective cultural production.

This complex interplay between the individual and the collective is, of course, a hallmark of jazz. On the one hand, jazz musicians strive to develop a highly individual, recognizable voice—Louis Armstrong's trumpet, for instance, is immediately distinguishable from, say, Miles Davis's. At the same time, it is imperative that in performance, improvisers be aware of the constantly moving, instantly changing musical environment and play with it rather than above it; one of the worst offenses one can commit on the bandstand is not to listen. This intricate dialectic between individual voice and collective interplay in cultural production is also problematized by the peculiar circumstances surrounding the genesis of *Treat It Gentle.* Bechet, not a fan of big band jazz or bebop, had toyed with the idea of writing a book as early as 1946, possibly much earlier that that, as he felt that jazz had developed in ways that distanced the music from its roots (Wilber 23). When he met American poet John Ciardi in November of 1950 during an engagement in Paris, he told him that he was writing his autobiography. Ciardi—by his own admission no jazz connoisseur—was immediately struck by the musician's storytelling abilities and recognized in him something "of a back-country Wallace Stevens" (83). Ciardi agreed to take a look at the manuscript and discovered that Bechet had not in fact written it himself, but had spoken into a tape recorder. The story of Omar and some early childhood reminiscences were then transcribed onto paper by Joan Williams, Bechet's secretary (Chilton 290). Ciardi was particularly distraught to see Williams's editorial interpolations, "vaguely scented purple passages" in "high-lilac college English," and his first task was to excise these easily identifiable passages (Ciardi 82). He also re-interviewed Bechet on several occasions, transcribing the tapes and editing the material. However, the project foundered when in 1952 Williams, insisting on receiving co-authorship credits, threatened to sue Ciardi and the publisher, Twayne, and so the manuscript was shelved and eventually put up for sale in a trade magazine. Desmond Flower, director of the British publishing firm Cassell and himself a passionate jazz fan, purchased it from Twayne and, having contacted Bechet, who agreed enthusiastically to more taped interviews, set out to complete Ciardi's work. *Treat It Gentle* was first published in England by Cassell in 1960, the year after Bechet's death, then by Hill and Wang in the United States (Chilton 292; Cifelli 153–55; Elman 79–81).

It is impossible to ascertain today what portion of the autobiography are Bechet's, and what parts are his various collaborators'. Unfortunately, Flower's tape recorder was defective and rendered Bechet's comments on the tapes barely audible, and Ciardi, prompted by Ralph Ellison in the 1980s, was unable to locate his original tapes in his files. What is clear, though, is that Bechet was directly involved with the manuscript at every stage, and the final version contains the Sidney Bechet he wanted to present to the world (Chilton 292–93; Ciardi 83). For his part, Ciardi later insisted that between 85 and 90 percent of the published book was the result of his collaboration with the saxophonist. At the same time, though, Ciardi in 1952 had written to the editor at Twayne in response to Williams's legal threats that "[i]n the finished manuscript, *no word of hers appears: not one.* It's all Sidney's talk and," he casually added, "talk I have put into his mouth" (qtd. in Cifelli 154).

The convoluted evolution of *Treat It Gentle* and Ciardi's own admission therefore raise the problem of authenticity. And yet, once again, the autobiography is emblematic of the *jazz* aesthetic precisely because its hybrid, collaborative aspects defy confirmation of one single, individual authorship. As Kathy Ogren points out, "[j]azz autobiographies are textual performances in which musicians, sometimes in concert with their amanuensis, create personas equally as fascinating as those developed musically" and concludes that "[t]hese verbal performances are conscious of a variety of storytelling methods that help communicate their persona, and many of their techniques are drawn from African American oral performance traditions that also relied on the understanding and participation of audiences" ("'Jazz'" 112, 118–19). Thus, *Treat It Gentle* not only occupies the fault line between oral storytelling and literary production, but also performs literary jazz as a collective enterprise. The fact that the book is not a solo performance aligns it with a characteristic of early New Orleans jazz, collective improvisation. The call and response between both Bechet and his collaborators as well as between *Treat It Gentle* and its readers hence posits the (literary) jazz aesthetic as a process in cultural time rather than the stable end result of a linear, historical development. The jazz aesthetic views neither Bechet's prevarications nor the editorial changes and additions of his (white) collaborators as somehow inferior, corrupted, or inauthentic; on the contrary: the perpetual exchange of meanings between fact and fiction, history and myth, oral storytelling and literary writing, the Old World and the New, black and white, slavery and freedom, creates a symbolic field of tension in which it is at least possible for a *human* self to be (re-)claimed. Since the demarcations of this field of tension are constantly changing—as is the musical environment of any jazz performance—this figurative territory must continuously be negotiated anew if the freedom afforded by the reclamation of a human self is to be retained. Or, as musicologist Ajay Heble observes, "improvisation's link with processes of identity formation and struggles for self-definition has less to do with a creative actualization of the self as a stable origin of meaning than it does with unsettling the very logic of identity. If anything, improvisation teaches us by example that identity is a dialogic construction (rather than something deep within us), that the self is always a subject in process" (95). Bechet's autobiography, especially the story of Omar, constitutes such a process of dialogic construction. Significantly, it is Bechet's voice that clearly dominates the book, not that of Williams, Ciardi, or Flower. Just as Bechet's immensely overpowering musical personality pointed the way from the New Orleans ensemble tradition of collective improvisation to the now standard conception of soloist-*cum*-accompaniment (even before Armstrong did so), so does Bechet's narrating persona eclipse the other voices (Schuller, *Early* 198). Thus, while *Treat It Gentle* is indeed a collaborative effort to a degree, its very refusal to separate clearly fact from fiction, written text from spoken word, history from myth, author from editor, creates a persona of Bechet that is the dynamic, unstable self of his (its) own story rather than the static, stable self of somebody else's history (Heble 110). The text's many hybridizations converge to turn the self from a narrated object of history into the narrating subject of story.[12]

The recognition of *Treat It Gentle* as an inherently unstable text also suggests a (partial) solution to one of the most difficult problems confronting the critic of literary jazz, namely how to align the *process* of musical improvisation in performance with the fixity of the printed word on the page.[13] This problem is defused somewhat if we demythologize what jazz improvisation is. It is a widespread misconception that the art of the improvising jazz musician simply involves an offhand playing of whatever comes to mind in the spur of the moment, or the tapping into some sort of mysterious divine force of inspiration. In reality, very few jazz solos are unmediated products of complete improvisation. As Paul Berliner's and Ingrid Monson's studies and their interviews with dozens of musicians prove, playing jazz entails the accumulation of a musical vocabulary that is carefully developed and rehearsed over years. As musicologist David Demsey summarizes it:

> The notes of an improvised jazz solo are no more spontaneously created than are the words of a spoken language. At this most integral level, sentences have been spoken before, in some form; individual words have been enunciated countless times until they roll smoothly off the tongue. In musical terms, melodic ideas are repeated and replayed for years until they become the individual vocabulary of a soloist; difficult chord progressions and awkward keys are endlessly practiced until they are mentally familiar and fall easily under the hands. In a great soloist's repertoire, every tune is like a familiar subject of conversation: although fresh ideas are always emerging, the language used to communicate them has a consistency for each individual. (780)

Pianist Dianthe Spencer seconds this when she describes jazz improvisation as "a language, a hard language, a very mathematical language, and at first, all you can think about is chords and not hitting the wrong notes. Then, once you know the language, you can begin to talk" (qtd. in S. Tucker, "'Where'" 28). This dynamic interaction between spontaneity and practice is consequently found not only in "Summertime," but in *Treat It Gentle* as well. In Bechet's solo on "Summertime," for instance, one such pre-rehearsed phrase occurs at the very beginning, as the first four measures of the second chorus consist of a direct quote from the "Miserere" scene in Verdi's *Il Trovatore.* Moreover, in the tenth measure of the final chorus Bechet weaves in a brief allusion, in double-time, to another Italian operatic aria, *I Pagliacci*'s "Vesti la giubba," a reference that he used time and again and that became something of a signature phrase of his.[14] It is also possible that the spectacular final break is at least partly pre-rehearsed, as Bechet was known to practice a host of different musical motifs that were guaranteed to elicit an excited audience reaction. Similarly, some bits and pieces of the fictional story of Omar in *Treat It Gentle* appear in interviews and article profiles as early as the 1930s, suggesting that this chapter in his autobiography was far from invented on the spot, but the latest and most detailed version of a story Bechet had, as it were, rehearsed in advance (Chilton 290–92). Thus, it is the very indeterminacy and tension between advanced planning and careful editorializing on the one hand, and oral storytelling on the other, that makes *Treat It Gentle* an improvised text in the *jazz* tradition.

What is more, Bechet's direct quotation of *Il Trovatore* and his use of a signature phrase derived from *I Pagliacci* in a session that explicitly sought to recapture the authentic spirit of early New Orleans jazz point to the jazz aesthetic's deconstruction of yet another binary pair: it suggests that in the jazz aesthetic hybridity and authenticity are not necessarily mutually exclusive. It also suggests that it is precisely this hybridity—of voices, cultures, stories, and histories—that infuses the jazz aesthetic with its peculiar power. Sidney Bechet's story thrives on dialectic tension, as we have seen, interrogating any and all received categories. Because of its inherent subversion and hybridity, the jazz aesthetic can question even itself and its own traditions. To Bechet, jazz is unquestionably a black art form. "White people, they don't have the memory that needs to understand it [jazz]," he judges at one point, and later reiterates, "I don't care what you say, it's awful hard for a man who isn't black to play a melody that's come deep out of black people. It's a question of feeling" (48, 114). Bechet repeatedly emphasizes also the centrality of New Orleans in the jazz canon, "a place where the music was natural as the air" (215). In his strong opinion, the further the music moves away from its roots in the Crescent City, the more diluted and inauthentic it becomes. This "long song that started back there in the South" is what he calls "the remembering song," and, as such, is implicitly the prerogative, the property, of Americans of African descent (202). At the same time, however, Bechet also knows full well that, certainly in the latter stages of his career, the vast majority of his accompanists were white Europeans, many of whom he commends on their expert musicianship. Moreover, like several other jazz luminaries—Billie Holiday or Charlie Parker come to mind—he harbored a lifelong ambition to perform in the setting of a classical European orchestra and in fact composed much of the music for an operetta and two ballets (all commercial and artistic flops) (Chilton 254–56, 279–80). An admirer of opera since childhood, he modeled his highly individual style, particularly his vibrato, partly on that of his hero, Enrico Caruso, and regularly quoted from the tenor's recordings (Chilton 5, 45–46). His discography, too, reveals a much more eclectic range and a more daringly experimental repertoire than his autobiography lets on.

Not surprisingly, it is once again the fictitious figure of Omar that Bechet enlists in the conclusion of the autobiography to probe this ostensible paradox between authenticity and hybridity: "I met many a musicianer in many a place after I struck out from New Orleans, but it was always the same: if they was any good, it was Omar's song they were singing. It was the long song, and the good musicianers, they all heard it behind them. They all had an Omar, somebody like an Omar, somebody that was *their* Omar" (202).[15] In other words, it is the history and origins of jazz as rooted in the black experience in America—synthesized by Bechet in the myth of Omar—that makes jazz black music, not necessarily the ethnic identity of its practitioners.[16] The promise of individual freedom within the collective to which Omar lays claim in Congo Square thus "comes into itself" in each jazz performance "if they was any good," be it the in telling of Omar's story or in the playing of "Summertime," where the import and duration of the original Free Day is perpetually reconfigured and redefined. Taking his cue from *Treat It Gentle*, musicologist Samuel Floyd also stresses the importance of what he calls "cultural memory," but adds that jazz "is not racially exclusive, for in absorbing the elements, practices, and transformations of a tradition, one also absorbs its cultural memory" (*Power* 140). Bechet himself attempts to explain this apparent paradox thusly:

> People come up to me and they say, "What's Negro music? What is it really being?" I have to tell them there's no straight answer to that. If I could give them a straight answer, just in one sentence like, I wouldn't have to say all this I'm saying. You can't say that

> just out straight. There's no answer to that question, not just direct. You could come up to me and say, "What's an American? What's a Frenchman?" How do you answer a thing like that? (204)

In more ways than one, *Treat It Gentle* is certainly not a "straight answer." The authenticity of jazz, Bechet states, transcends categories of race and nationality. Jazz deconstructs the legal, cultural, and social segregation of blackness from humanity. Ironically, in doing so it also recognizes simultaneously that these divisive categories continue to affect life in the (post-)modern world. As cultural historian Nicholas Evans tries to explain the paradox, jazz "always involves race, nationalism, and related concerns because it heightens the audibility, palpability, and even visibility of the cultural sameness and difference of whiteness and blackness" (18). In jazz, states critic Lee Brown, "what we really witness is, not the birth and death of essences, but a flux of values" (245). In this sense, *Treat It Gentle* implicitly asks for an epistemological shift from *what* (blackness, nationality) to *who* (the human individuality of the historical Sidney Bechet and of the cast of characters in his autobiography), from abstraction to concreteness. Still, since *abstraction* and *concreteness* are, of course, epistemological categories themselves, jazz interrogates these as well, riffing continuously at their juncture. Ultimately, only a *who* can assert individual freedom, whereas a *what* is always already defined by others to a degree.[17]

Significantly, the freedom asserted by the autobiographical self is a freedom constituted in and by story (oral narrative), in figurative space. The freedom of the *who* which Bechet claims for himself must continuously be asserted in the face of the exigencies of the *what*—race, nationhood, et cetera. It is thus crucial that Bechet's assertion of a free and human self is predicated in and by the *story* of a *who*—the mythical Omar—rather than in and by an *account* of a *what*—Jean Bechet. Therefore, *Treat It Gentle* contains all the ingredients for an aesthetic of African American fiction as literary jazz: the assertion of an at least temporary freedom in figurative space resulting from the persistent and often subversive narrative interrogation of the historical, cultural, social, and racial binaries that constitute the American landscape. Not coincidentally, it is precisely this assertion within a field of dialectic tension that the title character effects in his piano solo at the end of James Baldwin's "Sonny's Blues": "Freedom lurked around us and I understood, at last, that he [Sonny] could help us to be free if we would listen, that he would never be free until we did. . . . And I was yet aware that this was only a moment, that the world awaited outside, as hungry as a tiger, and that trouble stretched above us, longer than the sky" (1316). Here, too, just as in Bechet's performance at the Vieux Colombier, the jazz aesthetic navigates the literal space of contemporary social reality, traversing the diachronic time of American history in the synchronous time of performance and improvising a figurative space of at least temporary freedom.[18]

CHAPTER 2

"Swing It, Sister"

JAZZ TIME IN ANN PETRY'S *THE STREET*

Loving one who loves you
And then taking that vow;
Nice work if you can get it,
And if you get it,
Won't you tell me how?

GEORGE AND IRA GERSHWIN, "Nice Work If You Can Get It"

In Nathaniel Mackey's epistolary novel *Atet, A.D.*, multi-reedist N. is astonished by the dramatic improvement in the playing of his bandmate Penguin after the latter's prolonged stint of, in jazz parlance, 'woodshedding': that is, practicing in isolation. "It was," writes N., "as if the 'place' he'd gone off to prepare was not so much a place as a certain rapport, a 'place' neither wholly here nor wholly there. It was a 'place' which was more than one place at once, a utopic ubiquity which, though always there, was never all there" (15). It is precisely this kind of metaphorical space of at least temporary freedom toward which Sidney Bechet's poetics of place strives in forging an aesthetic of literary jazz. In enacting this literary jazz aesthetic, *Treat It Gentle* creates an unstable text that, jazz-like, asks to be continuously reinterpreted anew. It stands to reason, though, that the (oral) autobiography of a jazz musician is, of course, likely to avail itself of the same or similar aesthetic principles as the music itself. Thus, the question of what we stand to gain by reading African American narrative to the tune of jazz must necessarily be extended to prose fiction. Ralph Ellison's seminal novel *Invisible Man* has elicited a plethora of critical responses seeking to integrate jazz and literary-critical practice, primarily because the novel's prologue features Armstrong's "What Did I Do to Be so Black and Blue" quite prominently, and because of Ellison's own copious critical writings on jazz.[1] At the same time, Ellison's artistic biography practically demands such an approach, as Ellison was, of course, a trumpeter before he turned to writing, and even his own method of writing emulated the practice habits of the jazz musician (O'Meally, "Introduction" xxx). Thus, the validation of a jazz aesthetic in prose fiction demands that we turn to an author without any direct ties to the jazz community. It also suggests that we not only look at literary texts that are 'about' jazz, but that we apply such a critical reading to narratives in which jazz does not figure so conspicuously, or not at all.

Ann Petry's short story "Solo On the Drums" certainly is a literary text that both *is* jazz and is *about* jazz. In her novel *The Street,* on the other hand, jazz does not appear to be salient. Nor does Petry herself seem the kind of author whose work lends itself readily to a critical engagement with jazz: born into an upper middle-class black family—at the time, one of only two in the town of Old Sadybrook, Connecticut—she pursued a career in pharmacy initially, carrying on the family tradition. After her marriage and subsequent move to New York City, Petry switched to journalism, working for the *Amsterdam News* and the *People's Voice,* Harlem's biggest weeklies. Having published a number of short stories in the early forties, it was her experiences as a reporter for the *People's Voice* which furnished the inspiration for her first novel, *The Street,* published in 1946. Although an admitted "jazz buff" and hobby pianist, Petry did not have a direct connection to the jazz world (Petry, "Just" 102; Sanders Mobley 347–50; Ivy 200).[2] It is perhaps for this reason that—with the notable exceptions of Gayl Jones's and Johanna Garvey's analyses—Petry's fiction has generated very little criticism focusing on the role of music in general and jazz in particular. While the short story "Solo on the Drums" is saturated with the same jazz aesthetic that informs *Treat It Gentle, The Street* does not appear to be. Lutie Johnson, a single mother desperately trying to find the means to escape the poverty and despair of 116th Street in 1944 Harlem, is certainly no musician's musician, and her discovery as a singer is quite incidental. Even so, the novel's central event is Lutie's performance as a jazz singer. Her impressive rendition of the sentimental torch song "Darlin'" is located precisely in the middle of the book, in the ninth of a total of eighteen chapters. This strategic placement of an ostensibly minor scene, then, invites a reading of the text as a jazz text. "Narrative," as Ulfried Reichardt reminds us, is after all "the specifically human form of configuring time," and the compelling central positioning of Lutie as a jazz artist suggests that jazz plays a pivotal role as a structural device in *The Street* (474). While "Solo on the Drums" accedes to the same aesthetic principles as Sidney Bechet's autobiography, *The Street* extends the literary jazz aesthetic by swinging to a different time signature.

The 1947 short story "Solo on the Drums" features Kid Jones, star drummer in a swing orchestra, playing the solo of his career.[3] During the performance his mind wanders back to the morning of the same day, when his wife told him that she would leave him for the band's pianist. In the ensuing musical battle between drums and piano, Jones vanquishes his rival, the Marquis of Brund: "When he hit the drums again it was with the thought that he was fighting with the piano player. He was choking the Marquis of Brund. He was putting a knife in clean between his ribs. He was slitting his throat with a long straight blade. Take my woman. Take your life" (239). Just as Omar did playing his drum on Congo Square, Jones in his solo transcends reality by creating a figurative place for himself:

> The drums leaped with the fury that was in him. The men in the band turned their heads towards him—a faint astonishment showed in their faces. He ignored them. The drums took him away from them, took him back, and back, and back, in time and in space. He built up an illusion. He was sending out the news. Grandma died. The foreigner in the litter has an old disease and will not recover. The man from across the big water is sleeping with the chief's daughter. Kill. Kill. Kill. The war goes well with the men with the bad smell and the loud laugh. It goes badly with the chiefs with the round heads and the peacock's walk. (239)

As Gayl Jones points out in her comprehensive analysis, the drum solo "functioned as a kind of catharsis, a purgatorial ritual. Through his music, Kid Jones . . . has 'killed' the Marquis effectively in a musical ritual, so he won't have to do it in the world; the central confrontations have been transfigured" (97).[4] Just like Bechet's story of Omar, Kid Jones's solo, too, creates a figurative space out of lost love, deadly violence (at least the impulse for it), and Africanist memory. As with Omar and Bechet, transcending the pain and suffering of history is only temporary, lasts only for the duration of the song, for as Jones muses while bowing to the audience, "Yeah, he thought, you were hot all right. The jitterbugs ate you up and you haven't any place to go. Since this morning you haven't had any place to go. 'I'm leaving it's the guy who plays the piano I'm in love with the Marquis of Brund he plays such sweet piano I'm leaving leaving leaving—'" (241–42). Literally without "any place to go," the only place left is his music. It is that very same place to which Bechet's and Omar's stories strive. Even though Jones's figurative place, like Penguin's and Bechet's, is one of "utopic ubiquity," to use N.'s phrase again, at least his art—what psychologist Ferdinand Jones has called jazz's "challenge attitude" that is "crucial to the psychological survival of black Americans"—furnishes space for catharsis and, eventually perhaps, spiritual healing (127, 133). Thus, "Solo on the Drums" falls squarely within the jazz aesthetic as scored by *Treat It Gentle. The Street,* however, poses certain challenges to a jazz reading, not only because it is a text that is clearly not 'about' the music, but also because the "utopic ubiquity" of the metaphorical space that affords Bechet, Omar, and Kid Jones the opportunity of at least temporary transcendence only serves to accelerate the tragic downfall of *The Street*'s Lutie Johnson.

I. She's Got a Right to Sing the Blues: Jazz and Gender in *The Street*

Lutie Johnson, a single working mother in 1944 New York City, has one burning ambition: she is determined to find a way out of Harlem's dreary, depressing 116th Street for herself and her eight-year-old son Bub. Although she has never had any formal musical training, Lutie is a gifted singer. Boots Smith, the former sleeping car porter turned bandleader, overhears her one evening singing along with the jukebox in the Junto Bar and Grill and is struck not only by her exceptional beauty, but also by her innate musical talent. When Lutie accepts his offer to sing at the Casino with his orchestra, she thinks of the audition primarily as her best chance to escape 116th Street. Her rendition of the sentimental torch song "Darlin'" the following night occurs exactly in middle of the novel:

> The music swelled in the back of her and she began to sing, faintly at first and then her voice grew stronger, clearer, for she gradually forgot the men in the orchestra, forgot even that she was there in the Casino and why she was there. Though she sang the words of the song, it was of something entirely different that she was thinking and putting into the music: she was leaving the street with its dark hallways, its mean, shabby rooms; she was taking Bub away with her to a place where there were no Mrs. Hedges, no resigned and disillusioned little girls, no half-human creatures like the Super. She and Bub were getting out and away, and they would never be back. The last low strains of the melody died away and she stood holding onto the mike, not moving. There was complete silence behind her, and she turned toward the band, filled with sudden doubt and wishing that she had kept her mind on what

> she was doing, on the words of the song, instead of floating off into a day-dream. (222)

Lutie's apprehensions are unfounded, though, as her arresting performance not only commands the respect of the musicians, but also lands her the job. In Petry's description of this jazz performance, we find remarkable parallels to Kid Jones's drum solo: the juxtaposition of individual soloist and the band collective, the individual's ability to transcend in music the pain and suffering of history, the straining towards a metaphorical place of freedom. Even though Lutie's motivation is primarily economic rather than artistic, her performance is nonetheless the result of what Ferdinand Jones calls "the mental improvisational mode": "Black instrumentalists and jazz singers through the ages, like African American storytellers, exercise resistance and self-definition. . . . The parallel of jazz improvisation to the everyday mental processes of African American individuals is the stance that given reality is not a constant but is to be interpreted" (130, 133). And it is precisely this mental improvisational mode which resists and reinterprets a debilitating reality that we find in Sidney Bechet, Omar, Kid Jones, and also Lutie.

Her talent in harnessing this improvisational "challenge attitude" is also accentuated in the novel's very first chapter (F. Jones 127). Walking down 116th Street on a windy November day, Lutie espies a sign in front of a building advertising a vacancy:

> She read it rapidly. Three rooms, steam heat, parquet floors, respectable tenants. Reasonable. She looked at the outside of the building, Parquet floors here meant that the wood was so old and so discolored no amount of varnish or shellac would conceal the scars and the old scraped places, the years of dragging furniture across the floors, the hammer blows of time and children and drunks and dirty, slovenly women. Steam heat meant a rattling, clanging noise in radiators early in the morning and then a hissing that went on all day. (3)

One by one, Lutie accurately deciphers the meaning in or behind the words on the sign. This, however, still only constitutes interpretation, not improvisational re-interpretation. Nonetheless, when she enters the building, the names on the mailboxes and the narrow hallway, combined with her previous observations, inspire her to a jazz-like improvisation, to a reinterpretation of reality, on the spot:

> She stood there thinking that it was really a pity they couldn't somehow manage to rent the halls, too. Single beds. No. Old army cots would do. It would bring in so much more money. If she were a landlord, she'd rent out the hallways. It would make it so much more entertaining for the tenants. Mr. Jones and wife could have cots number one and two; Jackson and girl friend could occupy number three. And Rinaldi, who drove a cab nights, could sublet the one occupied by Jackson and his girl friend. (7)

The little story Lutie spontaneously composes out of the drab materials at hand is representative of Ferdinand Jones's mental improvisational mode in that it, too, "affirms the interpreter's subjective autonomy and therefore spares the individual from psychological dominance even when he or she cannot control the physical circumstances" (133). It is this very same talent for reinterpretation and improvisation that will later inform her performance as a jazz singer.

Even so, while this subjective autonomy of self, however temporary, at which Sidney Bechet, Omar, and Kid Jones arrive in and through music is a liberating one, Lutie's jazz performances only accelerate her fall. For at the very moment Lutie creates a liberating place of metaphorical freedom for herself and Bub in her reinterpretation of "Darlin'," she is observed by Old Man Junto, Boots's white employer, owner of the Casino, and all-powerful if inconspicuous slum lord. Junto "had never been known to look twice at any" of the girls employed in his many venues, but now, after Lutie's audition, he "wanted her for the same reason that he [Boots] had—because she was young and extraordinarily good-looking and any man with a spark of life left in him would go for her" (276). Ironically, it is Lutie's success as a jazz singer which allows Junto to order that Boots withhold her salary, which in turn sets in motion the events that lead to Boots's brutal murder and Lutie's flight. Ferdinand Jones's positivistic analysis of jazz omits the fact that, at least in the literary jazz aesthetic, the mental improvisational mode entails not only opportunity but also a significant *risk* in its struggle to transcend reality: Lutie's "day-dream" is destructive rather than redemptive precisely because it is an *illusion.*[5] As Lutie herself comes to realize eventually, "She had built up a fantastic structure made from the soft, nebulous, cloudy stuff of dreams. There hadn't been a solid, practical brick in it, not even a foundation. She had built it up of air and vapor and moved right in. So of course it had collapsed. It had never existed anywhere but in her own mind" (308). The collapse of her "fantastic structure" is caused by Boots's and Junto's male gaze of sexual desire that imprisons Lutie at the very moment she sings of liberation. Significantly it is jazz—Lutie's singing of "Darlin'"—which enhances her good looks. At the same time, jazz also enhances the danger confronting her because it invites the objectifying male gaze of desire in two key scenes, first when she sings along with the jukebox record at the Junto Bar and Grill, then at the audition in the Casino. Being 'too handsome' certainly never was a problem for the womanizing Sidney Bechet nor the fictional Omar, not even for the duped Kid Jones—but for Lutie Johnson, physical beauty is a curse rather than a blessing. Hence, Petry's take on the literary jazz aesthetic appears to emphasize its inherent dangers rather than its potential for self-definition and liberation.

These dangers, as many critics have pointed out, arise in a landscape shaped and regulated by the forces of white male capitalism personified in Junto (Garvey 135–37; Pryse 117–18; Wurst 18–20). The novel frames Lutie's performance at the Casino in these same symbolic terms as well: at the onset of her audition, Lutie "walked over to the microphone and stood there waiting for the melody to repeat itself. She touched the mike and then held onto it with both hands, for the silvery metal was cold and her hands were suddenly hot. As she held the mike, she felt as though her voice was draining away down through the slender metal rod, and the idea frightened her" (221). The phallic microphone—positioned by bandleader Boots and paid for by clubowner Junto—separates her body, the object of male sexual desire, from her voice, the instrument of individual human self-expression. Even though Lutie wins the respect of the musicians on the bandstand and hears "violent applause" from the crowd every time she sings later that night, the microphone transforms her individualistic art into that precious commodity of consumer capitalism, mass entertainment: "And she thought, It doesn't make much difference who sings or whether they sing badly or well, because nobody really listens. They're making love or quarreling or drinking or dancing" (224).[6] Moreover, after her first appearance with Boots Smith's orchestra has come to a close, a successful performance that has made her feel "so strong so confident," Lutie overhears one of the bouncers informing Boots that his employer wants to see him (226–27). After Boots has dropped his new singer off at her building on 116th Street, he learns that Junto wants to have Lutie for himself. But Lutie is also in more immediate danger: her successful first stint with Boots's band causes her to return home in the middle of the night, which leads directly to the sexual assault by Jones, the "cellar crazy" superintendent of her building (302). The attempted rape is foreshadowed earlier in the novel, for it is at the exact same time that Lutie sings "Darlin'" to the jukebox that Jones prowls through her apartment fondling her clothes.

Thus, for Lutie, the figurative territory of jazz is as dangerous as the literal territory of the unforgiving street, if not more so. The novel provides an interesting contrast between Lutie's musical endeavors and those of two unnamed male band members. One night soon after her debut, the pianist and a trumpeter remain on the bandstand during intermission:

> The trumpeter was experimenting with a tune that had been playing in his head for days. The pianist turned sideways on the piano bench listening to him. . . . The pianist groped for appropriate chords as the man with the trumpet played the tune over softly. Together they produced a faint melody, barely a shred, a tatter of music that drifted through the big ballroom. Conversation and the clink of glasses and roars of laughter almost drowned it out, but it persisted—a slight, ghostly sound running through the room. (302–3)

Unencumbered by the commercial demands of the venue and the artistic restrictions of pre-arranged scores, the two musicians play improvised jazz at its purest, spontaneously composing a new song, a new story, in the moment. While the musicians are engaged in the imaginative creation of art, Lutie asks Boots about her salary: "She waited for his answer, leaning toward him, straining to hear it and hearing the faint, drifting sound of music. It disturbed her because at first she thought it wasn't real, that she was imagining the sound. She turned towards the bandstand and saw that two of the boys were practicing" (304). For the two male musicians, jazz provides the opportunity for artistic self-actualization. For Lutie, "the thin, ghostly, haunting music" becomes in fact a prelude to tragedy and death: when she arrives at Boots's apartment towards the end of the novel in order to borrow money to secure a lawyer for Bub, she finds that Junto is present as well. Boots takes her aside to inform her that she can get all the money she needs if she agrees to "be nice" to Junto, to which she reacts with the barely controllable desire to kill the slumlord right then and there (421). Significantly, her homicidal impulses are accompanied by the memory of that faint tune she heard at the Casino: "She could still hear that floating, drifting tune. It was inside her head and she couldn't get it out. . . . If she hummed that fragment of melody aloud, she would get rid of it. It was the only way to make it disappear; otherwise it would keep going around and around in her head. And she thought, I must be losing my mind, wanting to hum a tune and at the same time thinking about killing that white man who is sitting, waiting, outside" (422). When her urge to kill finally erupts, she does kill the white man, but only by proxy, for it is the black man who has just attempted to rape her who receives repeated blows from the iron candlestick in her hand. At last, with Boots's body lifeless on the sofa, the thin, ghostly, persisting melody in her head disappears, and "[t]he room was perfectly still. There was no sound in it except her own hoarse breathing" (11). Just as the "slender metal rod" of the microphone drained Lutie's voice earlier, so does the candlestick now drain the room of even just the memory of music, haunting as it is. Surely then, the meaning the ghostly melody has acquired for Lutie diverges brutally from whatever meaning the two male musicians find in it. For them, jazz provides the freedom to explore artistically, to roam creatively—for Lutie, jazz in the end becomes the soundtrack for murder.

In her analysis of the subject, Sherrie Tucker avers that "in Black women's fiction, jazz pulls the individual back to the community," echoing the positivistic take of Ferdinand Jones and others ("'Where'" 38). Clearly, though, for Lutie jazz is the catalyst that propels her *out* of the (albeit dysfunctional) community, severing even the relationship to her son. In fact, the potentially liberating powers of jazz are rendered mute by the overwhelming male forces arrayed against her. It also underscores the fact that jazz "remains an enclave of machismo," as Francis Davis observed only recently (19). Historically, the only roles readily open to women have been those of vocalist and, less frequently, pianist.[7] Tucker's own historical study on women jazz musicians in the swing era in fact contradicts her findings in fiction: "In the gender division of jazz and swing labor, the normal configuration is for men to skillfully operate instruments and for women to perform privatized popular versions of femininity with their voices and bodies" (S. Tucker, *Swing* 6). The fate of *The Street*'s protagonist dramatizes that the jazz aesthetic can be as pernicious as it is liberating, for women more so than for men, even though—or, perhaps precisely because—Lutie inadvertently adheres to the gendered labor codes of jazz.

II. Swinging Time: The Mills Brothers' "Swing It, Sister," Lucky Millinder's "Darlin'" and Narrative Structure in *The Street*

Even though, or because, jazz hastens and accompanies Lutie's demise, the music also serves as a structural narrative device in the novel. Jazz or jazz-like improvisation appears in the beginning, the middle, and the end of the book. Both jazz and storytelling occur within time, after all, and the strategic placement of Lutie as a jazz artist hence suggests that 'jazz time' plays a significant role in structuring the narrative of *The Street* (474). The literary jazz aesthetic's striving towards a figurative space of freedom also entails the element of time, that is, narrative sequencing: in improvised jazz music, "there is no intent towards time as a period of *development*," observes multi-instrumentalist Leo Smith; "rather, time is employed as an element of space" (qtd. in Wilson 570; emphasis added).

This dynamic interaction of time and space, then, points to one of jazz's unique characteristics—one that sets it apart, to a degree at least, from other African American musics—namely its complex, multilayered manipulation of time, that elusive, mysterious quality called *swing*. Jazz musicians themselves often will define swing simply as that aspect of the music which is "making people's feet pat" (qtd. in A. Murray 174). Critics and musicologists, on the other hand, have made countless attempts over the years to define empirically this evasive phenomenon (Berendt 198–207; Berliner 244–47; Monson, *Saying* 26–29, 62–63). In his tome *The Swing Era,* Gunther Schuller even goes so far as to enlist computer-generated spectral graphs in his analysis, only to conclude that swing is a jazz element "which, I dare say, we do not yet fully understand" (225, 855–57). Nonetheless, what the various analytical investigations all share is the notion that swing results from a rhythmic manipulation of time combining seemingly opposite elements. Schuller designates these elements as "horizontal" and "vertical" relationships that merge in "the simultaneous integrated flow of performance energies" (225). For Schuller's colleague Wilfried Raussert, swing is derived from "a complex African sense of time in which recurrent and progressive elements intersect," and even though swing "postulates a regularity of temporal progression . . . it continuously disrupts and even negates such a regular movement" (521). And Samuel Floyd avers that swing is "a quality that manifests itself when sound events signify on the time line against the flow of its pulse, making the pulse freely lilt" (*Power* 115). It is precisely this combination of disparate time lines which informs both Lutie's jazz performances as well as the novel's narrative structure as a whole.

Lutie's vocal talent is first showcased when, treating herself to a glass of beer at Junto's Bar and Grill one night, she is inspired by a song blaring from the jukebox: "[T]he juke-box in the far corner of the room started playing 'Swing It, Sister.' She hummed as she listened to it, not really aware that she was humming or why, knowing only that she felt free here where there was so much space" (146). "Swing It, Sister" was a hit for the tremendously popular singing group and scat pioneers the Mills Brothers back in the 1930s (Friedwald, booklet 4–5).[8] The tune follows the Mills Brothers' standard recipe: accompanied only by guitar, Donald, Herbert, Harry and John Mills sing a bouncy, mid-tempo song imitating the voices of instruments—in this case, muted trumpet, trombone, saxophones, and tuba. Only the third chorus contains actual vocals, where Donald's lead implores the addressee to give in to that "crazy beat" and to "Swing it, sister, / Give it everything you've got." The rest of the performance, four choruses total, consists of the brothers' signature 'instrumentalized' scat-stylings. The song is not only significant in that it functions as a prelude to Lutie's rendition of "Darlin'," which she will sing next and, swinging it in jazz time, give it indeed everything she's got; Lutie hums along with the scat vocals while Junto himself, sitting at his usual table near the back, observes her reflection in the large mirror behind the bar. Thus, Lutie is not the only one who sees herself "look[ing] young, very young, and happy in the mirror" (145). Of course, Junto is too far away to hear Lutie's humming over the din of the customers, but then again Junto, like Boots, is interested in her body, not her voice. The music that he does hear is "Swing It, Sister," and so the Mills Brothers' song accompanies Junto's male gaze of sexual desire. As critic David Wills has observed, scatting is a peculiar variation of singing in that scat is not "a form of prediscursivity similar to the gesture and the cry, but rather the opening of utterance to a supplemental structure—of celebration, of invention, of complaint—whose site of production is nevertheless within the borders of the body. More articulate than a groan or a cry, less than a verbal utterance, the singing of a melody is something like a commentary upon the body issuing from within it" (138). Thus, Lutie's humming and the Mills Brothers' scatting both comment on her body not only as young and happy, but also as very desirable. Scatting, Wills continues, functions "as the vocal interface across which the language of the lyric departs and the sonic purity of the music returns to cement its relationship to the body" (139). Junto is enthralled not by the "purity" of Lutie's artistry, but by the "purity" of her physical beauty. Lutie's wordless, and to Junto inaudible, humming arouses his sexual desire, solidifying in his mind that Lutie is indeed one "swingin' sister," as Donald Mills's vocals and his brothers' scatting inadvertently confirm.[9]

But Lutie's artistic talent is not fully showcased until the jukebox plays the next tune. The song is "Darlin'," a sentimental ballad composed by Lucky Millinder and Frances Kraft Reckling. Recorded on May 26, 1944, six months prior to Lutie's arrival on 116th Street, "Darlin'" was Millinder's latest stab at the charts. Alabama-born and Chicago-raised Lucius Venable "Lucky" Millinder was an alumnus of the Mills Blue Rhythm Band of the 1930s before he organized a big band under his own name in 1940. A favorite at the famous Savoy Ballroom and other Harlem venues, Millinder's high-octane showmanship—he never played an instrument with the band, but sang occasionally—was designed to compete with the likes of Cab Calloway or Louis Jordan, and accordingly the band book contained many novelty numbers like "Who Threw the Whiskey in the Well" or "Big Fat Mama." The band's roster of the early forties nevertheless included musicians with exceptional jazz credentials—trumpeters Dizzy Gillespie and Joe Wilder, saxists Tab Smith and Lucky Thompson, bassist George Duvivier, or drummer Panama Francis, to name just a few.[10] The outfit's main attraction, however, remained Millinder's humorous antics and musical gimmicks as well as a string of singers. The first of the band's featured singers was Sister Rosetta Tharpe, whose highly expressive mezzo-soprano voice gave the new Lucky Millinder Orchestra several hits. Unfortunately, Tharpe left the band in 1944—quite possibly motivated in part also by the famously ribald antics of the other singing star, Wynonie "Mr. Blues" Harris, and of the bandleader himself—to return to her religious singing. Millinder replaced Tharpe with Judy Carol, a vocalist of stunning beauty but rather mediocre talent (Schuller, *Swing* 385–92; Schenker 4). While Harris, and occasionally Millinder, took on the driving jump-blues numbers that began to dominate the Orchestra's repertoire, Carol was primarily used as a balladeer or "canary," in the jargon of the swing era. Despite her musical limitations, her rendition of "Darlin'" became a hit when it was released in 1944.[11]

Typical of the countless sentimental torch songs popular in wartime America, "Darlin'" bemoans the absence of a dear lover. Basically a standard in AABA form, neither the composition itself nor the arrangement contains anything extraordinary—the first two A sections of the middle chorus were cut to accommodate the limitations of the 78 rpm discs—and the lyrics merely recycle a string of well-worn clichés. The first stanza alone summarizes the gist of the song nicely:

Darlin', where are you?
Darlin', how are you?
Darlin', my darlin,'
I'll wait for you.

The recording begins with Ellis Larkins's arpeggiated piano leading into (probably) Freddie Webster's trumpet introduction. Webster simply states the theme in a 'sweet' Harry James style before handing off to Carol. Other than some intonation problems, a few very slight melodic variations in the outgoing chorus (which might, however, be part of the arrangement as well), and a phrasing that occasionally lags behind the beat a bit—obviously, Carol has listened to Billie Holiday—Carol's singing adheres to the score. Taken at a leisurely pace of seventy-four beats per minute, Carol croons her way through the two A sections in D-flat, then arrives at the beginning of the bridge in ominous F minor that soon dissolves through a sunny A-flat major back into D-flat major. After the outgoing repeated A part, the arrangement has the five-man reed section play the melody of the bridge again, augmented by the seven brass for the second half, and driven throughout by an intensified back-beat in the rhythm section. Carol's repetition of the theme brings the performance back to the original languid groove, and things wrap up with a final trumpet flourish. Save for Larkins's occasional piano fills in the background, there is no improvisation, as the entire performance is carefully arranged and written out.

This, then, is the recording that prompts Lutie to sing along at the Junto Bar and Grill. Lutie begins singing "when the voice on the record stopped," that is, she superimposes her vocals on the instrumental bridge (147). Of course, we do not know what notes she sings, but we do know that she signifies on the original lyrics. On the bridge in the first chorus, Carol moans

> There'll be no play
> Until the day
> You're in my arms.
> This heart of mine is only
> Lonely for the one, the one I'll always love, ah—

Over the instrumental bridge in the second chorus, however, Lutie croons "There's no sun, Darlin'. [/] There's no fun, Darlin'" (147).[12] Rhythmically, this contrasts with the score's original "There'll be no play / Until the day." Because her lines are one syllable longer, Lutie must insert at least one additional note into each line, compared to the reed section's four notes per line. Regardless of what rhythmic value Lutie assigns to each of these notes, the meter of her extemporaneous lines must necessarily contrast with that of the original, and therefore with the rhythmic value of the notes played on the record by the saxophone section. Thus, Lutie does indeed 'swing' the song rather than simply sing along; her innate sense of jazz time recasts the original meaning of the lyrics and signifies, to borrow Samuel Floyd's terminology again, on the timeline against the rhythmic pulse of the recorded "Darlin'":

> The men and women crowded at the bar stopped drinking to look at her. Her voice had a thin thread of sadness running through it that made the song important, that made it tell a story that wasn't in the words—a story of despair, of loneliness, of frustration. It was a story that all of them knew by heart and had always known because they had learned it soon after they were born and would go on adding to it until the day they died. Just before the record ended, her voice stopped on a note so low and so long sustained that it was impossible to tell where it left off. (148)

Significantly, it is not the meaning of the lyrics, but the way Lutie recasts them, that makes her performance so exceptional. In other words, the quality of her performance stems not so much from her verbal signifying as from her *rhythmical* signifying, which "wasn't in the words," and which lends an entirely new emotional shade to the song. In short, it is *how* Lutie sings the song, rather than *what* she sings. This compelling shift from *what* to *how,* a shift predicated in and by rhythm, makes Lutie's version a true jazz performance—for, as pianist Bill Evans once put it succinctly, "Jazz is not a 'what,' it's a 'how,' and if you do things according to the 'how' of jazz, it's jazz" (qtd. in Kirchner 3).

Just as Lutie's sense of musical swing time transforms "Darlin'" from a saccharine ditty into a work of art, so does the novel as a whole avail itself of a similar complex layering of literary swing time. Gunther Schuller's attempt at an analysis of swing is again useful here. For Schuller, "the simultaneous integrated flow of performance energies" that generates swing consists of various elements: one of these is

> directed towards maintaining the horizontal flow from note to note. Another element of these energies . . . is involved with the vertical aspects of the music and feeding these up towards the horizontal line. A third part . . . is involved with the opposite: constantly reverting the horizontal line down towards the vertical. This complicated duct system must be maintained at an even flow and perfect balanced control over whatever period of time the performance is to cover. (*Swing* 224)

Thus, swing combines an inexorable forward motion with a loping circular motion. *The Street,* too, moves irresistibly towards the final catastrophe, but this horizontal movement constantly reverts back on itself in parallel plot lines in synchronous or vertical time.

On the one hand, the novel's action is clearly linear, teleological. Its naturalistic determinism is symbolized by the title subject itself: "No one could live on a street like this and stay decent. It would get them sooner or later, for it sucked the humanity out of people—slowly, surely, inevitably," as the protagonist eventually comes to realize (229). Even at the very beginning Lutie must acknowledge that she has "a choice a yard wide and ten miles long" when she muses whether or not to rent the tiny, drab apartment on 116th Street (19). And finally, when Lutie asks for a one-way train ticket to Chicago at Pennsylvania Station after she has killed Boots, she grimly thinks to herself, "Yes, a one-way ticket . . . I've had one since the day I was born" (434). Accordingly, Lutie's linear journey continues at the end of the novel "as the train roared into the darkness" (436). Thus, the text enacts that inevitable forward motion, and Ann Petry herself has said that she "tried to write a story that moves swiftly" (qtd. in Ivy 199).

Lutie's story is ironically accompanied by another teleological, linear narrative, that of the American Dream. Several critics have pointed to the significance of the figure of Benjamin Franklin and his archetypal American rags-to-riches story.[13] Other than a white skin, Lutie, "the All-American black girl" according to one critic, has all the assets needed to realize her own American Dream: talent, creativity, looks, determination, and an unwavering work ethic (Clark 496). Before she moved to 116th Street, she used to work as a maid for the Chandlers, a family of wealthy industrialists, and "[a]fter a year of listening to their talk, she absorbed some of the same spirit. The belief that anybody could be rich if he wanted to and worked hard enough and figured it out carefully enough" (43). And yet, all of these experiences and attributes converge only to produce tragedy for Lutie: her talent and creativity drive her into the insidious designs of Boots and Junto; her looks cause the sociopath Jones to attempt to rape her; and her determination and work ethic cause Bub to fall prey to Jones's ploy and be detained in a children's shelter. Lutie's linear journey toward disaster traces, in reverse, Ben Franklin's journey toward success: "All those years, going to grammar school, going to high school, getting married, having a baby, going to work for the Chandlers, leaving Jim because he got himself another woman—all those years she'd been heading straight as an arrow for that street or some other street just like it. Step by step she'd come, growing up, working, saving, and finally getting an apartment on a street that nobody could have beaten" (426). Lutie's identification with the myth of Ben Franklin, her firm belief "that if Ben Franklin could live on a little bit of money and could prosper, then so could she," and the tragedy this belief brings about only highlights that the myth of the American Dream, encoded and disseminated by white males, is designed to exclude her (64).[14] America's foundational myths of national identity governing its social, political, and economic evolvement—from the Puritan errand into the wilderness, to the western frontier, to manifest destiny, and so on—are all *teleological* myths (Bercovitch 7–8). They allow Ben Franklin, Junto, the Chandlers, and even the Italian immigrant family of the Pizzinis to pursue their American Dream; but for Lutie Johnson, black and female, they lead to an American Nightmare.

Precisely because the linear, horizontal trajectory of Lutie's life is accelerated by her jazz performances, leading not to the city upon the hill but to Chicago's South Side, the narrative flow constantly reverts back on itself. The novel's linear kinesis, analogous to the horizontal elements in Schuller's definition of swing, is continuously subverted by a narrative sequencing that appears momentarily to arrest the progress toward the story's inevitable destination—bringing to mind saxophonist Anthony Braxton's somewhat cryptic definition of swing as "gravitational intrigue" (qtd. in Lock 153). Therefore, just as in swing, the novel's horizontal elements are complemented by vertical elements, too, namely the parallel plot lines which time and again disrupt the linear teleology of the narrative.

Throughout the novel, the narrative point of view shifts between different characters, and almost all of their stories feature recurrent flashbacks. Moreover, especially in the first half of the book, the narrative structure repeatedly circles back to the same events, retelling them from a different character's perspective, or to different if related events that occur simultaneously. For instance, the first three chapters are narrated from Lutie's point of view, beginning with her deciphering of the wind-tossed sign and ending with her walking up to the Junto Bar and Grill. While chapter four focuses on Jones and begins with him watching Lutie leave the building, the entire chapter seems to arrest time: it narrates in flashbacks how Jones ended up on the street, but it also renarrates in unsettling detail the scene from the very first chapter in which Lutie inspects the apartment and senses the superintendent's sociopathic desire. After Jones has groped through Lutie's closet while Bub is out getting a bottle of beer for him, the chapter ends with Jones back in his own apartment, puzzled by the absence of Min, his submissive live-in girlfriend. Thus, in real time, chapter four advances the action for only a few hours at most. Chapter five once again circles back in chronological time, beginning with Min making supper earlier that evening. While Lutie is at the bar and Jones in her apartment, Min pays a visit to David the Prophet, a root doctor who provides her with the means to keep Jones at bay, and the chapter ends with Min's first successful rebuking of Jones. Chapters six through eight cover the time between Lutie's arrival at the bar and her preparation the next morning for the audition with Boots's band. Here, the narrative development is chronological, save for several long flashbacks, but much of it covers the same time span as did chapters four and five. In fact, the actual time covered by the narrative from the end of chapter three—Lutie leaving for the bar—through the beginning of chapter twelve—Jones returning to his apartment after the attempted rape of Lutie—amounts to little more than twenty-four hours. In the intervening almost two hundred pages, the narrative constantly rewinds the plot, developing the action in stops and starts, moving forward for at most a few hours at a time. And significantly, this time frame is demarcated by Lutie's two renditions of "Darlin'" in swing time: the first in the Junto Bar and Grill that leads to her introduction to Boots, the second one the following night at the Casino that gives rise to Junto's nefarious design and that leads to Jones's attempt to rape her later.

The sequencing of these parallel plot lines on the one hand creates the effect of arrested development (that is, vertical movement), suggesting that Lutie's efforts to escape the street and its pernicious influences are all in vain. On the other hand, each of the parallel plot lines pushes Lutie ever closer to disaster (that is, horizontal movement) by enhancing the inevitability of her eventual downfall. While the action in the last few chapters does pick up speed considerably, the novel's ending once again emphasizes the simultaneity of linear, horizontal, and circular, vertical, movement: the penultimate scene shows Lutie on the train to Chicago, a linear journey for the protagonist, but in the subsequent, last scene the novel closes with another snapshot image of the street that opened the book, a circular journey for the narrative. Moreover, Lutie's linear train journey into an unknown, foreboding future is accompanied by the motif of the circle:

> As the train started to move, she began to trace a design on the window. It was a series of circles that flowed into each other. . . . Her finger moved over the glass, around and around. The circles showed up plainly on the dusty surface. . . . The train crept out of the tunnel, gathered speed as it left the city behind. Snow whis-

> pered against the windows. And as the train roared into the darkness, Lutie tried to figure out by what twists and turns of fate she had landed on this train. Her mind balked at the task. It was that street. It was that god-damned street. (435–36)

The circular "twists and turns" of the narrative itself are accompanied by the deterministic teleology of the street's pernicious forces.[15] Significantly, Lutie's drawing of a series of circles at a time when the narrative propels her furthest into the future is occasioned by the flashback that reaches furthest into her past: the circles are occasioned by her memory of a writing exercise she and her peers were taught in grammar school so as "to get the proper slant to their writing" (435).[16] Yet again, the novel's exploration of swing time effects a kinesis that is at once linear and circular.

Thus, the novel's narrative sequencing is indeed Schuller's "complicated duct system" in jazz time, that complex interaction of the linear and circular elements of swing. Lutie's figurative one-way ticket to disaster is accentuated by a narrative sequencing that constantly circles back on itself, ensnaring her in ever-tightening circles of male desire. Musicologist Wilfried Raussert observes that swing time "subverts the idea of time as a linear, teleological process. Although it postulates a regularity of temporal progression—the influence of European marches becomes audible here—it continuously disrupts and even negates such a regular movement. A polyrhythmic effect—African sources manifest themselves—results from a flexible change of beat sequences" (521). Just as the action of *The Street* marches inexorably toward tragedy, so its own flexible change of narrative sequencing continuously disrupts the regular chronology of the events at whose very center is Lutie's performance of "Darlin'." Combining linear and circular, or horizontal and vertical elements, *The Street* is indeed a book narrated in swing time.

III. "Ornamenting the Passage of Time": Billie Holiday's "All of Me" and *The Street* as Jazz Text

"Time," notes Ishmael Reed in *Mumbo Jumbo,* "is a pendulum. Not a river. More akin to what goes around comes around" (218). And if jazz is "a way of ornamenting the passage of time," as Dick Hebdige once put it euphemistically, then so is narration, and *The Street*'s way of temporal ornamentation does indeed make it a jazz novel, even though it is not 'about' jazz per se (336). The reader experiences the same "slightly different sense of time" as Ellison's invisible man listening to Louis Armstrong: "you're never quite on the beat. Sometimes you're ahead and sometimes you're behind. Instead of the swift and imperceptible flowing of time, you are aware of its nodes, those points where time stands still or from which it leaps ahead. And you slip into the breaks and look around" (*Invisible* 8).

In terms of jazz music itself, the narrative sequencing of events in Petry's novel echoes, for instance, the dynamic layering of rhythmic time in Billie Holiday's famous 1941 recording of "All of Me" with the Eddie Heywood Orchestra.[17] Even though Holiday does not change Seymour Simons's lyrics at all, her melodic alterations (the vertical movement of harmony) and rhythmic modulations (the horizontal movement of rhythm) achieve a maximum of emotional expressivity. Heywood's arrangement takes the Gerald Marks score at a bouncy 110 beats per minute without reharmonizing the standard. Holiday, on the other hand, takes remarkable melodic and rhythmic liberties. Her vertical, harmonic alterations to the melody are characterized by a consistent lowering of intervals and by a downward bending of the pitch on central words like "goodbye" in her second chorus. The linear, rhythmic variations emphasize and enhance her characteristic behind-the-beat phrasing even more; for instance, in the second chorus Holiday both subtly delays and markedly elongates the "on" in the lines "How can I / Go on, dear, without you," contrasting noticeably with the underlying steady forward pulse provided by the band. Thus, the upbeat drive of Heywood's arrangement, akin to the linear teleology of *The Street,* is accompanied by Holiday's singing that consistently lags behind; her persona is literally left back refusing to be swept up by the orchestra's forward rhythm, persisting instead in its melancholy plea to "take all of me," analogous to *The Street*'s narrative that constantly reverts back on itself.[18] Clearly then, both "All of Me" and *The Street* derive their peculiar artistic power from the dynamic interaction between their respective horizontal and vertical elements.

To be sure, Petry's book is obviously a pre-arranged composition, as it were, and one that is most carefully executed; it does not contain an equivalent to Lester Young's tenor saxophone solo on "All of Me." Nor is it an unstable text like *Treat It Gentle,* or an improvisational story like Bechet's narrative of Omar. The lack of literary improvisation and textual instability, however, does not disqualify the novel as a jazz text. First of all, it is often forgotten that in the history of the music, improvisation did not become a *sine qua non* until the bebop revolution of the mid- to late 1940s. It was a common practice in earlier styles of jazz, especially big band swing, to have pre-composed solos, written out solos; Sidney Bechet, as I have pointed out, practiced set phrases in advance that later only sounded as if they were being invented spontaneously when he played them on stage. Quite frequently, too, star soloists in big bands would repeat a famous solo note for note, and sometimes it would not even be their own solo originally (Schuller, *Swing* 307–8; Berendt 161–64). Such solos, or entire performances even, may *seem* completely spontaneous, but they rely—albeit much more so than later styles of improvisation—on what Albert Murray has called "a very specific technology of stylization" (99).[19] Even in the second half of the twentieth century one can find numerous examples of jazz with little or no improvisation, for instance many of Duke Ellington's suites or Miles Davis's collaborations with arranger Gil Evans. Lucky Millinder's "Darlin'" also contains virtually no improvisation, yet it is still unmistakably a jazz performance. In general, the popular notion that the improvising jazz musician is a mere vessel of sheer talent or is struck by some bolt of quasi-divine inspiration at the outset of each solo is patently false. As the exhaustive studies of Ingrid Monson and Paul Berliner demonstrate—not to mention the countless interviews and memoirs of musician themselves—the art of jazz improvisation demands years, decades even, of constant learning and practice (much of it in isolation) of scales, chords, rhythms, licks, phrases, of studying harmony, of transcribing and memorizing recorded solos. Just as an everyday conversation consists largely of words, phrases, and entire sentences that we have 'practiced' or used before and hence of very little truly spontaneous extemporization, so does jazz improvisation consist also of elements of licks, solos, phrases, and melodies that the musicians have incorporated into their musical vocabulary before they go on stage each evening. "It is important to note," Gayl Jones stresses correctly, "that in jazz the concepts of 'improvisational' and 'extemporaneity' are only a manner of speaking: jazz is a mastery of technique, and a superb jazz text is as exacting a form as its musical counterpart. This technique is not like 'automatic writing,' because the jazz musician (and writer) . . . improvises upon traditional materials" (201).

Accordingly, for Petry—as for Ellington and Davis, for that matter—"a good story" and "good music" both retain a sense of spontaneity ("A Visit" 84). At the same time, both writing and music are also demanding crafts that exact much disciplined work from their respective practitioners: "It comes to you as you write," she simply said of the creative process, but also emphasized that she does not "freewheel" on the typewriter and revises constantly ("From" 72; "Visit" 82). Thus, the process of writing Petry describes also occurs, like jazz, within a dynamic field of tension framed by spontaneity and planning, inspiration and revision. As fellow writer Robert Creeley notes, improvisation is actually "the experience of possibility within the limits of his [the improviser's] material (sound and duration) and their environment" (qtd. in Mackey, *Discrepant* 9). Seconds Berndt Ostendorf: "Improvisation is not free in the sense of being arbitrary. It follows the difficult discipline of searching out the inherent curve of language as collective consciousness in finding the inherent rhythms and rituals of the vernacular" (115). And so, given its musical reference points and its literary translation of swing time, *The Street* does indeed constitute a jazz text, and Ann Petry is the consummate artist who makes it swing.

CHAPTER 3

Bopping Billy Clubs, Burning Cadillacs, and Wigged-out Aliens

JAZZ AND VIOLENCE IN SHORT STORIES BY LANGSTON HUGHES, RALPH ELLISON, AND AMIRI BARAKA

> As all Marines are riflemen, all members of the Arkestra are percussionists.
>
> SUN RA, personnel list of *Space Is the Place*

The very first short story Ann Petry published in the fall of 1939—under the nom de plume Arnold Petri—did not exactly intimate the trenchant interrogation of capitalism, race, and gender that was to inform *The Street*. "Marie of the Cabin Club" appeared in the pages of the Baltimore-based *Afro-American* and is an improbable mixture of romance and mystery. The title character works as a cigarette girl at the Cabin Club, a jazz venue. Trumpet virtuoso Georgie Barr gigs there on a regular basis, and "[t]he high, thin, sweet sound that came out [of his instrument] made her skin prickle and set her pulse to beating faster and faster" (14). Marie has not been able to approach Georgie, however, as he spends intermissions at the table of "an artificial looking white woman" (14). When Marie manages to save the trumpeter's life in a knife-fight, the two become friends. Soon she discovers that their every move, especially Georgie's, is monitored carefully by an Englishman (with requisite monocle). One night, Marie is kidnapped and taken to the stately mansion of the English mystery man, who threatens and beats her. He coerces Marie into telephoning Georgie, who arrives presently. It turns out that Marie's captor intends to exchange her for Rosa Marin, the white woman from the Cabin Club. Georgie refuses, and instead produces a squad of armed policemen storming the premises. The kidnapper is taken into custody, and Marie learns that Rosa Marin is actually a spy. Marin had recruited Georgie in France during his last

European tour, and after his return stateside she followed him, apparently to collect intelligence on the domestic espionage activities of the Axis powers. They agreed on the club as the least conspicuous place to exchange information, but the Englishman, spying for the Japanese, somehow got wind of it and intended to neutralize Marin. With all the mysteries resolved and the danger averted, Marie and Georgie pledge each other eternal love and "forgot all about Rosa Marin" until the day of the wedding, when they receive "by special messenger" a silver tea service courtesy of Marin and the French government (14).

Unlike *The Street* or "Solo on the Drums," "Marie of the Cabin Club" is not really a jazz text. The "unearthly" and "miraculous music" tumbling from the bell of Georgie Barr's trumpet has no function other than to inject an aura of (sexual) excitement into the goings-on and to allude to other popular stereotypes of jazz as an 'underground' music always on the edge (14). Of course, the figure of a trumpet virtuoso is more alluring than that of, say, a bartender or doorman, and the ancillary references to Georgie's music are designed simply to enhance his desirability for Marie as well as our suspense. Nonetheless, the short story is indicative of a rather curious theme in African American jazz narrative, namely the linkage between jazz, (political) power, and violence. The struggle between Omar and Marie's master in *Treat It Gentle* as well as Bechet's own violent outbursts, Kid Jones's fantasy of dismembering his rival in "Solo on the Drums," Lutie's surreal nightmare of the Super and her brutal killing of Boots in *The Street*, and, as we shall see, several bizarre acts of violence in Toni Morrison's *Jazz*—all of this suggests that there is more than a casual connection between jazz and violence. The suggestion deepens when we remember Langston Hughes's description of drowning out the sound of exploding artillery shells in besieged Madrid by playing his Ellington, Goodman, or Lunceford records at full volume (*I Wonder* 340–41); of Ralph Ellison's invisible man, who plays Armstrong's recording of "What Did I Do to Be So Black and Blue" as a prelude to the battle royal (*Invisible* 7–8); or of Amiri Baraka's Clay, who is fatally stabbed after he exclaims that Charlie Parker would have roamed the streets of New York City murdering white people had he not had a saxophone (*Dutchman* 97–98).

To be sure, physical violence has been a presence in the lives of many jazz musicians: one is reminded, for instance, of Sidney Bechet's famous shootout, Wild West-style, in the streets of Paris; of Charles Mingus's attraction to fire axes; or of Stan Getz's predilection for spousal abuse. Nonetheless, jazz is not (or is no longer) a musical genre readily associated with violent behavior. The excesses of rock 'n' roll and, later, hip-hop have long since eclipsed the association of jazz with vice and gangsterdom popular in the early days of the music (Ogren, *Jazz* 56–65).[1] And yet, pianist and jazz historian Ben Sidran insists that "Black music is a kind of 'ritualization' . . . which can channel black aggression toward constructive and creative ends. It does not drain away that aggression but redirects it, in a more highly articulated form" (139). Thus, jazz as a form of ritual violence is also a political tool. To Jacques Attali, music—all music—intrinsically contains violence and is a primary tool for the negotiation of political power: "*Noise is a weapon and music, primordially, is the formation, domestication, and ritualization of that weapon as a simulacrum of ritual murder*" (24). As a way of regulating and structuring noise, music "*creates political order because it is a minor form of sacrifice.* In the space of noise, *it symbolically signifies the channeling of violence and the imaginary, the ritualization of a murder substituted for the general violence, the affirmation that a society is possible if the imaginary of individuals is sublimated*" (25–26).[2] If Attali is correct, it should come as no surprise that this connection between music and violence is particularly salient in the United States. Sacvan Bercovitch sees in American history a perennial "simultaneity of violence and cultural formation" (9). And Ralph Ellison, for whom the black experience in the New World remained central to the project of the American democracy—and who, after all, *lived* this simultaneity of violent oppression and cultural production—observed in *Going to the Territory:*

> Indeed, a battle-royal conflict of interests appears to be basic to our conception of freedom, and the drama of democracy proceeds through a warfare of words and symbolic actions by which we seek to advance our private interests while resolving our political differences. Since the Civil War this form of symbolic action has served as a moral substitute for armed warfare, and we have managed to restrain ourselves to a debate which we carry on in the not always justified faith that the outcome will serve the larger interests of democracy. (595)

Ellison also stressed time and again that this symbolic action is, to invert Carl von Clausewitz's famous dictum, more than just the continuation of war by other means: "Any people who could endure all of that brutalization and keep together, who could undergo such dismemberment, resuscitate itself, and endure until it could take the initiative in achieving its own freedom is obviously more than the sum of its brutalization" (Ellison, *Going* 737; von Clausewitz 210). To Ellison, jazz musicians were "that most representative group of Negro Americans"—and hence, he might have added, representative of all Americans—in their everlasting quest not just to perfect their art, but to reinvent it (*Going* 749). The question now becomes how the jazz aesthetic negotiates violence: how does it critique, subvert, or lay claim to power within a political system that, historically, has disenfranchised African Americans? It is precisely this nexus between power, violence, and jazz that Langston Hughes's short story "Bop," Ralph Ellison's "Cadillac Flambé," and Amiri Baraka's "Answers in Progress" explore.

I. "MOP! MOP! . . . BE-BOP!": Sense and Nonsense in Langston Hughes's "Bop"

There can be no doubt that what Louis Armstrong was to jazz music, Langston Hughes was to jazz literature. Almost single-handedly, Armstrong created the basis for a jazz tradition—Hughes did the same for jazz literature. Curiously, African American writers produced virtually no jazz literature during the 1920s. In part, this was due to the fact that Armstrong, Bechet, Ellington, and others were at the time still creating what would become the foundation of the jazz tradition. In the age dubbed the Jazz Age, most Americans paradoxically did not recognize yet in jazz a distinct art form with its own antecedents and origins, nor did they necessarily recognize it when they heard it. After all, *The Jazz Singer,* like F. Scott Fitzgerald's short story collection, was about anything *but* jazz. In the 1920s, the word *jazz* was readily tagged on to just about any commercial and popular form of music (Evans 105–7; Ogren, *Jazz* 139–46; Sudhalter, "Hot" 149–51).

Another reason for the relative dearth of jazz narratives was that some of the most powerful Harlem Renaissance leaders were suspicious of this rowdy, hybrid, new art form. Men like Du Bois, Locke, or Johnson, always concerned with the 'respectability' of black American cultural production, saw in jazz (and blues) at best the source material for some higher, more refined art (Anderson 118–19; Brooker, "Modernism" 231–40; Floyd, *Power* 106–9; Ogren, "Controversial" 162–68). Consequently, they favored the symphonic concert music of a William Grant Still over the pioneering jazz of an Edward Kennedy Ellington. As Nathan Huggins concluded,

> Harlem intellectuals promoted Negro art, but one thing is very curious, except for Langston Hughes, none of them took jazz—the

> new music—seriously. Of course, they all mentioned it as background, as descriptive of Harlem life. All said it was important in the definition of the New Negro. But none thought enough about it to try and figure out what was happening. They tended to view it as a folk art—like the spirituals and the dance—the unrefined source for the new art. . . . [T]he promoters of the Harlem Renaissance were so fixed on a vision of *high* culture that they did not look very hard or well at jazz. (9–10)

Representative of this treatment of jazz as descriptive background in Harlem Renaissance fiction is Claude McKay's *Home to Harlem.* The references to jazz are numerous, but their primary purpose is to infuse the exotic-erotic soundtrack with a "primitive, voluptuous rhythm" (337) accompanying the protagonist's sexual conquests in a teeming, urban setting where

> the atmosphere was fairly bacchic and jazz music was snake-wriggling in and out and around everything and forcing everybody into amatory states and attitudes. . . . The women, carried away by the sheer rhythm of delight, had risen above their commercial instincts (a common trait of Negroes in emotional states) and abandoned themselves to pure voluptuous jazzing. They were gorgeous animals swaying there through the dance, punctuating it with marks of warm physical excitement. The atmosphere was charged with intensity and over-charged with currents of personal reaction. (107–8)

Similarly to Petry's "Marie of the Cabin Club," jazz in *Home to Harlem* simply charges the plot's backdrop with some added titillation but does not constitute an aesthetic that informs the text in its entirety.[3]

Hughes himself initially explored the literary potential of black music—not just jazz, but the blues, spirituals, and folk songs—in poetry.[4] Not until his first novel, the 1930 *Not without Laughter,* did Hughes begin to tap black music in a sustained fashion in prose. Even then, jazz was only one ingredient in a mélange of sounds reverberating through the narrative. Jazz in the Jazz Age was indeed still "waiting to be the music," in Sidney Bechet's words, and so Hughes's novel reflected a music that was only just beginning to gel from the collision of myriad styles, genres, and regional influences (Bechet 4): "Those mean old weary blues coming from a little orchestra of four men who needed no written music because they couldn't have read it. Four men and a leader—Rattle Benbow from

Galveston; Benbow's buddy, the drummer, from Houston; his banjoist from Birmingham; his cornetist from Atlanta; and the pianist, long-fingered, sissyfied, a coal-black lad from New Orleans who had brought with him an exaggerated rag-time which he called jazz" (Hughes, *Not* 78).[5]

By 1942, when Langston Hughes began writing his regular column "Here to Yonder" for the *Chicago Defender,* not only had jazz found itself, it had developed into America's pop music. But the country had just entered World War II, and the changing times seemed to call for a change in jazz as well. In that same year, 1942, Dizzy Gillespie left Lucky Millinder's band and joined Earl "Fatha" Hines, where he met a young saxophonist named Charlie Parker (Gillespie 162–63, 173–74). The bebop revolution was incubated. Bebop was everything the music of the grandiose swing orchestras of the previous decade was not: bebop was often politically conscious and self-assuredly black; it was frenetic, screaming, high-octane jazz at sometimes mind-boggling speeds. "Damn right!" exclaims Gillespie about the early days of bop, "We refused to accept racism, poverty, or economic exploitation, nor would we live out uncreative humdrum lives merely for the sake of survival. . . . If America wouldn't honor its Constitution and respect us as men, we couldn't give a shit about the American way. And they made it damn near un-American to appreciate our music" (287). Or, as Charlie Parker's alto saxophone famously declared, "Now's the Time" for a new music with a new attitude. It seemed indeed a music born out of the chaos of wartime. No wonder, then, that there was another voice that accompanied the bebop revolution, namely that of Jessie B. Simple. A year after Parker and Gillespie had joined forces, he made his first appearance in Hughes's "From Here to Yonder" column in 1943. At first identified only as "my Simple Minded Friend," Hughes had originally conceived Jessie B. Semple, eventually renamed Simple, as a propaganda tool to drum up black support for the war effort, but Simple soon proved this to be too simple of a role for him and took on a life of his own (Rampersad, *Life II* 61–64; Harper 23–44). Quick-witted, assertive, impatient, proud of his race, with a hipster lexicon all his own, Simple seemed in many ways the perfect literary foil to the beboppers at Minton's and Monroe's, just a few blocks away from Paddy's Bar, Simple's favorite hangout. Not surprisingly, Simple dug bop, too.

On November 19, 1949, Hughes published "Simple Declares Be-Bop Music Comes from Bop! Bop! Bop! Mop!" as one of his last *Defender* columns (Harper 242). As he did with his other Simple columns, Hughes revised it for inclusion in the 1953 collection *Simple Takes a Wife,* the second in the Simple series, and selected it for the 1961 *The Best of Simple* as well.[6] "Bop" is a vignette which follows the well-established call and response formula of pitting the somewhat obtuse narrator against the wily Jessie B. Simple. As the narrator walks past Simple's house on a Sunday, he finds him on the stoop scatting along Dizzy Gillespie's "Ool-ya-koo" emanating from the record player in an upstairs apartment[7]:

> "All that nonsense singing reminds me of Cab Calloway back in the old *scat* days," I said, "around 1930 when he was chanting, 'Hi-de-*hie*-de-ho! Hee-de-*hee*-de-hee.'"
>
> "Not at all," said Simple, "absolutely not at all."
>
> "Re-Bop certainly sounds like scat to me," I insisted.
>
> "No," said Simple, "Daddy-o, you are wrong. Besides, it was not *Re*-Bop. It is *Be*-Bop."
>
> "What's the difference," I asked, "between *Re* and *Be?*"
>
> "A lot," said Simple. "Re-bop was an imitation like most of the white boys play. Be-Bop is the real thing like the colored boys play."
>
> "You bring race into everything," I said, "even music."
>
> "It is in everything," said Simple.
>
> "Anyway, Be-Bop is passé, gone, finished."
>
> "It may be gone, but its riffs remain behind," said Simple. (*Early* 227)[8]

Despite Simple's subsequent edification of the narrator, the latter still maintains his opinion that bebop's scat vocals—the instrumentalization of the human voice—are devoid of meaning:

> "It all sounds like pure nonsense syllables to me."
>
> "Nonsense, nothing!" cried Simple. "Bop makes plenty of sense."
>
> "What kind of sense?"
>
> "You must not know where Bop comes from," said Simple, astonished at my ignorance.
>
> "I do not know," I said. "Where?"
>
> "From the police," said Simple.
>
> "What do you mean, from the police?"
>
> "From the police beating Negroes' heads," said Simple. "Every time a cop hits a Negro with his billy club, that old club says, 'BOP! BOP! . . . BE-BOP! . . . MOP! . . . BOP!'
>
> "That Negro hollers, 'Ooool-ya-koo! Ou-o-o!'

> "Old Cop just keeps on, 'MOP! MOP! . . . BE-BOP! . . . MOP!' That's where Be-Bop came from, beaten right out of some Negro's head into them horns and saxophones and piano keys that plays it. Do you call that nonsense?"
>
> "If it's true, I do not," I said. (227–28)

And, of course, it is not true. While the precise etymologies of the early, and soon largely obsolete term *rebop,* its synonym *bebop,* and the commonly used abbreviation *bop,* are unverifiable—as is so much else in the music's history—, jazz scholars agree that the terms derive from two of the most frequently used vocables in scat singing, that is, *rebop* and *bebop.* Recorded examples of the recurrent use of these vocables date back as early as Louis Armstrong's 1927 rendition of "Hotter Than That," for example (Baraka, *Black* 74–75; "Bop" 137–38; DeVaux, "Advent" 292; "Rebop" 403).[9] Hughes himself was very much aware of the actual etymology of the words *bebop* and *rebop* (*First* 59). At the same time, jazz lore is replete with stories of white musicians invading the uptown nightspots in the early 1940s to scribble down furtively on their shirt cuffs the brand new licks the black jazz artists on stage were inventing—part of what Amiri Baraka has accurately identified as "the Great Music Robbery"—or with the occasional assertion that the complexity of bebop harmonies was designed specifically to keep white players out of jam sessions (DeVeaux, *Birth* 351–52; "Advent" 295–302; Baraka and Baraka 331). Accounts of the participants in the birth of bebop vary. Predictably, white musicians tend not to recall any race-based discrimination and emphasize that the litmus test was always musical ability, while black artists—especially if they sense that their interlocutor is sympathetic—will sometimes intimate that the increasing chordal complexity was indeed a deliberate attempt to contain white imitators (Gerard 23–26). In jazz historiography, the issue of race is closely linked with the ongoing debate over the evolution of bebop: some students of the music, like Gunther Schuller for instance, see bop primarily as an aesthetic response to the worn-out clichés of the big band era, while others, like Amiri Baraka, insist that bebop grew out of a more explicitly militant political stance of its black creators (Gennari 475–98). Arguably, Scott DeVaux's analysis is the most nuanced:

> Entrenched patterns of segregation, both in the music industry and in society at large, automatically gave white musicians a nearly insuperable advantage in the mainstream market, blunting black ambition and forcing it into new channels. Bebop was a

> response to this impasse, an attempt to reconstitute jazz—or more precisely, the specialized idiom of the improvising virtuoso—in such a way as to give its black creators the greatest professional autonomy *within* the marketplace. Bop was the twin child of optimism and frustration, of ingenuity and despair. (*Birth* 27)

In any event, Simple's racial distinction between rebop and bebop is pure fabrication: no bebopper or jazz historian relates an ethnic distinction between bebop and rebop. In fact, Gillespie himself was commonly introduced as "Professor Rebop" in the 1940s before the term eventually fell into general disuse.[10] Simple's account of the origins of bebop in the sonic potential of billy clubs is therefore simply apocryphal.

But, as usual, nothing is that simple with Simple. His explanation that police brutality gave the music its name moves along very similar lines as Sidney Bechet's fictional story of Omar and the origins of jazz. Just as Bechet adduces the exigencies of American history, the historical context of chattel slavery in America, in order to explain jazz, so does Simple place bebop within a specific socio-historical context, the institutionalized violence inflicted upon African Americans by a political apparatus dominated by whites. And just as the telling of Omar and Marie's story of enslavement and murder allows Bechet to strive for a figurative space of at least temporary freedom, so does Simple's account of police brutality and black cultural production aim to assert African American identity and humanity, and to find in that imaginative assertion the freedom of artistic creation.

Jessie B. Simple's insistence on the politicization of bebop scatting recalls Lutie Johnson's humming to the Mills Brothers' "Swing It, Sister" in *The Street*. It also recalls David Wills's definition of scat as "the opening of utterance to a supplemental structure—of celebration, of invention, of complaint—whose site of production is nevertheless within the borders of the body" (138). Simple's appraisal—and practice—of bebop scatting is precisely that: not just a complaint, but simultaneously a celebration and an invention. Significantly, according to Simple, this at once plaintive and celebratory invention issues forth from within violated black bodies. Enhancing the blackness of black bodies, the "nonsense" vocables of scat are therefore a direct channelization of state-sanctioned violence. Attali's discussion of noise is once again useful at this point: to Attali, music is the result of an effort to impose order and structure on the disorder and chaos of noise. Thus, if music is meaning, noise is the absence of meaning, that is, nonsense (3–9, 122–24). At the same time though, precisely because noise is devoid of meaning, because it is nonsense, it contains the potential to create new meanings, to make sense: "the very absence of meaning in pure noise or in the meaningless repetition of a message, by unchanneling the auditory sensations, frees the listener's imagination" (33). The imaginative powers that are unleashed in and through noise can in turn create a new and different order (or, for that matter, find new ways to consolidate the existing one): "Listening to music is listening to all noise, realizing that its appropriation and control is a reflection of power, that it is essentially political" (6).[11]

Though historically inaccurate, Simple's explanation of the difference between rebop and bebop constitutes such a political act of reinscribing history through the free improvisation of the human imagination. First, there is indeed a lot of difference between *"Re"* and *"Be,"* as Simple elaborates: "Be-Bop music was certainly colored folks' music—which is why white folks found it so hard to imitate. But there are some few white boys that latched onto it right well. And no wonder, because they sat and listened to Dizzy, Thelonius, Tad [*sic*] Dameron, Charlie Parker, also Mary Lou, all night long, every time they got a chance, and bought their records by the dozens to copy their riffs" (*Early Simple* 228).[12] The difference between rebop and bebop, then, is that between *re*plication and *be*coming. For the white jazz musician, Simple suggests, bebop is matter purely of technique, a matter of craft: its riffs, licks, and chords can be learned from recordings—what Attali refers to as stockpiled use-time—and, once 'mastered,' are replicated in his or her own playing, thus becoming *re*-bop (Attali 124–27). For the black jazz musician, bebop is not just an abstract, technical art form: *be*-bop is also *living* use-time, an ontological process of negotiating and mediating the terrors of American history in striving towards a human identity of blackness.[13]

Secondly, Simple's *be*-bop is a political act of empowerment turning the hierarchical order of sense (music) and nonsense (noise) on its head. By labeling bebop scatting sheer nonsense—in other words, noise—the narrator echoes the cultural mainstream. Simple, on the other hand, by making sense of nonsense, music out of noise, exposes the ostensibly rational power structure as utterly nonsensical. "Bop comes out of them dark days," Simple affirms: "That's why real Bop is mad, wild, frantic, crazy—and not to be dug unless you've seen dark days, too" (*Early Simple* 228). In other words, to those unfamiliar with the black experience in America—"them dark days"—bop sounds indeed like noise. As Simple continues: "They think Bop is nonsense—like you. They think it's just *crazy* crazy. They do not know Bop is also MAD CRAZY, SAD CRAZY, FRANTIC WILD CRAZY—beat out of somebody's head! That's what Bop is. Them young colored kids who started it, they know what Bop is"

(228). In the concluding exchange between Simple and the narrator, the binary pair of sense/nonsense has become completely inverted: "'Your explanation depresses me,' I said. 'Your nonsense depresses me,' said Simple" (228). Simple has made sense out of nonsense (his "explanation") and thus revealed the narrator's initial charge of nonsensical noise as nonsense itself. Tapping into the potential of meaningless noise—the sound of the words *bebop* and *rebop*—Simple forges a life-affirming meaning that challenges and subverts the politics of the cultural mainstream. The political leadership of American society insists on the rationality of *de facto* or even legalized racial subjugation. This claim to reason is enforced and maintained through violence, symbolized here in the billy clubs of white police officers. Policing a political structure that claims to make sense legitimizes, even necessitates, the use of physical violence. The violence visited upon those who resist this claim to reason is channeled by and in the ostensibly unreasonable and nonsensical noise of bebop scatting. However, Simple's imaginative and improvisational channelization of violence unmasks the power structure's politics of implementing and maintaining what purports to be sensible order for what it is: utterly unreasonable, brutally irrational. Or, as R. Baxter Miller puts it, in the "blues fantasy" of Simple, "the wild leaps of contradiction and inconsistency pose no incongruity at all, at least none more ridiculous than those that take place in a society based on reason and morality yet still allowing racial segregation in the 1950s" (*Art* 112, 110). The violent irrationality of racism is exposed in a seemingly nonsensical tale of how noise becomes music: in Simple's story, the state becomes the purveyor of nonsensical noise, and the storyteller the purveyor of human sense, that is, music. "Part of the genius of black music," Nathaniel Mackey points out astutely, "is the room it allows for a telling 'inarticulacy,' a feature consistent with its critique of a predatory coherence, a cannibalistic 'plan of living,' and the articulacy that upholds it" (*Discrepant* 252–53). Hence, where the narrator of "Bop" hears jarring noise, Jessie B. Simple hears, and tells of, a sound will to live. Attali writes,

> The only possible challenge to repetitive power takes the route of a breach in social repetition and the control of noisemaking. In more day-to-day political terms, it takes the route of the permanent affirmation of the right to be different. . . . [I]t is the conquest of the right to make noise, in other words, to create one's own code and work, without advertising its goal in advance; it is the conquest of the right to make the free and revocable choice to

> interlink in another's code—that is, the right to compose one's life. (132)

And this, of course, is precisely what Simple practices, sitting on his stoop and scatting along with Dizzy Gillespie's "Ool-ya-koo." These "disc-tortions," as Hughes called them in the prefatory note to his bop-inflected *Montage of a Dream Deferred,* are therefore not only aesthetic claims to compose art, but also *political* claims to compose life (*Collected* 387).[14]

It is therefore certainly no coincidence that both the literary figure of Simple with his witty yet trenchant "disc-tortions" and the music of bebop with, as Eric Lott termed it, its "ritual dismemberment" of the pop music of the swinging thirties originated in an era ravaged by global violence on a heretofore unknown scale (601). The inspiration for Simple, as Langston Hughes tells us, was a man he met in a Harlem bar in the early 1940s who worked in a war plant making "cranks" (*Best* vii). America's involvement in World War II also had a decisive influence on the music of bebop, in a way. As Dexter Gordon, one of the original boppers, put it:

> I think all the cats were aware of the fact that what we were doing, what we were playing was new, was revolutionary . . . and it was accepted to a degree and then again, there was always somebody putting it down. I really think it was the start of the revolution, the civil-rights movement, in that sense, because that's what the music is talking about. This is all the young generation, a new generation at the time. And they're not satisfied with the shit that's going down. Because they know there should be changes being made. And actually it was a time of change because it was wartime and people were moving back and forth all over the United States and constantly traveling—armies, war jobs, defense jobs. It was a time of great flux. And it was a time of change, and the music was reflecting this. And we were putting our voice into what we thought was about to be the thing. (qtd. in Gitler, *Swing to Bop* 311)

No wonder, then, that these same violent times also gave birth to Jessie B. Simple, whose voice in the 1950s and '60s would come to speak out about the civil rights struggle just as eloquently.[15] And no wonder, then, that one former candidate for the US presidency—Dizzy Gillespie himself—copped a lick from Jessie B. Simple, as it were, and entitled his memoirs *To BE . . . or Not to BOP.*[16]

II. Jazz as Violent Performance Art: Ralph Ellison's "Cadillac Flambé"

In 1961, Langston Hughes published his collection *The Best of Simple,* which fittingly concludes with the short story "Jazz, Jive, and Jam." In it, Simple recalls how Joyce, his wife, recently dragged him to a lecture by a prominent black historian. The "Negro hysterian," as Simple renames him, "said we was misbred, misread, and misled, also losing our time good-timing. Instead of time-taking and money-making, we are jazz-shaking" (239). Offended and bored, Simple took the opportunity to rant about the ineffectiveness of all those civic improvement committees and conferences Joyce attends: "in my opinion, jazz, jive, and jam would be better for race relations than all this high-flown gab, gaff, and gas the orators put out. All this talking that white folks do at meetings, and big Negroes, too, about how to get along together—just a little jam session would have everybody getting along fine without having to listen to so many speeches" (242–43). To Joyce's indignant reply that meetings like these were not musicals, but serious efforts to further integration, Simple offered this counter:

> I said, "With a jazz band, they could work out integration in ten minutes. Everybody would have been dancing together like they all did at the Savoy—colored and white—or down on the East Side at them Casinos on a Friday night where jam holds forth—and we would have been integrated."
>
> Joyce said, "This was a serious seminar, aiming at facts, not fun."
>
> "Baby," I said, "What's more facts than acts? Jazz makes people get into action, move! Didn't nobody move in that hall where you were—except to jerk their head up when they went to sleep, to keep anybody from seeing that they was nodding." (243)

Simple proposes that future meetings include a band like Count Basie's or Lionel Hampton's so that the proceedings "open with jazz and close with a jam—and do the talking in between" (244). This way, he concludes, "Even I would stick around, and not be outside sneaking a smoke, or trying to figure out how I can get to the bar before the resolutions are voted on. *Resolved:* that we solve the race problem! Strike up the band! Hit it, men! Aw, play that thing! 'How High the Moon!' How high! Wheee-ee-e!" (244–45).[17]

Ralph Ellison would certainly have agreed with Simple's equation of jazz and democracy.[18] Because he saw what he often liked to call the drama of American democracy as fundamentally, intrinsically "jazz-shaped," jazz to Ellison was really a synecdoche for the American nation as a whole (*Going* 582, 595–96). Ellison, of course, had had formal musical training and aimed to make a career in music before he turned to writing. In his fiction, essays, and commentary, music, especially jazz and other African American musics, remained a constant source of inspiration, as it did for the long, monumental manuscript of his second novel. Even though this novel was only published posthumously as *Juneteenth*—a heavily edited version compiled by the executor of his literary estate, John F. Callahan—Ellison over the years had placed self-contained excerpts from the mushrooming manuscript in various literary journals. One of those excerpts was published as "Cadillac Flambé" in the February 1973 issue of the *American Review.*

The story is set in Washington, D.C., during the 1950s and is told from the point of view of a nameless narrator, a white newspaper reporter. The narrator is on his way home from a pleasant spring Sunday of bird-watching and is walking past the sprawling estate of Senator Sunraider, a powerful New England politician notorious for his virulent race-baiting. Suddenly he notices a white Cadillac convertible driven by a black man in a white suit coming to a stop beneath Sunraider's mansion. The driver, a jazz bassist named Lee Willie Minifees, proceeds to set his car on fire in an elaborate ceremony. As a stunned white crowd, including the senator, looks on and the car bursts into flames, Minifees launches into a lengthy mock-sermon. He recalls that driving home to Harlem from a lucrative engagement in Tennessee, he had turned on the radio and happened to hear the rebuttal to one of Sunraider's liberal colleagues, who had criticized Detroit's automobile industry for a lack of innovation. Sunraider retorted during this live broadcast that, on the contrary, American cars were the best-designed in the world. The only blemish on the reputation of the Detroit-made cars, Sunraider added derisively, was that Cadillacs had become rabidly popular among Harlemites: "We have reached a sad state of affairs, gentlemen, wherein this fine product of American skill and initiative has become so common in Harlem that much of its initial value has been sorely compromised. Indeed, I am led to suggest, and quite seriously, that legislation be drawn up to rename it the 'Coon Cage Eight'" (229). Therefore, Sunraider concluded, the recurrent complaints of African Americans about economic disenfranchisement were quite spurious: "Give your attention to who it is that is creating the scarcity and removing these superb machines from the reach of those for whom they were intended! With so many of these good things, what, pray, do these people desire—is it a jet plane on every Harlem rooftop?" (232). Listening to this speech, Minifees decided that he was obliged to return his luxury vehicle to one "of those for whom they were intended" and simply stopped by the Senator's house to make him a "present" (222). Topping Sunraider's infamous rhetorical hyperbole, Minifees ends his powerful mock-sermon, accompanied all the while by the crackling flames shooting forth from the car, by expressing his gratitude to the Senator:

> In fact, now I don't want anything you think is too good for me and my people. Because . . . if a man in your position is against our having them, then there must be something WRONG in our *wanting* them. So to keep you happy, I, me, Lee Willie Minifees, am prepared to WALK. I'm ordering me some club-footed, pigeon-toed SPACE SHOES. I'd rather save my money and wait until the A-RABS make a car. The Zulus even. Even the ESKIMOS! Oh, I'll walk and wait. I'll grab me a GREYHOUND or a FREIGHT! So you can have my coon cage, fare thee well! Take the TAIL FINS and the WHITE WALLS. Help yourself to the poor raped RADIO. ENJOY the automatic dimmer and the power brakes. ROLL, Mister Senator, with that fluid DRIVE. Breathe that air-conditioned AIR. There's never been a Caddy like this one and I want you to HAVE IT. Take my scientific dreamboat and enjoy that good ole GRACIOUS LIVING! The key's in the ignition and the REGISTRATION'S in the GLOVE compartment! And thank you KINDLY for freeing me from the Coon Cage. Because before I'd be in a CAGE, I'll be buried in my GRAVE—Oh! Oh! (228)

Just as Minifees rips into "God Bless America" for the fiery, dissonant finale, he is interrupted by police and fire engine sirens. Law enforcement eventually haul Minifees away in a straightjacket, leaving behind a thoroughly puzzled narrator and an incensed yet also frightened crowd of onlookers.[19]

Minifees's "duet with the expiring Cadillac" comprises the heart of the short story (229).[20] Significantly, the narrator implicitly likens the bassist's act of arson to a jazz performance: "a certain tension, as during the start of a concert, was building. And I had just thought, *And now he'll bring out the fiddle,*" but, of course, the crowd of onlookers is in for another kind of performance altogether, a performance which, the narrator recognizes, is largely "improvised" (218, 219). Minifees's 'concert' concludes when, "most outrageous of all, he threw back his head and actually sang a few bars before the noise of the short-circuited horn set the flaming car to wailing like some great prehistoric animal heard in the throes of its dying" (229). To the narrator, the sounds of Minifees's performance, including the mock-sermon, are sheer primeval noise that disrupts the harmonious setting of a late Sunday afternoon in the spring. Significantly, though, Minifees performs his concerto in the key of noise near Senator Sunraider's mansion in Washington, D.C., the hub of political power. The narrator is aware that he must have just witnessed "a crude and most portentous political gesture," but is incapable of seeing in the bassist's "noisy action" anything other than "a case of overreacting expressed in true Negro abandon, an extreme gesture springing from the frustration of having no adequate means of replying, or making himself heard above the majestic roar of a senator" (229, 232).[21]

What the narrator is missing—and he himself is prone, despite his professed liberal convictions, to regurgitate freely racialist stereotypes about blacks—is the fact that Minifees's improvised production of seemingly nonsensical noise within earshot of Sunraider is profoundly subversive: "Subversion in musical production," avers Attali, "opposes a new syntax to the existing syntax, from the point of view of which it is noise. . . . What is noise to the old order is harmony to the new" (34–35). Clearly, for the white onlookers, the bassist's actions are anything but harmonious: they disrupt Sunraider's barbeque, tarnish the narrator's bird-watching expedition, and generally unhinge the peaceful Sunday routine of the park-goers. Minifees's improvisation of noise directly opposes and challenges the existing syntax of harmony orchestrated by a political system condoning the continued subjugation of Americans of African descent, a system of which Senator Sunraider is the most vocal and visible representative. Just like Simple, Minifees, too, lays claim to the right to make ostensibly meaningless noise and, in doing so, unmasks the laws of harmony according to which society is arranged as truly meaningless themselves.

However, where violence remains figurative and contained within Simple's narrative in "Bop," violence here is enacted in the protagonist's torching of the white Caddy. The narrator recurrently likens the events he is observing to a sacrificial ritual, an "outlandish rite" of which Minifees is "the chief celebrant" (221): "I could hear the swoosh-pop-crackle-and-hiss of the fire," reports the narrator, and

> We watched with that sense of awe similar to that with which medieval crowds must have observed the burning of a great cathedral. We were stunned by the sacrificial act and, indeed, it

> was as though we had become the unwilling participants in a primitive ceremony requiring the sacrifice of a beautiful object in appeasement of some terrifying and long-dormant spirit, which the black man in the white suit was summoning from a long, black sleep. And as we watched, our faces strained as though in anticipation of the spirit's materialization from the fiery metamorphosis of the white machine, a spirit that I was afraid, whatever form in which it appeared, would be powerfully good or powerfully evil, and absolutely out of place here in Washington. (220)

The "terrifying and long-dormant spirit" which the narrator fears and which, he believes, shall issue forth from the destruction of the "gleaming white" automobile is the centuries-old yearning for self-determination and freedom for blacks in America; it is a spirit that has never been dormant really, just inaudible to the narrator until Lee Willie Minifees sets his Cadillac ablaze (215). Setting free this spirit of liberty and self-determination must indeed seem "absolutely out of place" at the center of a political system dedicated to curb, control, or render mute this very same spirit. But this pernicious, dehumanizing system is also so paranoid that it is convinced, as is the narrator subconsciously, that it may very well meet the same fate as Minifees's vehicle if it allows this spirit to find a voice.

The narrator's recurrent analogies to ritual and sacrifice point again to Attali's theory of music. Music, says Attali, is the channelization of noise, and every political system seeks to monopolize the codification of music because noise—chaos, death, violence—threatens the legitimacy and existence of this political system. Thus, the musician engages in a sacrificial ritual that either consolidates or subverts the existing social structure:

> The musician, like music, is ambiguous. He plays a double game. He is simultaneously *musicus* and *cantor,* reproducer and prophet. If an outcast, he sees society in a political light. If accepted, he is its historian, the reflection of its deepest values. He speaks of society and he speaks against it. . . . Shaman, doctor, musician. He is one of society's first gazes upon itself; he is one of the first catalyzers of violence and myth. . . . [T]he musician is an integral part of the sacrifice process, a channeler of violence, and . . . the primal identity *magic-music-sacrifice-rite* expresses the musician's position in the majority of civilizations: simultaneously *excluded* (relegated to a place near the bottom of the social hierarchy) and *superhuman*

(the genius, the adored and deified star). Simultaneously a separator and an integrator. (12)

Clearly, Minifees in Ellison's story is Attali's excluded musician-outcast whose performance of improvised noise issuing forth from the fiery sacrifice of the white Cadillac aims at unmasking, through a channelization of violence, the inhumanity of a political system that oppresses him. Sunraider's speech underscores Minifees's dual social status: the bassist has just returned from a financially successful engagement, but the politics of Sunraider and his ilk want to deny him the enjoyment of the fruits of his labor. And yet, Minifees's subversive action amounts to a characteristically Ellisonian *"tableau vivant"* that is thoroughly American: the "gleaming white" of the luxury vehicle mingles with "the leaping red and blue flames" ignited by the bassist's ingenious incendiary device, which he waves about like "a Fourth of July sparkler" (Ellison, "Cadillac" 219, 215, 220, 219). To Ellison, jazz musicians were "that most representative group of Negro Americans," and so the patriotic color imagery orchestrated by a jazz bassist again configures jazz as a metaphor for the ongoing drama of America and American democracy (Ellison, *Going* 749; H. Porter 95).[22] And hence, most ironic of all, the white spectators of Minifees's ritualistic murder-sacrifice of the vehicle are indeed also catching a glimpse of themselves.

However, while Minifees's act of arson is *analogous* in many ways to a jazz performance, it *is not* jazz itself. Just as much as the narrative thrives on the violence of noise, so it also separates it from the harmony of music: significantly, it is the Cadillac that is being sacrificed to noise, not jazz music itself. In fact, the narrator observes how Minifees removes his bass from the backseat of the automobile, carrying it "up the hill some thirty feet above the car, and placed it lovingly on the grass" before he proceeds to torch the car (218). To be sure, improvised jazz music informs Minifees's ritual sacrifice, but it remains at the same time safely removed from the conflagration that occurs. Symbolically, Minifees's unharmed instrument suggests the enduring relevance and power of jazz.

It is, therefore, no coincidence that the short story's protagonist is a bassist. The bass, says bebop legend Ray Brown, furnishes "rhythm with a good sound that can never be replaced by anything else. It's like a heartbeat," and Phil Bowler seconds, "[w]e're the foundation on which everything is built" (qtd. in Berendt 328; qtd. in Monson, *Saying* 29). To the lay listener, the bass may seem unobtrusive and at times even inaudible, but its function is absolutely crucial. As musicologist Joachim Ernst

Berendt summarizes, "[t]he task of the bassist is to provide the musicians of a jazz ensemble with a harmonic basis that they can traverse. He is the backbone of the group. Simultaneously, the bass has a rhythmic assignment. Since bebop, the bassist's four regular beats to the bar constitute often the only factor demarcating unwaveringly the fundamental rhythm" (320). Furthermore, the upright bass, or "bull fiddle," is the most physically demanding of all jazz instruments, even more so than the drum set (Crow 672–79; Berliner 130–31, 315–16). Because the development of the musical role and instrumental technique has been more sweeping and radical for the bass than for any other instrument, jazz historiography has sometimes referred to its "emancipation" from a strictly functional support instrument—often inaudible to the audience and, because of the limitations of early recording technology, often replaced by the tuba in studio sessions or left out altogether—to a fully-fledged solo voice on equal footing with horns, piano, and drums (Berendt 321–26; Crow 675–80). In "Cadillac Flambé," Lee Willie carefully removes his instrument from the immediate danger zone; he uses only the bow as part of the ritual sacrifice, and the bow is rarely used by jazz bassists. Thus, Minifees, the jazz bassist and representative American of African descent, embodies the black experience in the New World and, by extension, the project and promise of an American democracy that lives up to its own ideals. His bass, untouched by the flames and smoke, symbolizes the continuing vital importance of blacks as the actual "backbone" of the country as a whole. As Ellison concludes in "What America Would Be Like without Blacks," African Americans "are an American people who are geared to what *is,* and who yet are driven to a sense of what is possible for human life to be in this society. The nation could not survive being deprived of their presence because, by the irony implicit in the dynamics of American democracy, they symbolize both its most stringent testing and the possibility of its greatest human freedom" (*Going* 584). Minifees's sacrificial act certainly constitutes such a stringent testing; his bass, conversely, symbolically holds out the possibility for greater human freedom.

At the end of the short story, however, Lee Willie Minifees is overwhelmed by the police, forced into a straightjacket, and hauled off to jail. His impending incarceration appears to indicate a loss of freedom. Even so, the unharmed instrument as well as one of the milestones in the history of the "emancipation" of the bass reveal not only an echo of *Invisible Man,* but also offer a reading in which "Cadillac Flambé" retains the enduring *possibility* of greater freedom. In the fall of 1939, Duke Ellington hired a new and spectacular bass player for his big band: Jimmy

Blanton. Shortly after Blanton joined, Ellington made another addition in tenor saxophonist Ben Webster, and what has come to be known as the Blanton-Webster band is still considered by many to be the finest of all Ellington outfits. In the short time he spent with Ellington, Blanton—who died of pneumonia at the age of twenty-four—revolutionized the function of the bass in jazz. His agile technique and full, robust sound elevated the bass to a solo instrument (Lawrence 286–90; Polillo 368–70). Accordingly, Ellington decided to feature his new bass player and had his musical alter ego, arranger and composer Billy Strayhorn, rework an old tune, "Take It Away," for Blanton. The showpiece, retitled "Jack the Bear" and recorded for RCA Victor in early 1940, is a bluesy, exuberantly swinging tune and begins with an introductory bass solo of eight measures that positively shocked the jazz world and changed the role of the instrument forever, paving the way for the later innovations in bebop and beyond by the likes of Oscar Pettiford, Ray Brown, or Charles Mingus (Lawrence 292; Schuller, *Swing* 114–16).

Echoing the Ellington-Strayhorn composition, the invisible man in the novel's prologue asks, "[c]all me Jack-the-Bear, for I am in a state of hibernation," because "a bear retires to his hole for the winter and lives until spring: then he comes strolling out like the Easter chick breaking from its shell" (6). He defines hibernation as "a covert preparation for a more overt action" and concludes, "[b]ut I am an orator, a rabble rouser—Am? I *was,* and perhaps shall be again. Who knows?" (13, 14). Thus, it is as if Lee Willie Minifees is Jack-the-Bear returning from his invisible hibernation. Not only is the overt action of his ritual sacrifice set beneath "a clear blue springtime sky," he is most certainly also an orator and, at least in the eyes of the white onlookers, a rabble-rouser (220). The covert preparation for his fiery sacrificial ritual has taken place on stage and in the practice room as a jazz bassist, invisible and inaudible to Sunraider. Moreover, Minifees's incarceration is most likely going to be only temporary and thus constitutes but another hibernation from which he will eventually emerge. Because of his musical skills and name recognition at least within the jazz community—the narrator notices that the bassist wears "expensive black alligator shoes" as part of what Albert Murray calls the "special ceremonial costumes" of the jazz professional, who even off-duty "tends to remain in character much as does the Minister of the Gospel"—Minifees will without a doubt be in high demand upon his release and will continue to play his highly subversive yet simultaneously thoroughly American music (Ellison, "Cadillac" 230; A. Murray 230). As one of the "emancipators" of the bass extending Blanton's legacy in the 1940s, Oscar Pettiford identified four main criteria of meaningful bass-playing: "Humanity, expression, emotionality, and telling stories" (qtd. in Berendt 327). It is precisely these qualities which pervade portentously both Minifees's music and sacrifice, qualities to which he shall resort again after his state-imposed hibernation.

The connections to Ellison's novel do not cease here, for the white narrator of "Cadillac Flambé" himself is in many ways the invisible man's foil. *Invisible Man* ends with the famous sentence, "Who know but that, on the lower frequencies, I speak for you?" (581). Lee Willie, as we have seen, transmits his message on those selfsame frequencies. But where the invisible man is attuned to those frequencies, the narrator in "Cadillac Flambé" is not. Even though he professes to empathize with the bassist, he is as taken aback, as are the rest of the onlookers, because "burning an expensive car seemed so extreme a reply as to be almost metaphysical" (232). Nonetheless, the arson reverberates in his mind, and the story concludes echoing the final note of *Invisible Man:*

> What would be his fate? I wondered; and where had they taken him? I would have to find him and question him, for his action had begun to sound in my mind with disturbing overtones which had hardly been meaningful. Rather they had been like the brief interruption one sometimes hears while listening to an F.M. broadcast of the musical *Oklahoma!*, say, with original cast, when the signal fades and a program of quite different mood from a different wavelength breaks through. It had happened but then a blast of laughter had restored us automatically to our chosen frequency. (233)[23]

Whereas the invisible man deliberately sounds frequencies which the cultural mainstream seeks to suppress, the narrator here hopes to be returned from Minifees's violent if brief interruption of a Sunday spent catching birdsongs on tape "to our *chosen* frequency," a frequency, in other words, where white America is not inconvenienced by inadvertently having to face itself in black America. *Oklahoma!* the musical is set in the Indian territory at the dawn of the twentieth century and was a smashing success both with the critics as well as the public in its skillful fusion of romance, adventure, and folk materials, but it does not resemble the Oklahoma of Ralph Ellison's youth at all (Bunnett et al. 276–77; Wilk 257–62). Although the musical's *dramatis personae* includes, curiously, the Persian peddler Ali Hakim, it otherwise renders invisible the multicultural Oklahoma of Ralph Ellison's childhood celebrated in essays like "Remembering Jimmy" and in numerous interviews. No wonder, then, that the narrator of "Cadillac Flambé" prefers the fantasy world of *Oklahoma!* in which the Other in the person of Ali Hakim is conveniently married off to one of the minor characters without further complicating any of the amorous developments of the plot.

To the narrator's chagrin, the disruption of his "chosen frequency" hence consists of the translation into ritualistic violence of what Nathaniel Mackey calls "black music's infiltration of the dominant society" (*Discrepant* 6). The bassist's noisy sacrificial act—much like the invisible man's intended goal of his covert preparation—is an act of what Mackey terms "discrepant engagement": "Discrepant engagement, rather than suppressing resonance, dissonance, noise, seeks to remain open to them. Its admission of resonances contends with resolution. It worries resolute identity and demarcation, resolute boundary lines, resolute definition, obeying a vibrational rather than a corpuscular sense of being" (*Discrepant* 20). The narrator, on the other hand, clearly proud of his liberal stance yet unaware of his racial othering of Minifees, is inadvertently engaged in what could be termed conformist engagement.

This juxtaposition of discrepant and conformist forms of engagement also illuminates another salient feature of "Cadillac Flambé," connecting it to Ellison's non-fiction on jazz, namely the recurrent bird imagery. In the story, we are told that the narrator's "bird-watching expedition" has yielded a very satisfactory "tally of birds" enhanced by several glasses of a drink invented by the host called the "chicken-shot." He is also carrying a tape machine "to record bird-songs" (214). Later, he likens the rising top of Lee Willie's convertible to "the wing of some great, slow, grateful bird" and the burning automobile to "a huge fowl being flambéed in choice cognac" (217, 220). Minifees himself confesses that before he heard Sunraider's speech on the radio, he believed he was "as free as a bird—even though a black bird" steering his luxury automobile down the highway (224).

This conspicuous profusion of birds in the text strongly suggests one of Ellison's sly digs at the most important bebop revolutionary, Charlie Parker, nicknamed "Yardbird" or simply "Bird." For all his extolling jazz as a metaphor for America, Ellison, unlike Langston Hughes and Jessie B. Simple, never really reconciled himself with bebop and the more modern styles of jazz. In his eyes and ears, the boppers, these "disgruntled conspirators meeting fatefully to assemble the random parts of a bomb" as he described them in *Shadow and Act,* were not worthy to join Duke Ellington and Louis Armstrong in the pantheon of jazz (242). Ellison, who once blithely quipped that "style is more important than political ideologies," was deeply suspicious of the militancy of the beboppers and deplored what he perceived as bebop's move away from "the true jazz moment" always connected inextricably with blues and dancing (*Going* 743; *Shadow* 267). Although his public criticism of the music was muted, in private he could be scathing. Writing to his friend Albert Murray in the fall of 1958 with a summary of the Newport Jazz Festival—of whose board, like Hughes, he was a member—he describes the late Charlie "Bird" Parker's sound as "miserable, beat and lost" and deplores his pervasive influence on jazz musicians: "but hell, they believe in the witchdoctor's warning: If Bird shits on you, wear it" (Letter 244). He also ridicules "that poor, evil, lost little Miles Davis" along with John Coltrane, clearly expressing a lack of understanding, masked as disdain, for the experiments in modal jazz the Miles Davis Quintet was involved in at the time and would bring to perfection on *Kind of Blue* (245; O'Meally ed. 234–35).

The very opening of "Cadillac Flambé" that has the narrator return from a bird-watching expedition also hearkens back to Ellison's essay "On Bird, Bird-Watching, and Jazz." In this review of Robert Reisner's *Bird: The Legend of Charlie Parker,* Ellison points to "the pathetic comedy" of Parker's life and bemoans "the crabbed and constricted character of his style" as well as his "sound of amateurish ineffectuality" (*Shadow* 256, 264). The tragedy of Parker's life, as Ellison sees it, was that in rejecting the role of the entertainer so vehemently—a role which Armstrong, a hero to Ellison but a "moldy fig" to many boppers, embraced wholeheartedly—the alto saxophonist inadvertently conformed to the very image he was trying so desperately to escape, the image of a clown, "a sacrificial figure whose struggles against personal chaos, onstage and off, served as entertainment for a ravenous, sensation-starved, culturally disoriented public which had only the slightest notion of its real significance. . . . In the end he had no private life and his most tragic moments were drained of human significance" (261). Just as Parker's musical innovations and political militancy are just smoke and mirrors to Ellison, so is the freedom Lee Willie experiences driving his Caddy illusory. Consequently, the chirpy bird-chatter on the tape the reporter-narrator turns on instinctively is superseded by the bassist's profoundly political statements. Having moved his instrument away from immediate danger, Minifees speaks first and foremost as an American citizen rather than a jazz musician. Bird was "like a man dismembering himself with a dull razor on a spotlighted stage," but Lee Willie's immolation of the white car, that "huge fowl," is a raucous and much more effective sacrificial form of social protest (*Shadow* 261; "Cadillac" 217).

Thus, "Cadillac Flambé" explores the nexus between jazz, violence, and the right of African Americans to self-determination and freedom in their struggle to make their human voices heard. As Ellison himself wrote of his beginnings as a struggling artist, "[i]n those days it was either live with music or die with noise, and we chose rather desperately to live" (*Shadow* 227). For the established artist and consummate manipulator of sounds Lee Willie Minifees, on the other hand, the choice between music and noise is not an absolute one: in the ritual murder of his Cadillac to the tune of jazz, he decides rather desperately to live with the "noise" of his *own* music.

III. Black to the Future: Revolutionary Jazz in Amiri Baraka's "Answers in Progress"

In "A Coupla Scalped Indians," yet another short story lifted from his novel in progress, Ellison tells the coming-of-age story of two teenage boys. In the course of their adventures, they suddenly hear the sounds of a jazz band emanating from a nearby fairground. The narrator's companion, Buster, translates one by one how the soloists are "playing the dozens with the whole wide world" (186). Queried about the meaning of the trumpet player's solo, Buster explains:

> "Him? That fool's a soldier, he's really signifying. Saying,
>
> So ya'll don't play 'em, hey?
> So ya'll won't play 'em, hey?
> Well pat your feet and clap your hands,
> 'Cause I'm going to play 'em to the promised land. . . .
>
> "Man, the white folks know what that fool is signifying on that horn they'd run him clear on out the world. Trumpet's got a real *nasty* mouth."
>
> "Why you call him a soldier, man?" I said.
>
> "'Cause he's slipping 'em in the twelves and choosing 'em, all at the same time. Talking 'bout they mamas and offering to fight 'em. Now he ain't like that ol' clarinet; clarinet so sweet-talking he just *eases* you into the dozens." (186–87)

The trumpet's martial assertion here to blow the audience into "the promised land" echoes Jessie B. Simple's utopian recipe for social justice and reform by replacing the talk of politicians with the swing of Count Basie. Furthermore, where the violence in "Bop" remains contained within Simple's narrative and is situated, figuratively, in the past, where Minifees's concrete sacrificial violence is enacted by an individual and has no far-reaching consequences apart from the bassist's impending imprisonment, this passage from "A Coupla Scalped Indians" points to the revolutionary potential resulting from the interface between jazz and violence. As Ellison himself elaborated in *Going to the Territory* on the dramatic tug-of-war that is American democracy, "this contest (our *improvised* moral equivalent for armed warfare) proceeds as a war of words, a clash of styles, or as rites of symbolic sacrifice in which cabalistic code words are used to designate victims consumed with an Aztec voracity for scapegoats. Indeed, so frequently does this conflict erupt into physical violence that one sometimes wonders if there is any other viable possibility for co-existing in so abstract and *futuristic* a nation as this" (501; emphasis added). After all, America was born from revolution, and jazz, being a distinctly American art form, must therefore logically reflect the potential of revolution in the nation's continuing struggle to realize the *ideals* of American democracy. Thus, the jazz aesthetic's revision of the past—Sidney Bechet's invention of Omar, Jessie B. Simple's story of the origins of bebop—is accompanied not only by the possibility of violence and revolution. It also contains a utopian impulse in its struggle towards that metaphorical place of freedom, this "utopic ubiquity," to quote Nathaniel Mackey's N once more, an impulse that evinces itself in Bechet's description of slave songs as well as in Lutie Johnson's rendition of "Darlin'" (Mackey, *Atet* 15).[24]

More than Langston Hughes or Ralph Ellison, Jessie B. Simple or Lee Willie Minifees, Amiri Baraka has championed jazz music as a herald of revolution. Throughout Baraka's many transformations—from Bohemian Beatnik to Black Nationalist to crude Marxist Leninist—"one constant for me from the time of any consciousness in helping to define the world has been music," as he wrote in his *Autobiography* (65). Today, *Blues People* and *Black Music* remain indispensable texts for the jazz scholar. Baraka discovered bebop in his youth, and his association with Jack Kerouac and Allen Ginsberg early in his career in New York City fanned his desire to find a literary voice issuing from black music. In the early 1960s, he began to write numerous reviews, interviews, and articles for several jazz journals and was for a time a regular contributor to *Metronome* and *Down Beat* magazine, penning his short-lived column "Apple Cores" for the latter.[25] His anything but amicable departure from *Down Beat* was largely occasioned by the magazine's hostility towards the increasingly outspoken black nationalism of many musicians of the emerging free jazz movement (Kofsky 123–30). Baraka, however, was—and continues to be—free jazz's staunchest supporter. It is certainly no coincidence that his transformation from Greenwich Village Bohemian Beat to Newark Black Nationalist ran parallel with the rise of free jazz.[26] The "New Black Music," as he preferred to call it, signaled to Baraka a revolutionary call to arms, a rejection of and frontal attack on white America, and a return of jazz to its unadulterated sources in blues and bebop. The larger-than-life leader of the new "poets of the Black Nation," of the soldiers instigating this revolution, was John Coltrane (*Black* 176). As Baraka saw it, "Trane is a mature swan whose wingspan was a whole new world. But he also showed us how to murder the popular song. How to do away with weak Western forms. He is a beautiful philosopher" (*Black* 174).[27] The music of the "hatchet men" and "private assassins" around Coltrane, Ornette Coleman, and Cecil Taylor was the harbinger of a cultural and, eventually, social uprising of Americans of African descent as it spoke "of a world more beautiful than the white man knows" (*Black* 178, 175; *Blues* 228).

Baraka is arguably also the African American writer who exerted the most influence on jazz music. His frequent artistic collaborations, either as interviewer, concert organizer, or reviewer, in the 1960s with exponents of the "new music," especially with his downstairs neighbor Archie Shepp (an early Coltrane disciple), were manifestations of the increasing politicization of jazz (Baraka, *Autobiography* 256–57; Kofsky 243–44; Such 26–27). Looking back on that wild decade a bit ruefully, free jazz veteran Billy Bang for instance commented that "[m]usicians had no choice in the 1960s but to get into the political thing. A lot of the musicians did not have to get into the theoretical side of musicianship. . . . But they could pick up an instrument and it was like they were picking up an AK47. . . . They just started honking and screaming and the statements sounded like machine gun fire. This happened to me too" (qtd. in Such 71). For Baraka, there was no difference between jazz as aesthetic expression and jazz as revolutionary ideology. To him, jazz, real jazz, real *black* jazz, was *supposed* to sound like machine gun fire. His politics of aesthetics—or, for that matter, aesthetics of politics—as well as his staunch preference for the new free jazz therefore made his writings not all that palatable to Hughes or Ellison.[28]

The apocalyptic vision of Charlie Parker running down Fifth Avenue killing scores of white people that Baraka had conjured up in *Dutchman* seemed about to come true only a few years after the play's premiere. The year 1967 not only saw the publication of Baraka's collection of short stories, *Tales,* but also a series of bloody race riots that engulfed the nation. No wonder, then, that many of the stories in *Tales,* although written mostly in the first half of the 1960s, reflected the violence of the times, especially also since the young generation of black free jazzers saw in the jazz musician, in the words of Baraka's friend Archie Shepp, "a reporter, an aesthetic journalist of America" (qtd. in Baraka, *Black* 153; Watts 234). The collection's narrators, all to varying degrees autobiographical projections of the author himself, negotiate personal conflicts and alienation from the community. The last selection in *Tales* is not only different in that it bears the date of composition. Written after Baraka's transformation from the Beat Bohemian Leroi Jones to the Black Nationalist Amiri Baraka, the narrative voice of this story is clearly one that has been reborn into an unequivocally black identity. Consistent with the recurrent themes of transformation and revolt, *Tales* ends with the quasi-futuristic plot of "Answers in Progress," extending the premise of the earlier story "The Screamers," in which tenor saxophonist Lynn Hope spearheads a surreal black urban uprising that eventually fails nonetheless.[29] In this last tale, however, space aliens in search of records by jazz drummer Art Blakey, "long, blue wiggly cats, with soft liquid sounds out of their throats for voices," land amidst the violent, bloody chaos of a black upheaval in Newark:

> Space men wanted to know what happened after Blakey. They'd watched but couldn't get close enough to dig exactly what was happening. Albert Ayler they dug immediately from Russell's mouth imitation. . . . Red spam cans in their throats with voices, and one of them started to scat. It wigged me. Bamberger's burning down, dead blancos all over and a cat from Sigma Veda, and his brothers, hopping up and down asking us what was happening. (128)

The narrator, local organizer of the apparently nationwide black uprising now in its fifth day, discusses with "the blue leader" the revolution taking place, the paintings of Ben Caldwell, the poetry of Claude McKay, and together they debate "the changing reference, of our new world. As it stood already in the old ruins. And we all felt like Bird. The old altosaxophonist . . . but the limits opened out into the pure lyric tone of powerful beings" (131).[30] After another exhausting day, the revolutionaries agree on a new flag brandishing "[b]lack heads, black hearts, and a blue fiery space in the background" before the narrator goes home to his wife and children (132).

"Answers in Progress" departs deliberately from the conventions of storytelling—just as free jazz deliberately departed from the conventions of diatonic music. In the earlier, more conventionally modernist stories of *Tales*, "[t]he yearning for a functional and pragmatic theory of government *and* prose remains unfulfilled," as Werner Sollors has demonstrated, and consequently the depiction of a brutal, violent revolt against the political system in "Answers in Progress" comes in a style that revolts against conventional prose, too (156).[31] More like a snapshot—or sound clip—of the prolonged uprising, the story mixes prose, shaped poetry, and song, lacks any exposition or closure, and is generally allusive rather than descriptive. Stylistically, the short story is one of Baraka's "creative destructions," as William Harris has labeled them (18). It also draws on several different genres and artistic movements; most notably, of course, it parodies the science fiction genre.[32] Significantly, Baraka's aliens are not depicted as representatives of a technologically superior civilization: other than catching up on the latest jazz, the aliens seem to be interested only in "gettin' cooled out" on a space narcotic that tastes like carrots. "It was a cool that took you," the narrator comments approvingly. "You thought something was mildly amusing and everything seemed interesting" (131). Hence, "these blue dudes" visit earth not to conquer and colonize it with far advanced technology, but to expand their minds (131). But Baraka's use of the science fiction genre is not simply parodic. Musicologist Graham Lock points out that even in early slave songs, "[e]xtraterrestriality . . . encodes a heavenly site of order and justice that represents a vision of *greater sanity* than the terrestrial world of slavery, apprehended by the slaves as cruel, arbitrary, and irrational" (58). "Answers in Progress" clearly follows this tradition in that the full emancipation and empowerment of black people in America is possible only at a future (futuristic) time when blue space aliens land in Newark, New Jersey. Furthermore, the story encompasses the events of day five of the revolution: "That's the way the fifth day ended," concludes the narrator (132). The allusion to the book of Genesis suggests that on the next, the sixth day of the violent uprising, a new race, a new *black* race, will emerge, analogous to God's creation of the race of man, who shall have "dominion over the fish of the sea, and over the fowl of the air, and over the cattle, and over all the earth, and over every creeping thing that creepeth upon the earth" (Genesis 1.26). This parody of Genesis also limns another recurring motif in Baraka's prose and poetry, namely the idea of a black, or blacker, rebirth through music (Sollors 204).

It is not surprising, then, that these space aliens have heard first intimations of the emergence of a new black race in hard-bop jazz: "Art Blakey records was what they were looking for. . . . They wanted to know what happened to The Jazz Messengers. . . . 'You know where Art Blakey, Buhaina, is working?' We just about fell out" (127, 129). Drummer Art Blakey had been among the beboppers of the first hour. In the late 1940s, like many other progressive jazz musicians, he converted to Islam taking the name Abdullah Ibn Buhaina and traveled to Africa to study drumming and Islamic culture. He also formed the first of his various groups bearing the name the Jazz Messengers. Joining forces with pianist Horace Silver in the early 1950s, the Messengers quickly evolved into the archetypal hard-bop group (Gerard 63–64, 73–77). Hard-bop discarded the jagged lines, dizzying tempos, and complex harmonies of bebop in favor of a more pronounced reliance on the blues as well as on the spirituals of the black church. Hard-bop's redirection towards the more traditional rhythms and melodies of the (rural) black South, towards an emphasis of black "soul," evinced itself also in song titles like the Messengers' own "Moanin'" and other compositions like "Sunday Mornin'," "Back at the Chicken Shack," "Soul Station," "Greasin' Easy," and so on. Blakey was known as a loud, hard-hitting drummer famous for his intense press rolls, and his playing certainly expresses what literary critic William Harris has called "the jazz aggressive impulse" (16).

Surely, Blakey's religious conversion, the name of his band, his choice of instrument, and his incorporation of African drumming techniques appealed to Baraka.[33] At the same time, though, Baraka has always been very critical of hard-bop. In *Blues People,* for instance, he complained that hard-bop had become too formulaic, too commercial, and had degenerated into "the final meaninglessness of the popular" as "a mood music for Negro colleges" (220, 235). Even so,

> The direction, the initial response, which led to hard bop is more profound than its excesses. It is as much of a "move" within the black psyche as was the move north in the beginning of the century. The idea of the Negro's having "roots" and that they are a valuable possession, rather than the source of ineradicable shame, is perhaps the profoundest change within the Negro consciousness since the early part of the century. . . . The step from *cool* [jazz] to *soul* [jazz, i.e. hard-bop] is a form of social aggression. It is an attempt to place upon a "meaningless" social order,

> an order which would give value to terms of existence that were once considered not only valueless but shameful. *Cool* meant nonparticipation; *soul* means a "new" establishment. It is an attempt to reverse the social roles within the society by redefining the canons of value. (218–19)

In Baraka's opinion, however—perhaps not quite coincidentally, Herbie Hancock's gospel-tinged "Watermelon Man" had been a huge crossover hit in 1962, one year prior to the publication of *Blues People*—this valorization of black roots had unfortunately succumbed to commercial excess and artistic stultification. The redemption of black music was effected by the "new thing" of free jazz.

Accordingly, the blue aliens of "Answers in Progress" are keen to find out "what happened *after* Blakey. They'd watched but couldn't get close enough to dig exactly what was happening" (128; emphasis added). They are particularly impressed by the futuristic jazz of Sun Ra: "But when the Sun-Ra tape came on this blue dude really opened up. He dug the hell out of it. Perfect harmony these cats had too. Boooooo-Iiiiiiiioooooooooooooo . . . daaaa ahhhhhhhh aaaaahhhhhh . . . booooo OOOOOOOOOOOOO oooooooooaaaaaaaaaoooaaaaa" (131). Born in 1914, Sun Ra was easily the most colorful and controversial bandleader in jazz history. He initially made a living as a Chicago-based pianist first in the swing, then the bebop idiom, but at some point in the 1950s, Herman "Sonny" Blount transformed himself first briefly into Le Son'y Ra, then into Sun Ra. Claiming that he and his band, variously called the Myth-Science Arkestra, the Astro Intergalactic Infinity Arkestra, or similar such titles, had come to Earth from the planet Saturn, Sun Ra's ideology and multi-media performances combined this futuristic space narrative with Afrocentric Egyptian mythology, and standard jazz tunes with percussive, radically free collective improvisations that were quite often aleatoric and featured unusual instruments such as the synthesizer, violin, or piccolo, as well as the Arkestra's trademark "space chants" (Lock 13–74). "Space is the place" where, the Arkestra's "Space Ethnic Voices" intoned hypnotically, "Your bond / Is free / And your life is / Worthwhile."

The goal of the black uprising in "Answers in Progress" is a similarly utopian or futuristic one: the poem that disrupts the short story halfway through admonishes the revolutionaries to

> walk on out through sunlight life, and know
> we're on the go

for love
to open
our lives
to walk
tasting the sunshine
of life. (129–30)

"[W]e have / each other," the poem continues, and its utopian vision is virtually identical with the one Sidney Bechet described so eloquently in *Treat It Gentle:*

> My people, all they want is a place where they can be people, a place where they can stand up and be a part of that place, just being natural to the place without worrying how someone may be coming along to take that place away from them. There's a pride in it, too. The man singing it, the man playing it, he makes a place. For as long as the song is being played, *that's* the place he's been looking for. (203)

For Baraka, too, black music allows its practitioner as well as its audience to "visit another place. A place where Black People live. But dig, not only is this a place where Black People live, it is a place, in the spiritual precincts of its emotional *telling,* where Black People move in almost absolute openness and strength" (*Black* 168–69; emphasis added). As unlikely as it may initially appear, Bechet's and Baraka's jazz-poetics of place have the exact same destination.

Before reaching this Promised Land, however—the "Answers" of the title—the revolution "in Progress" must necessarily incur the detention or brutal killing of whites and the incineration of Newark. As Baraka wrote elsewhere, the "creation of a new reality" is only possible "after the destruction of the old" (*Daggers* 200). And that, too, is exactly what the free jazzers were doing: with "an almost *alien* power," Coltrane massacred the popular American song, and "to hear a man destroy all of it, completely, like Sodom, with just the first few notes from his horn, your 'critical' sense can be erased completely, and that experience can place you somewhere a long way off from anything ugly" (*Black* 57, 65). Clearly, then, the inherent hybridity of the jazz aesthetic, both in its literary and musical manifestation, is also a potential source of conflict that can erupt into brutal violence at any moment. Partly, that source lies in what Walter Göbel sees as "the tension between the deterministic form of blues and the utopian form of jazz" (72). In "Answers in Progress," the revolution's teleological determinism necessitates the shedding of blood, but the poem in the middle of the story as well as its soundtrack, courtesy of the Astro Intergalactic Infinity Arkestra, describe the peaceful utopia the current, gory violence strives to effect. And so Baraka was perhaps not merely facetious in declaring, "[i]t is science-fact that Sun-Ra is interested in, not science-fiction" (*Black* 199).

But even the "science-fact" that Baraka hears in Sun Ra's music, and to which he himself lays claim in "Answers in Progress," is after all still utopian. The story gives its date of composition as March of 1967. After the dissolution of the short-lived but influential Black Arts Repertory/Theater School (BART) in Harlem, Baraka had returned to his hometown of Newark, where he established the School's successor, the Spirit House. He also became directly involved in local politics, founding the Black Community Development and Defense Organization intended to further the interests of the city's African American community. "Answers in Progress" is eerily prophetic—Attali's remark that music "has always been in its essence a herald of times to come" rings ominously here—because only four months after its composition, the country's worst race riot since Watts engulfed Newark (Attali 4). For almost a full week, from July 12 to 17, a broad and extremely violent racial uprising turned the city literally into a war zone. The National Guard was mobilized to quell the revolution; over 1,500 people were injured, and police reported 1,300 arrests, not to mention the excessive property damage (Watts 348–56; Woodard 78–84). This massive riot solidified Baraka's resolution to topple the political establishment of Newark. While its mayor, Hugh Addonizio, had been elected partly due to support from African American voters, he proved to be rather impervious to the black community—in "Answers in Progress," "[t]he dead mayor and other wops [are] carried by in black trucks" (128). The forays of Baraka and his fellow black nationalists in the Committee for a Unified Newark (CFUN) into power politics were initially unsuccessful, but in 1970, Kenneth Gibson, whose candidacy was endorsed by the CFUN and whose campaign was engineered in part by Baraka himself, defeated Addonizio in a runoff election (Watts 356–63; Woodard 143–55). Bursting with confidence, the black nationalist-poet-activist declared, even before the runoff, that the Gibson mayoralty would turn Newark into "New Ark . . . an example upon which one aspect of the entire Black nation can be built" (qtd. in Watts 363). But Baraka's romantic vision of a unified black nation grooving to the space chants of Sun Ra's Arkestra was not to be. Gibson turned out to be a hard-nosed pragmatist and technocrat, and before long the mayor's office and Baraka's black nationalists were bitter political enemies. Of course, Baraka and the CFUN could not openly oppose Gibson's reelection, and Baraka in the course of the following years became so disillusioned with black electoral politics that he discarded the utopia of New Ark altogether and transformed himself once more, this time into a primitive Marxist-Leninist (Watts 364–67, 420–21).

Just as Baraka the would-be politician romanticized the public sphere of New Ark, so does "Answers in Progress" romanticize the private life of the narrator. The end of the short story releases the narrator into domestic bliss: "I knew after tomorrow's duty, I had a day off, and I knew somebody waitin' for me at my house, and some kids, and some fried fish, and some carrots, and wow" (132). In reality, Baraka's private life was in a state of turmoil in the spring of 1967. After his failed marriage to Hettie Cohen (white and Jewish), he had been in a series of less than committed relationships with black women. Shortly before his departure to Newark, he had impregnated eighteen-year-old Bumi, member of an African dance troupe affiliated with BART. Bumi, intent on seeing Baraka fulfill his responsibilities as father of their child, followed him to Newark, which did not, however, prevent the poet-activist from entering into a relationship with actress and dancer Sylvia Robinson. He even attempted to persuade the two women of the righteousness of a polygamous marriage, justified, so he claimed, by the tenets of Maulana Karenga's Kawaida ersatz-religion that he had espoused. Conveniently for Baraka, already the disinterested father of three children, Bumi fell suddenly ill and died in the hospital. Even though this freed him to marry Robinson, who adopted the name Amina, later that same year, their relationship, too, would prove to be rather calamitous at times, mostly due to Baraka's virulent sexism (Baraka, *Autobiography* 320–35; Watts 291–95, 345–47).

Thus, both Baraka's private life and public career in the late 1960s and early 1970s resembled a dystopia much more closely than the family idyll to which the narrator of "Answers in Progress" retreats, or the New Ark the black revolutionaries and their blue alien allies seek to build. The fact that *Tales* features thinly veiled autobiographical first-person narrators and ends with a romantically idealized fiction of the private self, but with an unresolved revolution organized by the public self, not only raises certain ethical questions.[34] It also highlights that, ultimately, "Answers in Progress" is not discrepant engagement in Mackey's sense of the term, but rather discrepant escapism—unlike Langston Hughes's "Bop" or Ralph Ellison's "Cadillac Flambé"; or Sun Ra's "Space is the Place," for that matter.[35] Where Sidney Bechet's fictional autobiography serves to illuminate the jazz aesthetic, Amiri Baraka's autobiographical fiction, in the end, only serves to aggrandize the author's fictional alter ego.

Published in 1967, the same year as *Tales*, Baraka's collection of music criticism, simply titled *Black Music,* also ended on a utopian note regarding the future of jazz: "But there is a theory stated just before. That what will come will be a *Unity Music.* The Black Music which is jazz and blues, religious and secular. Which is the New Thing and Rhythm and Blues. The consciousness of social reevaluation and rise, a social spiritualism. A mystical walk up the street to a new neighborhood where all the risen live. Indian-African anti-Western-Western (as geography) Nigger-sharp Black and strong" (210–11). These predictions have not come to pass, either: the demise of free jazz, accelerated by the premature death of John Coltrane in 1967, was succeeded by the crass commercialism of much of fusion and, later, smooth jazz in the 1970s and 1980s, while the last decade of the century saw the consolidation of the museological zeal of the neo-conservatives around Wynton Marsalis. If there exists a black "unity music" today at all, it is arguably hip-hop. Even so, the recurrent materialism and hedonism of hip-hop is obviously not the kind of "social spiritualism" Baraka had in mind.[36] Baraka, certainly in his Black Nationalist phase, had to dismiss and suppress the hybridity inherent in both literary and musical jazz; he therefore could not and would not acknowledge the jazz aesthetic's recognition that complete transcendence is, ultimately, impossible—hence the escapism of "Answers in Progress" and the illusive prophecy at the end of *Black Music.*

Nonetheless, the "unearthly" and "miraculous music" of Ann Petry's Georgie Barr does indeed echo through Amiri Baraka's short story, if on another frequency to be sure (Petry, "Marie" 14). "Answers in Progress" clearly sounds many of the same blue notes as Langston Hughes's "Bop" and Ralph Ellison's "Cadillac Flambé." Nathaniel Mackey points out that black music avails itself of "a liminality that situates it somewhere between the reality from which it recoils and the ideal to which it aspires (and thereby makes it suggestive of both)," and the often grotesque violence in these stories is the result of the eruption of the perpetual tension between the ideal and the real (*Discrepant* 46). Free jazz tenor saxophonist Albert Ayler, on the other hand, insisted that "One day, everything will be as it should be" because jazz was "the healing force of the universe" (qtd. in Lock 212, 59). Until then, though, the exigencies of American history and reality suggest that Dizzy Gillespie's admonishment, to be or not to bop, may express a more viable stance.

CHAPTER 4

Kinds of Blue

TONI MORRISON, HANS JANOWITZ, AND THE JAZZ AESTHETIC

> Play it, jazz band!
> You've got seven languages to speak in
> And then some. . . .
>
> LANGSTON HUGHES, "Jazz Band in a Parisian Cabaret"

"There are," says Nathaniel Mackey's N., "musics which haunt us like a phantom limb" (*Bedouin* 1). Clearly, Hughes's "Bop," Ellison's "Cadillac Flambé," and Baraka's "Answers in Progress" are haunted, and violently so, by jazz. The crossroads these stories traverse are a figurative place where, Mackey explains, "[i]mmanence and transcendence meet, making the music social as well as cosmic, political and metaphysical"—violent and spiritual (*Discrepant* 235). The violence in these stories is also part and parcel of the "double paradox," or crossroads, Walter Göbel discerns in the uses of music by the contemporary African American novel: "thematically it fuses engagement with escapism, formally the revolution of poetic language with the devaluation and transcendence of linguistic expression. . . . The interpretations of the music thus oscillate between syncretic utopia, subversion of the dominant culture, and nostalgic projection, three elements which . . . can coexist" (Göbel 80–81). The tenor of this critical discourse of literary jazz is, again, the negotiation of binary pairs that the jazz aesthetic in fact thrives on, engaging seemingly disparate, opposite elements. Jazz is, after all, a decidedly hybrid music, but its very hybridity therefore also raises the question of how viable a tool a literary-critical jazz aesthetic can be for the examination of a distinct African American literary tradition. For the history of literature written by blacks in America has always consisted of the struggle to establish an 'authentic' voice against a dominant culture that has sought to silence, distort, or ignore that voice.

In 1951, James Baldwin wrote that "[i]t is only in his music . . . that the Negro of America has been able to tell his story" (*Notes* 24). But that same year, British jazz critic Leonard Feather published in the pages of *Down Beat* magazine a blindfold test with jazz trumpeter Roy Eldridge. Throughout his distinguished career, Eldridge had repeatedly expressed his firm belief that white and black jazz musicians had distinctly different styles and that he could easily distinguish between them. When Feather took him at his word and administered the test, the results were somewhat astonishing: the musician, nicknamed "Little Jazz" by his peers, was either noncommittal or wrong much more often than he was right (Feather, *Book* 47). Listening to Billy Taylor's recording of, ironically, "All Ears," the seventh of ten selections, Eldridge's irritation mounted: "I liked the pianist. Couldn't tell who was colored and who was white. They could be Eskimos for all I know," he admitted and had to concede defeat in the end (Feather, "Little" 12).[1] Eldridge's blindfold test again raises the old yet still provocative question: can white folks play the blues? If, indeed, the end product of a jazz performance transcends what W. E. B. Du Bois called "the problem of the color-line,"can jazz itself still provide a useful critical framework for the study of black American cultural expressions (v)? To be sure, music, instrumental music at least, is a much more abstract art form than literature, but the contemporary critic still faces the same dilemma that confronted Roy Eldridge: the apparent paradox that jazz music is at once a distinctly black American art form as well as a cultural hybrid.

Some of the ways in which the literary jazz aesthetic negotiates this tension between authenticity and hybridity may be clarified by the comparison of two novels, both of which bear the title *Jazz.* The first one, published in 1992, is Toni Morrison's *Jazz,* set during the Harlem Renaissance. The second one was originally published in 1927, a year after Morrison's Violet Trace mutilates the face of a dead girl at a Harlem funeral. Also entitled *Jazz,* that novel's plot is set in London and Paris, does not contain any major characters who are black, and was written by Hans Janowitz, a German-speaking Jew born in southern Bohemia.[2] Despite the obvious and enormous differences between Morrison and Janowitz and their books, both employ virtually identical techniques to achieve "the translation of the world into jazz music," as Janowitz puts it (24).[3] In theme, cast of characters, and setting, the two novels diverge dramatically: Morrison's grand, epic sweep interrogating the meanings of history and identity contrasts sharply with Janowitz's short, lighthearted comedy of errors. It is therefore all the more significant that both texts, in striving to forge an aesthetic of literary jazz, employ the same narrative strategies of style and structure. This suggests the need for a critical practice that is not predicated solely on form and language, as most contemporary jazz critiques are. The tendency of structuralist approaches to privilege literary text at the expense of historico-cultural context is not really in tune with the jazz aesthetic.

Toni Morrison's novel *Jazz* is not, strictly speaking, about jazz at all. Its very first paragraph sounds the basic theme: a woman named Violet went to a funeral to mutilate the face of a dead eighteen-year-old girl, who had been shot by Violet's husband in a desperate act of misguided love. This, then, is the melody on which the disembodied first-person narrative voice improvises a story, or several stories, constantly adding, revising, inventing, shifting back and forth between various characters, going back in time as far as antebellum Virginia. The various stories and voices the narrator evokes are, as Morrison explains, designed to reflect "a jazz performance in which the musicians are on stage. And they know what they are doing, they rehearse, but the performance is open to change, and the other musicians have to respond quickly to that change. Somebody takes off from a basic pattern, then the others have to accommodate themselves. That's the excitement, the razor's edge of a live performance of jazz" ("Toni" 41). How important jazz is for her writing she underscored already in 1983, when she described her style as "hanging on to whatever that ineffable quality is that is curiously black. The only analogy that I have for it is music. John Coltrane does not sound like Louis Armstrong, and no one ever confuses one for the other, and no one questions if they are black. That is what I am trying to get at . . ." ("Interview" 153).[4]

Hans Janowitz's *Jazz,* on the other hand, sprang from a completely different cultural environment. Janowitz was born in the Czech town of Podebrady in 1890. Studying in Prague, the bilingual Janowitz—he was fluent in Czech and German—associated with the Prague Poetry Circle, where he met Franz Kafka, Max Brod, Karl Kraus, and others, and began to publish essays and poetry. After the war, he eventually settled in Berlin, where he co-wrote the script for the German silent movie classic *Das Cabinet des Dr. Caligari* and became an overnight celebrity, finding ample work in the movies and the theater. It was in the cabarets of Berlin where he encountered this new, exciting music from America that appeared to furnish the perfect soundtrack for life in the chaotic Weimar Republic. Thus inspired, he began to write a novella entitled *Jazz,* which was published in 1927 to great critical acclaim (Brady 468–70; Kracauer

62–66; Riess 125–28). Much like Morrison's novel, Janowitz's book is not strictly about jazz either, although the narrative voice consciously and overtly emulates jazz music. Like the former, the latter, too, tells a love story that turns out differently than anticipated. Its basic theme or melody is the chance encounter on a train from Liverpool to London between Lord Henry, a young English playboy and would-be jazzer, and Madame Mae R., a beautiful aristocrat and flapper. Henry and Mae are smitten with each other but are separated before they learn the other's identity. For the rest of the book, the first-person narrator traces Lord Henry's rise to fame in Paris as the leader of the hugely successful "Lord Punch's Jazz Band" and Madame Mae's efforts to track down Henry. In the process Janowitz's narrator also adds, speculates, invents, improvises, moving back and forth between Paris and London, the past and the present, introducing new characters and musing about their motives. And in order to make his world jazz, a world so different from Morrison's, Janowitz nevertheless deploys the same structural and stylistic devices.

I. Jazzing Up the World: From Harlem to Paris

Toni Morrison's jazz critics have primarily focused on two aspects of her novel in order to assess the aesthetic at work, namely narrative structure and language. Perhaps the most jazz-like aspect of the novel's technique of storytelling is its narrative voice, and Paula Gallant Eckard goes so far as to claim that "[t]hough unnamed, jazz is the essential narrator of the novel" (13). Critics have correctly pointed out that the narrator resembles a jazz soloist who improvises on a basic theme—the novel's first paragraph—and in the course of the solo constantly invents, re-harmonizes, elaborates, digresses, and explores.[5] Significantly, it is a narrative voice engaged in the creative *process* of storytelling, reacting against and responding to other voices, other sounds, picking up new motifs on the way, correcting itself, even contradicting itself:

> Risky, I'd say, trying to figure out anybody's state of mind. But worth the trouble if you're like me—curious, inventive, and well-informed. Joe acts like he knew all about what the old folks did to keep on going, but he couldn't have known much about True Belle, for example, because I doubt Violet ever talked to him about her grandmother—and never about her mother. So he didn't know. Neither do I, although it's not hard to imagine what it must have been like. (137)

The narrator's storytelling is truly improvisational: "I watched them through windows and doors, took every opportunity I had to follow them, to gossip about them and fill in their lives" (220).

Janowitz's narrative voice, like Morrison's, is not only gossipy and judgmental, but also forgoes linear narration by switching back and forth in time and place, invoking new voices, finding and elaborating new motifs, improvising scenes and dialogue—in short, it too is a narrative voice engaged in the creative process of storytelling: it revels in interrupting its own storyline "because it brings me delight to disrupt syncopationally the so-called course of the action once again and always again. For do not forget, ladies and gentlemen: it is a jazz novel that is developing here. After all, the jazz character must finally erupt somewhere. And because much has been ruptured in this chapter already, it shall therefore erupt in the next one" (19). Where Morrison's narrator improvises and leaves the basic melody of the storyline behind to elaborate on the beauties of the city sky or explain the significance of Thursdays (35–36, 49–51), Janowitz's narrator improvises as well, elaborating on the characteristics of Hungarian aristocrats in exile or explaining the history of a hotel room mirror, for instance (19–22, 32). And like Morrison's narrator, Janowitz's too remains unnamed, disembodied, running the same risks the jazz soloist runs in the act of creation, correcting itself when necessary in order to maintain a connection between the melodic line of the solo and the underlying chord progression of the song, contradicting itself when that connection ruptures, and, also typical of jazz according to Morrison's critics, eschewing closure[6]:

> A jazz-novel has the right to fade softly in the middle of a motif's repetition and simply come to an end. To safeguard this inalienable right in the first jazz-novel having unfolded according to the laws of jazz music—well, this should naturally be granted to me. If I still take the liberty to afford, say, the saxophone a coda, softly accompanied by violin, piano, and drum, then you may be displeased with this or not: I have to leave it at that. The jazz-instrument is difficult to control, it likes to go its own soundways, and so I let it speak here once again, although I cannot entirely suppress the fear it could pull a prank on the jazz-character, its own innate character, you see. But I cannot avail anything against this either; for I am, after all, fully and completely at the mercy of my instruments, in the scope of this narrative. (Maybe I should rather be doing chamber music next time?) (112)

Thus, the narrative voice in Janowitz's *Jazz* is also, in a way, jazz music itself, creating and reinventing itself in the moment.[7]

But it is not only in terms of narrative structure and technique that Toni Morrison's *Jazz* is jazz, but also on the level of language itself, as many critics have pointed out.[8] Eusebio Rodrigues has put forth perhaps the most detailed stylistic analysis of Morrison's language, as for example with the following passage:

> Dorcas lay on a chenille bedspread, tickled and happy knowing that there was no place to be where somewhere, close by, somebody was not licking his licorice stick, tickling the ivories, beating his skins, blowing off his horn while a knowing woman sang ain't nobody going to keep me down you got the right key baby but the wrong keyhole you got to get it bring it and put it right here, or else. (60)

Rodrigues argues that in its use of onomatopoeia, repetition, and punctuation, this passage enacts the sounds and the structure of jazz music:

> The syllables "ick" and "ing" act in counterpoint. The "ick," first sounded in "t*ick*led," continues to sound, like a pair of drumsticks clicking, in l*ick*ing, l*ic*orice, st*ick*, t*ick*ing . . . The participal "-ing" (set up by the first "knowing") is repeated to maintain a continuous flow of movement: licking, tickling, beating, blowing, knowing, going. Internal echo-rhymes ("where," "somewhere") and balanced repetition ("somewhere," "somebody") quicken the tempo. The tiny riff ("where somewhere, close by, somewhere") with its deliberate commas, placed to compel the voice to pause, enacts a slow shimmy. The three song titles, unpunctuated, are made to run on together. . . . The whole passage ends with a period that is no period, for the voice does not drop but continues to sound. "Or else" is indefinite, incomplete, it is a warning, or else a promise. It resonates, and how does one punctuate a resonance? (735)

It is to be added here that towards the end of the passage, the language is not only polyvocal—we hear, in fact, two voices, the narrator's and the singer's, at one and the same time—but the quickened tempo is also reminiscent of what jazz musicians call double-time, an apparent increase in tempo creating a polyrhythmic effect.

Eusebio's analysis of Morrison's jazz style, however, fits Janowitz's own style almost perfectly. For instance, the second half of the novel's opening paragraph, a tour de force describing the jazz age in Europe, uses the same stylistic devices:

> . . . es war die Zeit der historischen Dissonanzen zwischen Ost und West: das erste Jahrzent des Kommunismus in Russland war bald überstanden, eine neue Menschheit war unter den Sowjets in der einen Welthäfte herangewachsen, streng abgegrenzt vom bürgerlichen Westen des verarmten, zwieträchtig gespaltenen Europa, vom West-Westen des über und über vergoldeten Amerika, eine Kluft von noch nie erlebter Tiefe war aufgerissen zwischen den beiden Hälften der Menschheit, mitten durch die einstige Zivilisation der Demokratie ging jetzt ihr roter Grenzstrich, hinter dem die proletarische Kultur ihr Zukunftsreich baute; diese Dissonanz zwischen Ost und West klang grell durch alles Leben der Erde, ja, es war die Zeit eben dieser grellen Dissonanz, aufgewühlter Kontraste, es war die Zeit der wilden Kindereien, Schattenwürfe nur der tragischen Verwilderungen, die noch bevorstanden, es war die Zeit der wilden Freude an wilder Lausbüberei, an wildem Unfug im Ordnungsbereich, kurz: das wahre Programm der Zeit hiess:
>
> Jazz,
>
> und Jazz ist es natürlich auch, womit wir uns hier beschäftigen wollen. (6–7)
>
> . . . it was the time of historic dissonances between East and West: the first decade of Communism in Russia was soon survived, a new mankind had grown up under the Soviets in one half of the world, strictly demarcated from the burgeois West of the impoverished, discordantly split Europe, from the West-West of the all over overgilded America, a chasm of heretofore unprecedented depth was ripped open between the two halves of mankind, straight through the former civilization of democracy its red borderline went, behind which the proletarian culture built its future empire; this dissonance between East and West sounded shrilly through all life on earth, yes, it was the time of just this shrill dissonance, of stirred-up contrasts, it was the time of wild kiddie games, only shadowshapes of the tragic wilderness yet to come, it was the time of the wild joy in wild tricksterishness, in wild mischief in

> the area of law and order, in short: the real program of the time was:
>
> Jazz,
>
> and it's of course jazz that we shall be dealing with here.

The vowels *o* and *e* in the words "Ost" and "West" at the beginning act in counterpoint, and they continue to sound, for example, in the accentuated middle syllable of "Eur*o*pa" and "Am*e*rika" respectively; the contrast in sound is linked twice to the historical dissonance of the time. The consonant cluster *st*, reminiscent of the sound of a hi-hat, continues to sound as well, in "ers*t*e," then again in "eins*t*ige" and "Kontras*t*e," thus repeated to create a flowing rhythm that quickens (as when "West-Westen" is complemented by "über und über," rhythmically constituting double-time) or relaxes (as after "eine Kluft"). The sequencing of the root *wild* has the same effect. Moreover, the consonant cluster *st* of the hi-hat is complemented by the voiceless alveolar fricative *ss* of the sizzle cymbal accentuating the flow of the language: the fricative in "Di*ss*onanzen" recurs in "Ru*ss*land," "aufgeri*ss*en," "hie*ss*," and finally in "Jazz" toward the end.[9] Here, the fricative resonates across the physical boundaries of pagination and spacing as well as the grammatical boundaries of punctuation: " . . . hie*ss:* Jazz, und Jazz . . . ," a combination of syncopation, semantics, grammar, syntax, and spacing, which has a polyrhythmic effect. Because the opening paragraph does not really deal with the music itself, jazz functions, much like in Rodrigues's analysis, as both a warning (of the ostensibly chaotic nature of these jazzy times) and a promise (jazz as the "program" that can make sense of these "wild" times). The passage also contains two riffs, the recurring phrase "es war die Zeit" and "Dissonanzen zwischen Ost und West." Moreover, a call and response pattern emerges, with "es war die Zeit" the call, the historical elaborations the response. Lastly, the word "Jazz" is polyvocal too, as it is both the narrator's voice we hear and the voice of the time declaring itself the Jazz Age, another instance of call and response. Clearly, then, what Rodrigues says of Morrison's jazz also pertains to Janowitz's jazz: "What we experience is language trying to become music as it tries to capture the flow of human time" (751).

Thus, if we are to adopt the theoretical framework of literary jazz put forth by Morrison's jazz critics, we must also concede that Janowitz's novel is, in fact, a jazz novel—and perhaps it very well is. But what is more, many of Morrison's jazz critics reference jazz as a marker of authentic blackness: for example, Alan J. Rice concludes that "Morrison's jazzy prose style is . . . an aesthetic device to foreground her blackness," while Robin Small-McCarthy emotes that "[i]n her consistent use of selected conventions of the jazz aesthetic, and in concert with our African ancestors, Morrison seems to sing out that 'The [holy] spirit will not descend without song'" (A. Rice, "Jazzing" 432; Small-McCarthy 295). Both of these statements are emblematic of the fact that "[i]f we think of 'jazz' not only as a music but as a relatively self-contained and identifiable culture, we are unlikely to discover other cultures as consumed with the idea of authenticity," as E. Taylor Atkins points out (23). This, then, forces the provocative question: since Janowitz's *Jazz* fits so neatly into the critical framework demarcated by Morrison's jazz critics, is it also a 'black' novel? Obviously, it is not. And yet, the challenge that the preceding comparative analysis poses is this: if indeed the *literary* jazz aesthetic transcends culture, race, and even language itself, how can a *critical* aesthetic of jazz still be useful for the study of African American literature? Part of the problem is the theoretical template that Morrison's jazz critics use in their efforts to make *Jazz* jazz, as most of their interpretations avail themselves of a primarily structuralist approach. That is, they argue that because the text's structure and style contain certain elements derived from jazz music—improvisation, the riff, call and response, et cetera—Morrison's novel becomes, thus, jazz literature. What these critics either misrepresent or ignore altogether is how the novel's aesthetic gesture connects with jazz history. Clearly, the critical investigation of a literary jazz aesthetic must hence be grounded much more firmly in the history of jazz music and cannot rely on an analysis of form and structure only. A more fruitful approach, perhaps, may be initiated by examining how Toni Morrison's novel—a novel in which the word *jazz* occurs only once: on the title page—is grounded in the history of the music, specifically the aesthetic of the jam session and the cutting contest.

II. Cutting to the Chase: Dexter Gordon and Wardell Gray, Morrisonian Cracks and Ellingtonian Breaks

The jam session was, as Ralph Ellison called it, "the jazzman's true academy" (*Shadow* 245). In an art form that for the first half-century of its existence knew no formal schooling and was not represented in academia, informal gatherings of musicians improvising with each other free from the demands of producers, agents, promoters and club owners provided both the training ground and the experimental laboratory for jazz musicians. The cutting contest is a particularly competitive variety of this jazz tradition and arose out of early New Orleans jazz. In the first decade of the twentieth century, there were roughly thirty bands active in the Crescent City. As a form of advertising, bands would routinely ride through the streets of Storyville on horse-drawn wagons promoting various events and products. When a chance meeting between two rival orchestras occurred, quite often a so-called "bucking contest" would ensue: their wagons were tied together by a rope to prevent escape, and each band would try to outplay the other in a contest of skill, endurance, and volume. Later, in the heyday of the swing era, the so-called battle of the bands pitted two orchestras against each other in a similar fashion; the victory of Chick Webb's orchestra over the "King of Swing," Bennie Goodman, at the Savoy Ballroom in 1936 is perhaps the most famous such battle (Bechet 63–68; Berendt 22–24; "Cutting"; Polillo 72–73, 127–28, 146–48). Unlike the bucking contest or the battle of the bands, the cutting contest is waged between individual musicians. In a cutting contest, two or more soloists alternately improvise on the same tune with the ultimate goal of "cutting" or outplaying the opponent by countering, subverting, expanding, and ultimately topping the opponent's musical ideas. Solo space is allotted in accordance with the success or failure of the improviser as adjudicated on the spot by both the musicians on the bandstand and the listeners in the audience. Often, the formula for such a competition will pit two musicians who play the same instrument against each other, according one chorus to each player at the beginning before steadily decreasing solo space to four measures each (hence the term "trading fours"), occasionally even to two or one. The cutting contest thus constitutes the musical variety of African American oral traditions like signifying, playing the dozens, or other call and response patterns (DeVeaux, *Birth* 210–12; Townsend 56–60). While the informal jam session had always been a vital ritual in musicians' circles, the cutting contest began to acquire even more significance with the demise of the swing big bands starting in the late 1930s: as job opportunities in larger orchestras steadily decreased, jazz musicians were forced to compete for jobs in small combos or found their own band. Thus, although held mostly in a congenial atmosphere, the purpose of cutting contests was to establish and maintain a hierarchy of professional ability and competence. As such, they constituted not only the breeding ground of what would become the bebop revolution, but they also carried potentially wide-ranging economic implications for all involved: newcomers just might land a gig with a big name in the business or even secure a recording contract if they managed to "cut" their opponents, whereas arrived players had to protect their reputation as well as their market value and, if possible, enhance it by cutting particularly tenacious upstarts or well-established rivals (DeVeaux, *Birth* 208–10). On this "musical dueling ground," Ellison, himself a trumpeter, noted that "even the greatest can never rest on past accomplishments, for, as with the fast guns of the Old West, there is always someone waiting in a jam session to blow him literally, not only down, but into shame and discouragment" (*Shadow* 246). Trombonist Dicky Wells remembers some of the cutting contests at the countless basement clubs in Harlem in the early 1940s:

> Anyone could go, but mostly performers went, mostly musicians. . . . All the musicians would be sitting around the walls, all around the dance floor. Maybe there would be forty guys sitting around there. The floor was for dancers only, and they would be cutting each other, too, while we were cutting each other on the instruments. Everybody would be blowing—maybe six trombones. Now Hawk [tenor saxophonist Coleman Hawkins] would always come by the session . . ."I just happened to stop by and had my horn," he would say. You knew he'd come to carve somebody. (24)

Coleman Hawkins was one of the most feared opponents in cutting contests, and tenor saxophonists proved to be particularly combative; some of these battles have acquired near-mythical status in jazz lore. The bartender at the legendary Minton's Playhouse remembers the frequent bouts fought between Ben Webster, a tenorist in the swing tradition, and Lester Young, whose style became the model for many emerging beboppers: "Lester Young and Ben Webster used to tie up in battle like dogs in the road. They'd fight on those saxophones until they were tired out; then they'd put in long-distance calls to their mothers, both of whom lived in Kansas City, and tell them about it" (qtd. in Ellison, *Shadow* 246–47).

Among the many young players sowing the seeds of bebop and challenging the older, established generation of Hawkins and Webster was a tenor saxophonist from California, Dexter Gordon. Gordon, an inveterate jammer, had been a member of Lionel Hampton's and Billy Eckstine's big bands, but after he left Eckstine in 1945, his reputation grew when he immersed himself in New York City's after hours jazz scene, honing his craft alongside the likes of Lester Young and Charlie Parker (Gitler, *Jazz* 202–3; Britt 63–68). When he returned to his native Los Angeles a year later, he quickly became the star on the local jam session circuit. Known for his extraordinary harmonic awareness, his big, gutsy sound, and his uncanny ability to weave fragments from campy pop tunes into his solos, he was the perennial winner in cutting contests. Only one other tenorist could hold his own next to Gordon, and that was Wardell Gray. Born in Ralph Ellison's hometown of Oklahoma City, Gray came to the West Coast in 1946—the same year as Gordon, and the same year Charlie Parker collapsed during a recording session and spent six months recuperating in Camarillo State Hospital. Parker's presence was giving the jazz scene around Central Avenue a tremendous boost, and the inconspicuous, soft-spoken Gray, "who couldn't have weighed more than a hundred pounds and wouldn't hurt a flea," who "[r]ead French philosophers and talked about Henry Wallace," as fellow West Coast bopper Hampton Hawes remembered, soon became known as the only saxophonist in town who could make Bird turn his head on the bandstand in disbelief (Hawes and Asher 80; Morgan, liner notes; Gitler, liner notes).[10] As Gordon recalled,

> . . . the jam-session thing was going on very heavily at that time, at several different clubs. At all the sessions, they would hire a rhythm section along with, say, a couple of horns. But there would always be about ten horns up on the stand. Various tenors, altos, trumpets and an occasional trombone. But it seemed that in the wee small hours of the morning—always—there would be only Wardell and myself. It became a kind of traditional thing. Spontaneous? Yeah! Nothing was really worked out. It was a natural thing. (qtd. in Britt 18)

While the two tenorists established a relationship of mutual professional respect and personal friendship, their musical battles were nonetheless a very serious business indeed, as Gordon was quick to point out: "It wasn't somebody would say, 'I can play better than you man,' but actually . . . that's what it was. It was serious—shit, dead serious. You'd think, damn, what the fuck was he playing? You'd try to figure it out, what was going on. To a degree, that was one of the things, to be the fastest, the hippest. The tenor player with the biggest tone—that takes balls, that takes strength" (qtd. in Gioia 35). Thus, cutting contests are not simply won or lost on sheer power and stamina alone; they also entail the vital attempt "to figure it out," to decode, transform, and extend meaning. The competitive juxtaposition of two different interpretations of the same song paradoxically also presupposes a collaborative interface of meaning. The cutting contest, in other words, constitutes a framework in which different meanings both compete and collaborate, where competition and collectivity are interdependent.

Gordon's cutting contests with Gray quickly accrued so much fame that they caught the interest of record producer Ross Russell, owner of the Dial record label. Russell put Gordon and Gray into the studio in the summer of 1947 and accorded them the then uncommon luxury of a six-and-a-half minute recording—so long in fact that it would take up both sides of a 78 rpm disc when it was released—with the express intent of recreating the fire and excitement of a cutting contest. The tune selected, aptly entitled "The Chase" and penned by Gordon, had evolved out of the spontaneous battles between Gordon and Gray. The title was chosen as a reference to the two chasing the competition off the bandstand as well as subsequently chasing each other (Gitler, *Jazz* 209–10; Wiggins 315–16). "The Chase" is a standard thirty-two bar song with an AABA structure and derives from the time-honored New Orleans vehicle "High Society." After stating the introduction and theme in unison, Gordon leads off with one full chorus of improvisation and is followed by Gray, then another chorus by Gordon, then back to Gray again. After Jimmy Bunn's piano solo of one chorus, it is Gray who leads off, this time for sixteen measures, followed by Gordon's half. The next chorus is subdivided even further, Gray and Gordon alternating every eight bars before "trading fours"—alternating solos of four measures—in the final chorus of improvisation. This is followed by a riff section in which Gordon and Gray, switching the sequence once again, continue to trade fours. The steadily decreasing solo space accorded to the soloists as well as their alternating order heightens the intensity of the improvisations and has Gordon and Gray literally chase each other.

This was not only the first studio recording that sought to put the cutting contest into a commercially viable format, it also became Dial's best-selling record, outpacing by far the sides Charlie Parker had cut for the label. The sales figures were so encouraging that Russell called Gordon back into the studio a mere six months later to pair him with another tenorist, Teddy Edwards, on a tune entitled "The Duel" in an (unsuccessful) attempt to capitalize on the commercial success of "The Chase." It was the success of this recording, too, which helped in no small measure to popularize the two-tenor-battles, which just around that time evolved into the ritualistic centerpiece of impresario Norman Granz's highly profitable Jazz At The Philharmonic concert series (Britt 16–21; Gitler, *Jazz* 209–10). But as one of the veterans of the early days of the cutting contests recalled, it was Gordon's commanding presence on the

West Coast jam session scene that paved the way: "he did a lot of beautiful things. Like he and Wardell Gray—'The Chase.'. . . They actually started the two-tenor thing" (qtd. in Britt 26). In fact, the term *chase* made its way into the jazz lexicon and has become synonymous with *cutting contest* ("Chase").

One of these unrehearsed chases was captured on record in July of 1947 at the Elk's Club on Central Avenue, and the tune showcasing the vaunted battle between the two tenor saxophonists is appropriately enough entitled "The Hunt."[11] It opens with solos by trumpeter Howard McGhee and alto saxophonist Sonny Criss, each followed by polite applause. Next is trombonist Trummy Young, a veteran of the Earl Hines and Jimmy Lunceford orchestras and the only representative here of the older generation of the swing era. It is probably Wardell Gray who starts the spontaneous riff behind Young, signaling the other musicians' encouragement as well as respect (4:59–5:32).[12] Young is followed by another up-and-coming bebopper, guitarist Barney Kessel. First the audience, then his fellow musicians react favorably to his solo, spurring him on—"go, go!" (7:09–7:10)—by shouting and clapping (6:37–6:38, 7:55, 8:10, 8:16–8:20). Consequently, Kessel's solo is the longest to that point. Then, however, the concluding duel between Gray and Gordon turns what has heretofore been a congenial jam session into a no-holds-barred, take-no-prisoners cutting contest over a total of seventeen choruses. Gray's initially somewhat hesitant opening chorus—it sounds as if he is walking up to the front of the stage as he begins to play—is followed by Gordon, who is encouraged by rhythmic clapping (9:22–9:26). He responds by tapping into his encyclopedic knowledge of popular song and weaves a brief quote from "The Wedding March" into his improvisation, only the first of many such quotations (9:33–34). Gray not only answers in kind, but raises the bar as if to taunt Gordon by firing off one of his signature licks, derived from the Oscar-winning Bing Crosby hit "Swinging on a Star" from the musical *Going My Way* (9:56–9:59), and building much of his chorus on that motif, seemingly determined to beat the master of musical quotations at his own game.[13] No wonder that Gordon in turn seems overeager to initiate hand-to-hand combat as he cuts into the solo of Gray's third full chorus, creating a brief moment of confusion that is resolved when Gordon, in a gesture of chivalry, quickly retreats and lets his opponent finish his turn (11:10–11:12). However, Gordon starts his next turn by 'signifying' at the beginning of his improvisation on the concluding phrase of Gray's, the musical equivalent of throwing down his gauntlet (11:34–11:42). Gray, not to be outdone and probably out to avenge Gordon's disruption in his own solo chorus, first plays a quick flurry of notes behind Gordon (11:44–11:46) and then signifies on the concluding motif of Gordon's solo when he opens the eighth total chorus of the battle (12:05–12:13). This begins the reduction of the exchanges from one full chorus each to eight measures, then later to four in the ninth chorus. As each tenorist tries to outdo the other in an intense and prolonged call and response section of trading fours that whips the audience into a frenzy, Gordon is clearly at a loss twice as to how to respond to Gray's ceaseless, zigzagging lines of eighth-notes in unusual intervals (14:02–14:06, 14:18–14:22) before he finally resorts to a stock blues riff (14:26–14:31) and subsequently recovers. Still, Gray seems to come out of this particular bout slightly ahead—this time. As Ross Russell remembers, these battles were like a "contest between evenly matched boxers of contrasting skills, a Dempsey against a Joe Louis, a Marciano against a Muhammad Ali" (liner notes).

The parallels between the cutting contest, "The Chase," and "The Hunt" on the one hand and Toni Morrison's *Jazz* on the other are numerous.[14] First of all, motifs of cutting, hunting, and chasing permeate the novel. The very first paragraph, the paragraph whose content furnishes the basis for the narrative voice's improvisations, mentions that Violet "went to the funeral to see the girl and to cut her dead face," which is in a sense a cutting contest, albeit a tragicomic one, between Violet and her rival and challenger, the girl who had stolen her husband away (3). Later on, the narrative voice provides a more detailed account of the funeral, ascribing Violet's inexplicable deed to the aggressive, violent half of her split consciousness, "*that* Violet": "She had been looking for that knife for a month. Couldn't for the life of her think what she'd done with it. But *that* Violet knew and went right to it. Knew too where the funeral was going on . . ." (90). Although "the blade she had not seen for a month at least and was surprised to see now aimed at the girl's haughty, secret face" does not do much damage at all, Violet struggles against the young, brawny ushers trying to restrain her because "[m]aybe she had more than one cutting in mind," as the narrative voice surmises (91).

Violet's split consciousness that leads to her cutting her rival foreshadows Joe's hunt for his mother and his chase after his lover, Dorcas. The novel's Golden Gray section ends with alternating parallel plot lines: in the first, Joe is hunting after the mysterious woman the locals in rural Vesper County, Virginia, have dubbed Wild, whom he believes to be his mother. Joe has been trained in woodsmanship by Henry Lestory, also known as Hunters Hunter.[15] Not only is Wild the sort of woman who "made men sharpen her knives," her presence is usually announced by a flock of "redwings, those blue-black birds with the bolt of red on their wings"—surely no coincidence in a novel that early on alludes to Charlie "Bird" Parker in the figure of a "colored man" who "floats down out of the sky blowing a saxophone" (178, 176, 8). Even though Joe makes three attempts to find Wild and comes very close once, he is unable to ascertain whether she is in fact his mother. The second of these two parallel plot lines finds Joe in New York City three decades later chasing his girlfriend, who has just left him for a man her own age, and his search for Dorcas reminds Joe of his past:

> Joe is wondering about all this on an icy day in January. He is a long way from Virginia, and even longer from Eden. As he puts on his coat and cap he can practically feel [his childhood friend] Victory at his side when he sets out, armed, to find Dorcas. He isn't thinking of harming her, or, as Hunter had cautioned, killing something tender. She is female. And she is not prey. So he never thinks of that. He is hunting for her though, and while hunting a gun is as natural a companion as Victory. (180)

Joe follows Dorcas and two girlfriends to a jazz party where Joe, out of misguided love, shoots her fatally. Not only do both of these plot lines tell the story of a chase, they alternate in such a way that they resemble the structure of "The Chase," or any cutting contest: the narrator's voice, narrating the rural chase after Wild, alternates with Joe's own voice, narrating the urban hunt for Dorcas, in passages that progressively decrease in length. The next section is structured according to the same principle, only here the narrator's voice alternates with Dorcas's interior monologue. Not only is the narrative strategy here reminiscent of the jazz term *double-time* in that the text literally moves back and forth between two 'times,' the past and the present; in terms of the dialogic structure of these passages, the narrative voice, in that sense, is the Dexter Gordon to the characters' Wardell Gray or Teddy Edwards.[16] Just as in a cutting contest where the opponents improvise over the same chord changes, so are the two parallel plot lines based on the same theme: the chase after a loved one. And just as in a serious cutting contest, someone is left for dead at the end. Furthermore, Joe's hunt for his mother and later for Dorcas is paralleled by Golden Gray's chase after his biological father, Hunters Hunter. Golden Gray likens his own chase to the search for an amputated arm: "I will locate it so the severed part can remember the snatch, the slice of its disfigurement. Perhaps then the arm will no longer be a phantom, but will take its own shape, grow its own muscle and bone, and its blood will pump from the loud singing that has found the purpose of its serenade" (159). Here again, the narrative voice in its improvisation links the motif of cutting to identity, meaning, and music.

Yet the narrative voice itself concedes defeat toward the end of the story; in a novel filled like a jam session with contesting, contrasting, and competing voices, the narrator appears to be the loser of this particular cutting contest:

> So I missed it altogether. I was sure one would kill the other. I waited for it so I could describe it. I was so sure it would happen. That the past was an abused record with no choice but to repeat itself at the crack and no power on earth could lift the arm that held the needle. I was so sure, and they danced all over me. Busy, they were, busy being original, complicated, changeable—human, I guess you'd say, while I was the predictable one, confused in my solitude into arrogance, thinking my space, my view was the only one that was or that mattered. (220)

However, the novel does not end there—the narrator in effect pulls off a musical save (Berliner 210–16, 379–83; Grewal 135–36). As a music created in the moment, all jazz, the jam session and the cutting contest in particular, relies on the interplay between the musicians themselves and between the performers and their audience. Like jazz, *Jazz* too depends on that interplay between voice and listener, narrator and reader, more so than any of Morrison's other novels. It ends with a plea for our response to the narrator's call: "If I were able I'd say it. Say make me, remake me. You are free to do it and I am free to let you because look, look. Look where your hands are. Now" (229). We are asked to participate in the performance of the narrator's story; after all, as Violet points out toward the end, "[w]hat's the world for if you can't make it up the way you want it?" (208). Thus, the narrator's improvisation is a failure only if we fail to answer its call and refuse, in Dexter Gordon's words, to "try and figure it out," if we decline to participate in what is a process of creating meaning collectively. *Jazz* without a reader is like "The Chase" without Dexter Gordon, or "The Hunt" without Wardell Gray.[17] As jazz critic Ajay Heble observes, "improvisation teaches us by example that identity is a dialogic construction, that the self is always a subject-in-process" (95).

Significantly, Violet and Joe's fragmented lives become meaningful and whole again when jazz is reintroduced into their home—literally in the form of the Okeh records Felice brings with her, and figuratively in the form of the bird they purchase, a bird for whom "nothing was left to love or need but music" (224). Thus, jazz propels the novel's happy end—rather unusual in the Morrison canon. Joe and Violet, together with the appropriately named Felice, indeed arrive at, in Sidney Bechet's memorable phrase, "a place where they can be people, a place where they can stand up and be a part of that place, just being natural to the place without worrying how someone may be coming along to take that place away from them" (203). The couple's journeys (if not the narrative voice's) from fragmentation to wholeness are prefigured by the only jazz composition referenced explicitly, the "Trombone Blues." It is this record which, at the beginning of the novel, affords Violet the opportunity to kidnap a little baby boy in a misguided if unconscious effort to atone for her own inability to bear children and to win Joe back. When the baby's older sister leaves him in his stroller on the sidewalk so that she can procure a copy of said record, Violet seizes the moment. Fortunately, she is apprehended right away, but part of the onlookers' ire is also directed against the irresponsibility of the sister:

> "Will you just look at what she has left that baby for."
> "What is it?"
> "'The Trombone Blues.'"
> "Have mercy."
> "She'll know more about blues than any trombone when her mama gets home." (21)

The "Trombone Blues" was recorded by Duke Ellington's Washingtonians in early September of 1925 in the Pathé Studios on East 53rd Street in New York City, released as Pathé 3633. The other side contained a tune recorded on that same session, significantly entitled "I'm Gonna Hang Around My Sugar" (M. Tucker 263). Thus, the symbolic placement of the record in the baby carriage foreshadows the trajectory of the book's narrative arc: just as the onlookers are focused on the blues, so the narrator in the beginning can see only a tale of loss and violence and a "scandalizing threesome" in the Trace household (6). The theme of familial and personal fragmentation is reversed in the end when, to the narrative voice's own great astonishment, Violet decides to hang around her sugar, as it were. The irony of this prolepsis is deepened by the fact that the "Trombone Blues" is not, strictly speaking, a blues. This also points to a salient narrative strategy in Morrison's fiction: as Trudier Harris has shown, one of the primary techniques Morrison employs is one of "reversal, where outcomes consistently fall short of expectations" (11).

The strategic positioning of the "Trombone Blues" serves to strengthen the connection between the novel and the music even further. Jazz historians agree that this particular session for Pathé does not exemplify the Washingtonians' best work (Schuller, *Early* 320; M. Tucker 153–55). The main shortcoming, especially of the "Trombone Blues," is the inordinate number of breaks—brief suspensions of the accompaniment for one or two measures, during which only one instrument (sometimes two) carries on the melodic or rhythmic line. The eighteen breaks during a total of a little over three minutes of music result in a somewhat strained and choppy performance.[18] However, these recurrent musical breaks in the arrangement of the "Trombone Blues" reappear as psychological breaks, "private cracks," when the narrative voice seeks to explain the "public craziness" of Violet snatching the baby out of the buggy: "I call them cracks because that's what they were. Not openings or breaks, but dark fissures in the globe light of the day. . . . Sometimes when Violet isn't paying attention she stumbles onto these cracks, like the time when, instead of putting her left heel forward, she stepped back and folded her legs in order to sit in the street" (22–23). Furthermore, the aural breaks of the "Trombone Blues" are also mirrored by the visual breaks of blank pages dividing *Jazz* into different sections.

And finally, Mark Tucker's analysis of the breaks in "Trombone Blues" also pertains to the narrative voice's storytelling: "Frequent breaks were characteristic of dance tunes of the time, but the best players—say, a Louis Armstrong or Sidney Bechet—could seize the moment of rhythmic suspension, spin out a phrase or two, then set up the band's entrance in such a way as to make the interruption dramatic . . . The breaks on 'Trombone Blues' do not serve this function. Instead they make an already fragmented structure even choppier" (154). In addition to the narrative voice's weaving together fragmented storylines, its (ostensible) improvisational failure to bridge convincingly the gap between the tales of loss and violence that comprise the majority of the narrative and the image of domestic bliss at the end is emblematic of the fact that as an improviser, the voice is a Pike Davis rather than a Louis Armstrong, a Prince Robinson rather than a Sidney Bechet—a Toby Hardwick rather than a Dexter Gordon or a Wardell Gray.[19]

Nevertheless, the narrator's fragmented story ultimately becomes *Jazz*—and thus also jazz by default—only in the collective interplay with the reader. Hence, the aesthetic gesture of Morrison's novel is identical with the aesthetic gesture of jazz music to such an extent that Ellison's description of the jam session is essentially a description of *Jazz* too:

> The delicate balance struck between strong individual personality and the group during those early jam sessions was a marvel of social organization. I had learned too that the end of all this discipline and technical mastery was the desire to express an affirmative way of life through its musical tradition, and that this tradition insisted that each artist achieve his creativity within its frame. He must learn the best of the past, and add to it his personal vision. Life could be harsh, loud and wrong if it wished, but they lived it fully, and when they expressed their attitude toward the world it was with a fluid style that reduced the chaos of living to form. (*Shadow* 229)

The lives that Morrison's narrator witnesses, narrates, and invents are also harsh, sometimes loud, and sometimes wrong. But from the first word to the last, and even beyond, the narrative voice is engaged in this very struggle, to reduce the chaos of living to form with a fluid style.

III. Octopi and Phantom Limbs: Jazz and Intertext

Thus, the aesthetic gesture in Morrison's novel is explicitly inventive, just like African American jazz has always been. At the same time, the jam session and the cutting contest, as well as the Washingtonians' "Trombone Blues," provide the reference points that ground her literary jazz firmly in the history of jazz music. Here, then, is also the difference to Janowitz's *Jazz.* The aesthetic gesture in his novel is, ultimately, *imitative:* "You will allow me to use the circumstance that I am writing a jazz-novel as an excuse, because this book is not going to be a novel of the usual stripe. Other laws, I think, govern this book, just like other laws govern a jazz piece instead of a sonata for piano and violin" (25). Janowitz's jazz narrator copies the "laws" of jazz music, just like European jazz musicians of the 1920s and later copied African American jazz. Friedrich Hollaender for instance, pianist of the Weimar Republic's best jazz combo, the Weintraub Syncopators, remembers the youthful enthusiasm this new, exciting music elicited: "Yass! Yass! everybody shouts, as if someone had forgotten to turn off the faucet. It's 'Jazz' they mean, and everyone wants it and no one can play it. You run and buy yourself the new discs from America, schlep them home, bang them onto the turntable as if to fry eggs and then let them spin, ten times, twenty times, until they get so hot that the needle gets stuck in the melting wax" (qtd. in Rotthaler 135). In other words, Janowitz and Hollaender emulate;

Morrison and Gordon innovate. Janowitz's narrator seeks to transpose the rhythms and sounds of jazz onto the written page, sounding what Jessie B. Simple would call *re*bop, whereas Morrison's narrator, truly a story*teller* of *be*bop, strives in the end to escape the fixed boundaries of the page (or, in musical terms, the notation of the staff). But the difference between Janowitz's and Morrison's jazz is not one of 'racial' essence, nor is it one of calculated reasoning (musical "laws") versus mere feeling (the popular cliché of jazz improvisation): the difference lies in *following* the "laws" of jazz—or, for that matter, those of a violin sonata—and *creating* or *writing* them. While almost nothing is known about Janowitz's exposure to jazz in the Weimar Republic, his novel clearly evinces an appreciation for and understanding of the music as an aesthetic construct. Unlike Morrison half a century later, though, Janowitz simply did not have access to a jazz *tradition* because that tradition was only beginning to be forged on the other side of the Atlantic. Hence, the difference between his literary jazz and that of Morrison is that their aesthetics arise out of very different socio-historical contexts. European jazz remained basically an imitation of the American model, and it was not until the 1960s that it arguably began to speak with a voice of its own. For example, pianist Michael Naura, a pioneer of German modern jazz, remembers that

> [w]hat the regularly employed dance bands played after 1945 were juvenile, really heartwarming and pitiful attempts to copy certain things. I was listening to *Flying Home* played by a radio orchestra . . . that was a wonderful try, but rhythmically it's totally off. . . . We [Naura and vibist Wolfgang Schlüter] formed a quintet with bass, drums, piano, guitar and vibes. We were basically just aping back then, you know. We were like a piece of blotting paper that had to somehow soak up the American ink first. (qtd. in Knauer 160–62)

Because European jazz musicians developed their craft in a completely different economic and cultural context and practiced it within a different social network, cutting contests were a rarity. And even when musicians did participate in informal jam sessions, this setting was always already by necessity an imitation of the American model.[20] As Amiri Baraka explains, "[m]usic, as paradoxical as it might seem, is the result of thought. It is the result of thought perfected at its most empirical, *i.e.* as *attitude,* or *stance.* Thought is largely conditioned by reference; it is the result of consideration or speculation against reference, which is largely arbitrary. There is no *one* way of thinking since reference (hence value) is as scattered and dissimilar as men themselves" (*Blues* 152–53). Literature surely is as much a product of thought as music is, and so the two novels discussed here differ in their "*stance*." Janowitz's *Jazz* refers to the same art form as Morrison's, but its aesthetic gesture, its stance, is by default imitative, lacking a grounding in musical traditions that simply did not exist in Europe. Consequently, the jazz aesthetic demands attention not just to literary and musical form, but, equally important, also to the history of the (predominantly) African American musicians who invented, shaped, and innovated it.

Tenor saxophonist Benny Golson makes a related point that echoes Baraka's notion of different stances: "People talk about music. 'Music is ethnic,' they say. Music in and of itself is *not* ethnic. Notes are merely servants. They only do what we tell them to do. If we know how to write something that's ethnic, then it becomes ethnic. Music in and of itself is not ethnic. Notes are only tonal documentations of pitch, that's all. But what we do with them, now, that's something else" (78).[21] In other words, it is the stance from which these otherwise neutral words are sounded which imbues them with relevance. Yes, jazz is indeed "the great octopus" that will do and use anything, to adduce Dexter Gordon's memorable image once more (qtd. in Gerard 37). At the same time, the octopus's tentacles, however far they may reach, all protrude from the animal's head; that is, the tentacular prey—Golson's "tonal documentations of pitch"—is sought out by the octopus's head—Baraka's concept of stance or attitude. Morrison's *Jazz* is just such an octopus, whose tentacles nab a vast variety of literary cross-references. Its cryptic epigraph already foreshadows the eclectic range of intertextual connections that follow: it is taken from "Thunder, Perfect Mind," considered by scholars to be the most enigmatic of the large body of fourth-century Gnostic texts discovered in 1945 near Nag Hammadi, Egypt (H. Rice 133–35). Octopus-like, the novel itself points to, among others, Dante, Kate Chopin, F. Scott Fitzgerald, Virginia Woolf, William Faulkner, Charles Dickens, Herman Melville, and Nathaniel Hawthorne.[22] And yet, two crucial elements of *Jazz,* the narrative voice and the seemingly minor character of Wild, align it not only firmly with jazz music, but also situate it clearly within the greater context of the black experience in America—that is, the octopus's head.

Jazz's narrative voice harks back most clearly to two literary ancestors, Ralph Ellison and Ann Petry. Morrison's unidentified, disembodied narrator recalls Ralph Ellison's observation that

> There is . . . a cruel contradiction implicit in the art form itself, for true jazz is an art of individual assertion within and against the group. Each true jazz moment (as distinct from the uninspired commercial performance) springs from a contest in which each artist challenges all the rest; each solo flight, or improvisation, represents (like the successive canvasses of a painter) a definition of his identity as individual, as member of the collectivity and as a link in the chain of tradition. Thus, because jazz finds its very life in an endless improvisation upon traditional materials, the jazzman must lose his identity even as he finds it. . . . (*Shadow* 267)

As tenor saxophonist Sonny Rollins, one of the most uncompromising improvisers in jazz, confirms: "I want to get into my own world and create my music," but getting there also has the opposite effect, "[b]ecause when I really concentrate while I am playing, I lose myself" (qtd. in Nisenson, *Open* 12–13). The narrative voice, too, is losing its identity even as it invents, amends, and mingles with all the other voices in the book, and sometimes even corrects its own. Furthermore, the voice's solo flight, rising out of a choir of other contentious voices, echoes both the tradition of jazz music and the African American literary tradition and becomes itself one of its links.

In fact, Ellison's and Rollins's observation concerning the musician's lost-and-found identity and the simultaneity of severance and unity is taken one step further by Nathaniel Mackey, whose concept of black music as a "phantom limb" extends the notion of fragmentation to figurative amputation. To Mackey, the "meeting of transcendence and immanence" in African American musics effects a constant tradeoff between the extant and the imagined, the factual and the fictional: "the phantom limb is a felt recovery, a felt advance beyond severance and limitation that contends with and questions conventional reality, that is a feeling for what is not there that reaches beyond as it calls into question what is" (*Discrepant* 235). This confluence of observation and projection, doubt and revelation, is expressed in the narrative voice's self-reflectivity:

> Pain. I seem to have an affection, a kind of sweet tooth for it. Bolts of lightning, little rivulets of thunder. And I in the middle of the storm. Mourning the split trees, hens starving on rooftops. Figuring out what can be done to save them since they cannot save themselves without me because—well, it's my storm, isn't it? I break lives to prove I can mend them back again. And

> although the pain is theirs, I share it, don't I? Of course. Of course. I wouldn't have it any other way. But it is another way. I am uneasy now. Feeling a bit false. What, I wonder, what would I be without a few brilliant spots of blood to ponder? Without aching words that set, then miss, the mark? (219)

Suffused with images of violence, the narrative voice's uneasiness stems from the realization that the reason for the voice's existence are its own words, and yet those words are also "false." Not only do the (speculative) events the narrative voice describes constitute Mackey's phantom limb, but so does the voice itself: the voice is unquestionably there, observing events from the window, and yet the voice is immaterial, beyond the grasp of the characters—and ultimately beyond our grasp, too. The union with the other characters' lives the narrative voice accentuates here is offset by its admission of alienation: "I ought to get out of this place. Avoid the window; leave the hole I cut through the door to get in lives instead of having one of my own" (220). The severance from the other characters the voice laments is in turn mirrored in them. They all suffer some form of figurative amputation, be it cultural, familial, political, or social. For example, Golden Gray explicitly uses the analogy of amputation—couched in a terminology virtually identical to Mackey's—after he discovers that Hunters Hunter was his biological father:

> Only now, he thought, now that I know I have a father, do I feel his absence: the place where he should have been and was not. Before, I thought everybody was one-armed, like me. Now I feel the surgery. The crunch of bone when it is sundered, the sliced flesh and the tubes of blood cut through, shocking the bloodrun and disturbing the nerves. The dangle and writhe. Singing pain. Waking me with the sound of itself, thrumming when I sleep so deeply it strangles my dreams away. There is nothing for it but to go away from where he is not to where he used to be and might be still. Let the dangle and the writhe see what it is missing; let the pain sing to the dirt where he stepped in the place where he used to be and might be still. . . . This arm that never held itself out to give me balance as I walked thin rails or logs, round and slippery with danger. When I find it, will it wave to me? Gesture, beckon to me to come along? Or will it even know who or what I am? It doesn't matter. I will locate it so the severed part can remember the snatch, the slice of its disfigurement. Perhaps then the arm will no longer be a phantom, but will take its own shape, grow its own

> muscle and bone, and its blood will pump from the loud singing that has found the purpose of its serenade. (158–59)

Golden Gray's analogy of the amputated phantom arm not only echoes the various quests of all the other characters—Joe in search of his mother and Dorcas, Violet in search of an explanation, Dorcas in search of love, Felice in search of her ring—it contains the related theme of orphanhood as well. "Sometimes I feel like a motherless child," the famous spiritual mourns, and so *Jazz*'s phantom limbs are also singing a serenade of the plight of the African diaspora. The novel's ending with its impassioned, sensual plea to the reader indicates that the narrative voice itself is just another one of the many orphans, literal and figurative, that people the narration; without a reader, the book itself and its voice are orphans.

The motif of the phantom limb in turn mutates into a tentacle that points back in the direction of *The Street*. There, the pain of Golden Gray's amputated arm that chokes off his dreams is foreshadowed by Lutie's nightmare. Instead of dreaming of a lucrative singing career with Boots's band after being invited to audition, she has a horrific nightmare of Super Jones snapping at her with "wolfish mouth":

> She reached out her hand toward the padlock and the long white fangs closed on her hand. Her hand and part of her arm were swallowed up inside his wolfish mouth. She watched in horror as more and more of her arm disappeared until there was only the shoulder left and then his jaws closed and she felt the sharp teeth sink in and in through her shoulder. The arm was gone and blood poured out. She screamed and screamed and windows opened and the people poured out of the buildings—thousands of them, millions of them. She saw that they had turned to rats. The street was so full of them that she could hardly walk. They swarmed around her, jumping up and down. Each one had a building chained to its back, and they were all crying, "Unloose me! Unloose me!" (192–93)[23]

Unlike Violet, Joe, or Felice, Lutie will not be able to mediate the terror of the nightmarish phantom arm; its serenade will drown out her own song of escape, independence, and self-determination. For her, there is no transcendence after the murder of Boots and the severance from Bub, just a train ticket to Chicago—quite an ironic unloosening.[24]

In addition, Morrison's narrative strategy constitutes a logical extension of Petry's experiments with point of view, as *Jazz*'s disembodied narrative voice bears some resemblance to *The Street*'s Mrs. Hedges. Although she rarely leaves her apartment, Mrs. Hedges is the undisputed patroness of 116th Street who knows everyone and everything. "Early in the morning she was there in that window like she'd been glued to it," remarks a resentful Super Jones (288). Perched at the open window of her apartment, nothing escapes her scrutiny, and her detailed knowledge about the street and its denizens, even more than her partnership with Junto, makes her the single most influential person on the block with the power to route the course of people's lives. Mrs. Hedges is continuously "staring out of the window, brooding over the street like she thought, if she stopped looking at it for as much as a minute, the whole thing would collapse" (121). Even though both are stationary, reclusive and seemingly all-knowing and employ this as a defense-mechanism, *Jazz*'s narrative voice is in some ways Mrs. Hedges's foil: Where Morrison's disembodied narrator occasionally contemplates the possibility that leaving her window and actually venturing into the outside world would alleviate the loneliness, Petry's Mrs. Hedges, monstrously obese as well as bald and scarred from incurring severe burn wounds in an apartment fire, is determined "never to expose herself to the prying, curious eyes of the world" and is quite content with running a brothel in her apartment (247).

And lastly, *Jazz*'s phantom limbs also have a precursor in Sidney Bechet's *Treat It Gentle.* "Omar," asserts Bechet at the very outset, "he'd have these dreams about things. There was one time he had a dream about his right arm, about losing it at the elbow. After that, he'd only practice shooting with his left hand" (6). The dream's message is realized much later, during the first confrontation between Omar and Marie's master, when the latter "fired at my grandfather. And that ball, it hit in the arm my grandfather had had that dream about. Maybe you won't believe it, but that's how it happened" (16). To be sure, this is but one minor detail with which Bechet spices up his tall tale. At the same time though, the fictional Omar and his equally fictional story—a story about slavery and freedom, love and hate, death and redemption, transcendence and tragedy—become themselves a phantom limb: Omar never really existed, but his figure haunts the entire autobiography. Even *Treat It Gentle*'s narrative voice points, tentacle-like, to Mrs. Hedges in *The Street* and to Morrison's narrator in *Jazz,* for it contains also the phantom limbs of the various narrative voices of Bechet's collaborators—voices that we know are there, but cannot differentiate from Bechet's own. In a sense, then, Omar floats through all of these narratives; in fact, the phantom-like Omar is, perhaps, himself the head of the octopus. Bechet's words are worth quoting again here: "I met many a musicianer in many a place after I struck out from New Orleans, but it was always the same: if they was any good, it was Omar's song they were singing. It was the long song, and the good musicianers, they all heard it behind them. They all had an Omar, somebody like an Omar, somebody that was *their* Omar" (202). Without a doubt, the jazz narratives of Ann Petry, Langston Hughes, Ralph Ellison, Amiri Baraka, and Toni Morrsion all have their own "Omar" behind them, the black experience in the New World and the struggle to transcend the pain and suffering of history. Like the musicians on Congo Square Bechet describes, these jazz narratives, too, are "climbing up in the music like it was a tree and they wanting to shake it down and talk to the moon" (11).

Toni Morrison's *Jazz* actually has its very specific Omar in Wild. Just as Omar stands at the beginning of the events chronicled in *Treat It Gentle,* so the phantom-like Wild stands at the beginning of the events narrated in *Jazz.*[25] Amiri Baraka points out that blues and jazz "could not exist if the African captives had not become American captives," and likewise, *Jazz* could not exist if it were not for Wild (*Blues* 17). Wild, mysterious, elusive, and silent, is a pregnant "naked berry-black woman" who "is covered with mud and leaves are in her hair," huddling beside the road in the night rain when Golden Gray first sees her (Morrison, *Jazz* 144). She in fact embodies what Morrison elsewhere calls "the dark, abiding, singing Africanist presence" in America (*Playing* 5). And while she never actually sings, Wild figures very much as that Africanist presence in the novel, the embodiment of the 'blackness' Morrison seeks to capture in her language, a blackness that is mysterious, elusive, and yet unmistakably 'there,' and that lies at the core of the maze of stories which make up the book: Wild is "[e]verywhere and nowhere" because she is "not a story of a used-to-be-long-ago-crazy girl whose neck cane cutters liked to imagine under the blade, or a quick and early stop for hardheaded children. She was still out there—and real" (179, 167). Perhaps, then, Wild is the embodiment, too, of that most enigmatic problem confounding musicologists: how to describe and define that similarly mysterious, elusive quality called "swing." The novel really don't mean a thing without Wild's swing, and, reminiscent of the narrative sequencing of *The Street,* swing's combination of circular and linear movement is echoed by a structural evolution in *Jazz* where the further the narrative voice progresses with its story, the further back into the past it has to delve.

In fact, *Jazz* also delves into Morrison's own literary past: Wild may very well be the metamorphosed title character of *Beloved* finally having emerged from the woods behind 124 Bluestone Road on the outskirts of Cincinnati—not coincidentally, a road indeed reverberating with blues tones, just like Bechet's bend in the road, Petry's 116th Street, the street in front of Jessie B. Simple's stoop, Lee Willie Minifees's highway, or Baraka's Newark avenues. Beloved is pregnant and naked when she escapes at the end of the novel, leaving behind only footprints in the sandy bed of the creek behind Sethe's house. Wild, too, is naked and pregnant on the rainy night Golden Gray sees her for the first time. The timeline, geography, and characterization strongly suggest that Beloved, who is among many other things also the Middle Passage turned flesh, has transformed into Wild (Aguiar 12; Kubitscheck 159–60). And like the story of Wild, which is more than just a story, the story of Beloved is much more than itself as well in that it is inspired by the infamous case of Margaret Garner, the fugitive Kentucky slave who killed her daughter rather than seeing her returned to slavery.

The figures of Omar and his relatives Wild and Beloved signal one important stipulation for the analysis of jazz narrative: literary-critical practice cannot be divorced from the history and histories of black people in America, and it therefore cannot be reduced to mere linguistic or structural elements. For even if Omar, as his inventor describes him, did not in fact exist, Bechet is still correct because "somebody like an Omar" surely did. Yet Omar, any Omar, could be conceived only in the New World—not in the Weimar Republic of Hans Janowitz. To be sure, Janowitz's book has its own tentacles, too—tentacles nabbing references to *Sturm und Drang,* Cubism, or *Jugendstil.* But there is no Omar, no Wild, that propels his *Jazz.* For Hans Janowitz, jazz is an exciting, novel music, music that offers fresh ways of writing, that inspires a literary game of structure and sound; to him, as to the rest of the European avant-garde, jazz functions as what Jed Rasula terms a "decal" (14–15). But for Toni Morrison—as for Bechet, Petry, Hughes, Ellison, and Baraka—jazz is a way to negotiate the meanings of history and to probe what it means to be black in America. The fictional character Omar is, in a way, the historical conscience behind all of these texts. Thus, Benny Golson is correct: in and of themselves, Morrison's and Janowitz's jazz variations are indeed mere literary translations of "tonal documentations of pitch"; but what each does with the available notes is "something else" after all. And so one question remains: clearly, Hans Janowitz's *Jazz* is not a 'black' novel—but is it a 'jazz' novel? Perhaps, the jazz of Hans Janowitz and the jazz of Toni Morrison are merely two different kinds of blue.

CODA

Waiting to Be the Music

HYBRIDITY, AFRO-MODERNISM, AND CRITICAL PRACTICE

You got some of all of us in you, dontcha? What you gonna do with all that Colored from all over creation you got in you? Better be something good."

PAULE MARSHALL, *The Fisher King*

Instance he's playing now. Improvising. Might be what you like, till you hear the words. Want to listen sharp. Hard. Begin all right: then hear chords a bit off: feel lost a bit. In and out of sacks, over barrels, through wirefences, obstacle race. Time makes the tune.

JAMES JOYCE, *Ulysses*

"The music called *jazz*," insisted James Baldwin, began out of the necessity "not only to redeem a history unwritten and despised, but to checkmate the European notion of the world. For, until this hour, when we speak of history, we are speaking only of how Europe saw—and sees—the world" ("Of the Sorrow" 326). This certainly delineates Toni Morrison's artistic endeavor, too. At the same time, jazz is also "an American language" where, as Sterling Brown contended, "the performer's color does not matter": "Of all the arts, jazz music is probably the most democratic. Mixed units of Negroes and whites have recorded for well over a decade, and most of their records are jazz classics" (24). And thus, the literary jazz of Toni Morrison and Hans Janowitz alerts us to the paradox that jazz music is both: a distinctly black American art form and 'world music.' The jazz aesthetic is inextricably grounded in the black experience in America—and yet, precisely because it challenges the received binary pairs of white and black, the New World and the Old (both Europe and Africa, even Asia), imitation and authenticity, jazz and 'non-jazz,' it is also by necessity a hybrid. As Nicholas Evans reminds us again, jazz "always involves race, nationalism, and related concerns because it heightens the audibility, palpability, and even visibility of the cultural sameness and difference of whiteness and blackness" (18).

What the preceding chapters suggest is that authenticity and hybridity are not, in fact, mutually exclusive. 'Authentic blackness' actually thrives on hybridity: it harnesses the energies inherent in the tension-filled process of cultural production and its myriad possibilities while simultaneously affirming and extending, not diluting, the African American tradition. The jazz aesthetic appears a very viable way to describe and interrogate this ostensible paradox. But if, as David Wills posits, jazz is indeed "a music born of the impossibility of absolute racial definition," it is certainly not impossible to situate jazz within a historical context (139). After all, the texts of Petry, Hughes, Ellison, Baraka, and Morrison all hearken back to their own Omar, and so literary-critical practice must always also be grounded in the history of jazz music and the people who have been making it. But, we remember, Sidney Bechet went to France, not to Africa, to be closer to Omar. Thus, it seems that a jazz critique of African American literature cannot help but be a hybrid, just as jazz itself was and is a hybrid, drawing on and transforming sources from outside the black American experience. To one young music student at Tuskegee who would soon switch from the trumpet to the typewriter, Ellington and Eliot swung to a very similar tune. Ralph Ellison later remembered how jazz had prepared him for his discovery of literary modernism:

> Now, the jazz musician, the jazz soloist, is anything if not eclectic. He knows his rhythms; he knows the tradition of his form, so to speak, and he can draw upon an endless pattern of sounds which he recombines on the spur of the moment into a meaningful musical experience, if he's successful. I had a sense that all of these references of Eliot's, all of this snatching of phrases from the German, French, Sanskrit, and so on, were attuned to that type of American cultural expressiveness which one got in jazz and which one still gets in good jazz. (*Going* 520)

For Ellison, it was this reveling in eclectic fragmentation that linked jazz and modernism. His analogy, however, also alludes, if only faintly, to an important difference between the jazz aesthetic's modernism and literary high modernism. In the jazz aesthetic, the modernist impulse to make it new is not limited to technique only and does not end with finding novel ways to syncopate narrative time. The jazz aesthetic is also aware of "tradition," of a communal past whose meanings have not dissolved completely. In other words, the jazz aesthetic is modernism with a historical conscience.

Of course, "modernism with a historical conscience" is really just another paradox. And the term *modernism* has been just as hotly contested as the term *jazz*.[1] To be sure, the mythical Omar, Lutie's mental improvisations, Simple's revisionist oral history, or the disembodied voice's narrative flights of fancy in Morrison's *Jazz*, all revolve around the key modernist themes of fragmentation, alienation, and epistemology.[2] Even so, the modernism of Bechet, Petry, or Morrison does seem to swing to a different beat than Eliot—or, for that matter, Janowitz—after all. According to Craig Werner, Afro-modernism recognizes

> Afro-American expressive practices as intricate adjustments to a world fragmented by the communal experience of slavery and racial oppression. . . . [T]he central problem confronted by Afro-American culture closely resembles that confronted by mainstream modernism: the alienated individual experiences a profound sense of psychological and cultural dislocation in a world characterized by an accelerating rate of change; he or she subsequently attempts to regain some sense of coherence. The primary difference between Afro- and Euro-American responses to this dilemma can be seen in the tendency of many Euro-American modernists to experience their situation as individual and, to some extent, ahistorical, while Afro-American modernists generally perceive a communal dilemma deriving from historical and political forces. (186–87)

Thus, Afro-modernism also acknowledges what Werner calls the "the practical imperatives of mythological awareness"—or what Bechet simply calls "Omar" (134). As Edward Pavliç seconds, "African American modernist quests are grounded in a distinct historical experience of modernity in which increasingly refined, rigid, and oppressive identity logics of racial segregation played a central role" (83). The "liberation from history" Hugh Kenner has identified as an aspiration of much of (white) American modernism is, in the jazz aesthetic, not only impossible, but perhaps even undesirable (218).

But, again, Bechet resurrected the African slave Omar at the Vieux Colombier in Paris, and he summoned the spirit of authentic New Orleans jazz by quoting a Verdi opera. The octopus-like nature of the jazz aesthetic is related to what Pavliç sees as the "disruptive improvisations" of African American literary modernisms because jazz history, too, is after all replete with just such disruptions (10). To Gary Giddins, for instance, the ultimate modernist disruption occurred with the bebop era:

> Jazz modernists . . . of the era immediately following World War II ignored the traditional repertory, and when they did pay homage to the ancients (ragtimers and New Orleans-style players), whatever regard they may have felt was often soured by condescension. Modernism, after all, was a rallying point, and a political movement—a transformation of mere entertainment into art. The genius-leaders of the movement—Charlie Parker, Dizzy Gillespie, and Thelonius Monk—knew better, of course; the traditions live in even their most volatile experiments, whereas their disciples, more obsessed with the propaganda of the new, were inclined to dismiss as passé the sweetness of Johnny Hodges or the showboating of Louis Armstrong. Still, what both the geniuses and their disciples propagated *was* new. (*Rhythm* xiii)

Yet Giddins also emphasizes that bebop was not really such a radically modernist rejection of the old: "It is now commonplace to view modern jazz as a logical outgrowth of the past, an evolution rather than a revolution. Hindsight is a great peacemaker, especially since no one can mistake the obvious debts Parker, Gillespie, Monk, and [Kenny] Clarke owed such predecessors as [Lester] Young, [Roy] Eldridge, Teddy Wilson, and Jo Jones" (*Celebrating* 66–67).

The modernist tension between tradition and change Giddins diagnoses in bebop is not the only one the music brought to the fore. Bop's "improvisational disruptions," to use Pavliç's phrase again, also interrogated received notions of authentic blackness. We recall that Sidney Bechet had adored Caruso; Charlie Parker, the "genius-leader" of the new movement, begged Edgar Varèse for lessons in music theory and eagerly drank in everything from the tinny brass of a Salvation Army band around the corner to the fiddler in a Romanian restaurant to twangy country and western from the jukebox (Giddins, *Celebrating* 104–13; Reisner 138–39, 229–30). But to Ellison the self-conscious modernist, bop did not sound like "good jazz" at all. Ironically, he heard in bebop something more akin to Euro-American high modernism, namely its severance from the authentic jazz and blues impulse grounded in black vernacular blues culture. "The thinness of much of so-called 'modern jazz' is especially reflective of [a] loss of wholeness," he lamented (*Shadow* 275).[3] Amiri Baraka heard in the same music the exact opposite, an Afro-modernism that paved the way for the next generation of avant-gardists to return to the authentically black roots of jazz: "the moderns, the *beboppers,* showed up to restore jazz, in some sense, to its original separateness, to drag it outside the mainstream of American culture again" with its "willfully harsh, *anti-assimilationist* sound" (*Blues* 181). To both writers, jazz music's hybridity is a threat: Ellison decries it, Baraka suppresses it.

What, then, are the demands the jazz aesthetic as modernism with a historical conscience places on literary-critical practice? Musicologist Ingrid Monson rightly points out that "the heterogeneity of musical elements found in jazz improvisation is deeply related to the heterogeneity of African American cultural experience. The jazz experience has always been more varied and cosmopolitan than many of the narratives that have been written about it" ("Doubleness" 311). Baraka's and Ellison's takes on bebop are precisely such partial narratives, but what they share, disparate as they may be, is the stipulation of authentic blackness as a stable, fixed category that is either normative (implicit in Ellison) or essentialist (explicit in Baraka). As Madhu Dubey notes of more recent trends in African American literary criticism, "[t]he academic production of the vernacular [e.g. blues and jazz] as the ultimate sign of African American cultural difference works along a contradictory circuit, participating in the commodification of black culture as a distinct area of expertise, while redressing anxieties about 'mulattoization' that inevitably attend the commodification of black culture" (310). Take, for instance, how literary criticism has commodified the music of John Coltrane. To Baraka, as we have already seen, Coltrane was the blackest of all black revolutionaries of the sixties, the undisputed leader of the "poets of the Black Nation" (*Black* 176). To Henry Louis Gates, whose tremendously influential theory of Signifyin(g) was explicitly devised, at least in part, to redress the fallacies he perceived in the tenets of Baraka and others in the Black Arts Movement, Coltrane's music of around 1960 is still a "stellar example" of Signifyin(g), the epitome of authentically black cultural practices grounded in the vernacular, and therefore "fundamentally black" (*Figures* xxiv–xxix, 274–75; *Signifying* 104, 64).[4]

In fact, Coltrane, who had journeyed from blues to bebop to hard-bop, had grown dissatisfied by 1960 with the harmonic cycles that had defined jazz improvisation up to that point, and jazz, he felt, had become stagnant. He started to express an increasing interest in the traditional music of India, especially in the patterns and scales of the Indian raga (L. Porter 202–3, 209–11; Kofsky 424–25). He was also beginning to collect recordings by Indian sitar master Ravi Shankar and told a French critic,

"I'm certain that if I recorded with him I'd increase my possibilities tenfold" (qtd. in Polillo 602–3). Furthermore, Coltrane's intense practice regimen had included for quite a few years the *Thesaurus of Scales and Melodic Patterns* by Russian-born maverick lexicographer and musicologist Nicolas Slonimsky, an occasional collaborator of Varèse's, and there are even direct quotations from Slonimsky's tome on some of Coltrane's recordings (L. Porter 149–50).

Thus, Coltrane was clearly looking for inspiration from outside African American culture to reinvigorate his art, and even though his growing interest in Indian music coincided with his immersion in traditional African musics, he was never interested in shaping a musical expression of 'authentic blackness,' as he stated explicitly in many interviews as well as album liner notes (Nisenson, *Ascension* 94, 109–11; Gerard 67–69; Kofsky 418–19).[5] "Labels, I don't bother with," he said a year before his death (qtd. in Kofsky 433). Significantly, when pressured to settle on one label after all, he did not choose 'jazz' or 'black music': "As far as types of music, if you ask me what *we* are playing . . . I feel it is a music of the individual contributors. And if you wanted to name it anything, you could name it a 'classical music'" (qtd. in Kofsky 454).

But what is ultimately at issue here is not whether, say, Archie Shepp is 'blacker' than John Coltrane, nor whether Bechet's "Summertime" is any less authentically jazz than Gordon and Gray's "The Chase." Bechet and Coltrane are great jazz artists precisely because they push the envelope by synthesizing seemingly disparate musical styles and traditions. Literary criticism has tended to ignore or distort jazz's inherent hybridity in order to posit a program of authentic blackness—or, indeed, in order to eschew probing the relationship of whiteness to blackness. Jazz suggests that any notion about and expression of 'authentic' blackness is a *process,* a process that, like jazz improvisation, occurs in time and therefore asks to be continuously negotiated anew. And precisely because an authentic blackness embedded in time must necessarily also react to impulses from 'outside' the African American tradition, the resulting hybridity does not dilute authenticity, but it *is* that authenticity: the jazz aesthetic in fact encourages the usage of extraneous material, *as long as that material is brought into some sort of negotiation with the tradition's historical conscience*—its Omar. As Sidney Bechet muses at the outset of his autobiography, "all my life I've been trying to explain about something, something I understand—the part of me that was there before I was. It was there waiting to be me. It was there waiting to be the music" (4). Perhaps, then, there is also still much more African American narrative that is there waiting to be the music.

Notes

Notes to Prelude

1. Then again, that a drummer would describe his craft through the metaphor of storytelling is not so unusual after all, considering that in the antebellum South, Haynes's ancestors were forbidden from playing the drums for fear of the powerful, seditious messages the instrument could convey.

2. For instance, in the 2002 special issue of *Callaloo* on jazz poetics, only one out of eighteen literary-critical articles (Fritz Gysin's essay on the works of Xam Wilson Cartier, Leon Forrest, and Nathaniel Mackey) focuses exclusively on jazz and prose fiction.

3. Gates's critical practice, however, betrays a certain unfamiliarity with jazz. See chapter 4 and the Coda as well as Stephan Richter's essay "Magic Books and a Jam Session."

4. The interested reader is invited to consult the Works Cited list, which, while not presuming to be representative in the least, includes many indispensable monographs by Amiri Baraka, Scott DeVeaux, Ira Gitler, or Gunther Schuller, to name just a few.

Notes to Chapter One

1. Mention must be made here of the improbably named James Reese Europe. Before jazz became jazz, so to speak, Europe's Harlem-based Clef Club Orchestra was, in 1913, the first black American ensemble to make a recording. After leaving the Club, Europe led the famous 369th US Infantry "Hell Fighters" Band, which became tremendously popular in dance-starved, war-torn France. Tragically, Europe was stabbed to death in 1919 in the middle of his glorious homecoming tour by a demented drummer (D. Lewis 30–34; Polillo 95–97; Schuller, *Early* 247–52).

2. The dedication of Bechet's bust on Congo Square was arranged to coincide with the city's annual Jazz and Heritage Festival. The centennial celebrations also included a mass at St. Augustine's Church, a scholarly conference hosted by the University of New Orleans, and many tribute concerts (Persica A-15).

3. The "Old World" in this case refers not only to Europe, but also to Africa, as Congo Square was, of course, an important slave market. Furthermore, Bechet had been honored years before the centennial in his hometown by the issuance of postage stamps bearing his portrait in the Republic of Gabon as well as the Republic of Chad (Chilton 290).

4. Like so many other musicians—Miles Davis, Duke Ellington, Max Roach, and John Coltrane among them—Bechet, too, rejects the term *jazz:* "But let me tell you one thing: Jazz, that's a name the white people have given to the music. . . . That doesn't explain the music. There's two kinds of music. There's classic and there's ragtime. When I tell you ragtime, you can feel it, there's a spirit right in the word. . . . But Jazz—Jazz could mean any damn thing: high times, screwing, ball-room. It used to be spelled *Jass,* which *was* screwing. But when you say ragtime, you're saying the music" (3). Accordingly, Bechet prefers the word *ragtime*—or simply refers to "the music"—throughout his autobiography, even though the term as he uses it clearly designates what is still called jazz today.

5. Jazz scholars have been in agreement for a long time, though, that designating New Orleans as the origin of jazz is an oversimplification that excludes similar developments elsewhere in the South and Midwest (Baraka, *Blues* 70–71; Schuller, *Early* 59–60; Polillo 60–63).

6. See for instance the biographical sketches in books by Rudi Blesh, Martin Williams, and Whitney Balliet, as well as the *Times-Picayune*'s front page article on the Sidney Bechet Centennial Celebration in the summer of 1997 (Blesh 35–36; Williams 136; Balliet 39–40; Persica A-14). In his study of African retentions in African American musics, Samuel Floyd enlists the ostensibly historical Omar prominently to elucidate his interpretive framework (*Power* 8–9). And in her article on jazz musicians' autobiographies, Kathy Ogren is fully aware of the extent of Bechet's liberties with facts, but curiously says of Omar's story that it was "*most likely* apocryphal" ("'Jazz'" 119; emphasis added). In what borders on a postmodernist twist, Bechet himself alludes to the fictional nature of the story he is telling. Commenting on Marie's master, who fabricates the lie that Omar had raped Marie to cover his own craven desire for his slave, Bechet warns:

> And when you start one of those lies, there's nothing you can do but go about getting it finished. It gets all out of your hands, and you're trying to catch at it every which way. But there's nothing you can do once it has got started. All the mending and repairing you do to it, trying to keep it where it started, trying to keep that one lie from becoming a thousand lies. But you can't do anything about it. You're just like a dog that's chasing rabbits when there's so many of them he doesn't know which one he's after. (27)

The difference between Marie's master and Bechet is, of course, that the latter is a 'master' improviser, whereas the former is not.

7. It is not clear whether Bechet had actually visited Senegal, and if yes, when. Chilton does mention a few brief tours through North Africa in his biography, but no visit to Dakar specifically. Even so, after grudgingly granting the country interior autonomy in 1955, the status of Senegal continued to be debated in France. President Leopold Senghor's name appeared quite frequently in the French press,

which by and large echoed the government's deep-seated suspicions of Senghor's brand of African socialism. However, the continuing presence of French troops on Senegalese soil never led to anything near the bloody quagmire of the Algerian struggle for independence (Gildea 20–29; Yansané 309–14).

8. In this sense, Bechet's narration of the fictional story of Omar echoes what Ralph Ellison wrote in his introduction to *Invisible Man:* "I knew that I was composing a work of fiction, a work of literary art and one that would allow me to take advantage of the novel's capacity for telling the truth while actually telling a 'lie,' which is the Afro-American term for an improvised story" (xxii). Both texts in turn are reminiscent of Sun Ra's incomparable epistemology: "They say that history repeats itself; but history is only his-story. You haven't heard my story yet. My story is different from his story. My story is not part of history because history repeats itself. But my story is endless, it never repeats itself. Why should it? The sunset does not repeat itself. Neither does a sunrise. Nature never repeats itself. My story is close to mystery. My story is better for man than history. Mystery is better than history. What's your story?" (qtd. in Szwed 317).

9. *Treat It Gentle,* however, also contradicts Andrews's critical framework to an extent. First, Andrews claims that African American autobiography began to diverge more and more from the model of the slave narrative after the Civil War. Second, Andrews's quasi-structuralist approach emphasizes the intertextual elements in the slave narratives by privileging "the dynamics of signification" in their "rightful participation in *logos*" (23, 7). That the semi-literate Sidney Bechet, who never had a regular education, consciously modeled his autobiography on slave narratives is virtually impossible; his favorite reading in later years consisted of a steady diet of *Mad Magazine.* Even though he could, with effort, read musical notation, his aversion against written arrangements or musical transcription was well known (Chilton 219, 286). (It is unlikely, nor is there any indication to that effect, that any of Bechet's three literary collaborators were familiar with the African American slave narrative.) The interface between *Treat It Gentle* and the slave narrative therefore seems to corroborate Samuel Floyd's concept of cultural memory—his gaffe regarding the historicity of Omar notwithstanding—which Floyd defines as "a repository of meanings that comprise the subjective knowledge of a people, its immanent thoughts, its structures, and its practices; these thoughts, structures, and practices are transferred and understood unconsciously but become conscious and culturally objective in practice and perception" (8). As literary jazz, *Treat It Gentle* hence constitutes, like the music itself, what Stephen Henderson has called "the 'Soul Field' of the Black Experience," or what Jim Merod refers to as a "cultural archive" (S. Henderson 49; Merod 12–14). William Kenney's and Thomas Carmichael's critical readings of the autobiographies of Louis Armstrong and Charles Mingus also point to this connection between the slave narrative, cultural memory, and jazz music (Kenney 29; Carmichael 30).

10. It is possible that this is a result of the recording equipment being used—Meade Lux Lewis's piano is barely audible throughout—especially since Blue Note did not acquire the reputation for high fidelity recording techniques until Rudy Van Gelder became the label's engineer of choice a few years later. However, repeated listenings to the other tracks from that same session indicate that Bechet employed a dark timbre deliberately on "Summertime." A highly unusual squeak, for Bechet, in measure ten of the first chorus, on A1 nonetheless, suggests that he might have been using a harder reed. (The soprano saxophone is tuned B-flat, so playing an A

actually produces a concert G. Since the focus of this discussion is on Bechet's solo, I shall not transpose his notes into concert key.) I do not agree with Martin Williams's contention that the saxist was plagued by a bad reed on that session (150). The impeccable glissandi, slurs, growls, and microtonal inflections would surely have produced more than one minor squeak on a severely chipped or otherwise damaged reed. But then again, Bechet was famous for a truly titanic embouchure as well as an utter indifference to his equipment; he was observed, on more than one occasion, whittling reeds from the cover of cigar boxes in emergencies, only to perform flawlessly thereafter (Chilton 122).

11. The reference to Langston Hughes's trumpet player is intriguing on another level as well. Hughes was exposed nightly to jazz music when he worked as a dishwasher at the famous Le Duc club in 1924, managed by the even more (in)famous 'Bricktop,' in Paris, and the musicians he heard on a regular basis included the likes of Frank Withers and Cricket Smith, with whom Bechet would jam regularly only a short time later (Rampersad, *Life I* 84–85; Chilton 77). There is no indication that these two giants ever met in person; however, Hughes is likely to have heard Bechet at some point in late 1924 or early 1925, when the latter was a semi-regular member of Noble Sissle's orchestra—which played at the grand *Crisis* gala (ostensibly honoring Jessie Fauset), with Hughes in attendance—and otherwise did free-lance work in New York (Chilton 67–68, 77; Rampersad, *Life I* 84–85, 96–97).

12. This is precisely the aspect of *Treat It Gentle* which Nicholas Gebhardt's otherwise illuminating analysis of what he calls the remythologizing jazz act as also a social act suppresses (74–75). Gebhardt's reading is a teleological one which approaches the autobiography as a homogenous, stable text that reaches its culmination in the last chapter. Such a reading must necessarily ignore the multiple authorship and convoluted editorial processes of which *Treat It Gentle* is the result.

13. In his study *Understanding the New Black Poetry,* for example, Stephen Henderson contends that "[t]he central problem is . . . the printed page" and worries that "[i]n their insistence upon jazz as a model and inspiration for their poetry, these writers were and are confronted with enormous technical problems, some of which may be insoluble if they continue to write that poetry down. For their model is dynamic, not static, and although one can suggest various vocal and musical effects with typography, an extensive use of these rather mechanical devices may be ultimately self-defeating" (30). However, Henderson's concerns diminish when we remind ourselves that most of us, be it as poets or critics, encounter jazz improvisation more often than not as sounds fixed on recordings, sounds that are hence 'readable' much like a text.

14. Perhaps not quite coincidentally, both operas are also basically unmitigated tragedies of untimely death. Enrico Caruso, Bechet's hero, recorded both "Miserere" and "Vesti la giubba."

15. Bechet's improvisation of the story of Omar in order to explain jazz music finds an uncanny parallel in the narrative voice of Toni Morrison's *Jazz,* who feels compelled to narrate the antebellum story of Golden Gray—also a story about slavery and freedom, love and lust, racial identity and individual ancestry—in order to explicate an event in the present. (See chapter 4.)

16. Bechet's reminiscences of Mezz Mezzrow, the controversial white reed player, underscore this as well: as far as Bechet is concerned, the problem with Mezzrow was not that he wanted to play 'black' music, but that he wanted to *be* black: "But

still, when a man is trying so hard to be something he isn't, when he's trying to be some name he makes up for himself instead of just being what he is, some of that will show in his music, the idea of it will be wrong" (168–69). Over the last few years, a revisionist school of jazz criticism has emerged, represented by James Lincoln Collier's *Jazz: The American Theme Song,* Gene Lees's *Cats of Any Color,* and Richard M. Sudhalter's *Lost Chords,* which questions the primacy of African American innovators in the jazz canon and/or the presence of African retentions in the music. In my view, the arguments and documentation these critics put forth do not convincingly refute in its entirety Gunther Schuller's premise that "*every* musical element—rhythm, harmony, melody, timbre, and the basic forms of jazz—is essentially African in background and derivation" (*Early* 62). Sudhalter, for one, implicitly retracted at least parts of his argument at a panel discussion organized by the San Francisco Jazz Organization in the spring of 2001 ("Jazz and Race"). Collier's work is representative of this revisionist school of jazz historiography in that it appears to weigh "direct evidence" of written documentation or recorded performances more heavily than oral histories of the kind Art Taylor or W. Royal Stokes have compiled (Collier 189). What Schuller's thesis does fail to take into account is the simple fact that jazz—excepting free jazz—is organized around the concept of *diatonic* music, which is, of course, European in origin. (For a critique of Schuller's premise, see for instance Youngren 20–21.) Even Samuel Floyd, one of the most vocal proponents of the theory of African retentions in jazz, concedes that "African American musical practices in the United States cannot be traced directly to specific populations in Africa with any degree of certainty" ("African" 7). At the same time, however, that same lack of certainty also pertains to efforts to trace retentions of various European folk musics.

17. My terminology here derives from James Baldwin's essay "Equal in Paris," which recounts Baldwin's arrest for allegedly stealing bed sheets from a rundown hotel. Sitting in the police station that December evening, waiting to be processed,

> I was not a despised black man. They would simply have laughed at me if I had behaved like one. For them, I was an American. And here it was they who had the advantage, for that word, *Américain,* gave them some idea, far from inaccurate, of what to expect from me. In order to corroborate none of their ironical expectations I said nothing and did nothing—which was not the way any Frenchman, white or black, would have reacted. The question thrusting up from the bottom of my mind was not *what* I was, but *who.* And this question, since a *what* can get by with skill but a *who* demands resources, was my first real intimation of what humility must mean. (*Notes* 146)

18. I draw here on R. Baxter Miller's discussion of diachronic and synchronic time in the short fiction of Langston Hughes ("Race").

Notes to Chapter Two

1. See for instance Cataliotti (156–57), Göbel (70–73), Harding (138–58), Jarrett (83–88), Jimoh (130–54), Marvin (599–604), O'Meally (*Craft* 78–104), Ostendorf (110–18), H. Porter (72–76), or Raussert (527–34).

2. It is intriguing, though, that Petry's first published short story, "Marie of the Cabin Club," features Georgie Barr, a jazz trumpeter (see chapter 3). Interestingly, Petry chose the male pseudonym Arnold Petri.

3. In her article on the function of music in Petry's fiction, Johanna Garvey claims that Kid Jones plays "jazzy blues" in a blues combo (123). While Jones may indeed be playing the blues—most certainly he is playing blues-influenced music—Petry's description of the orchestra's personnel as well as the song performed makes it highly unlikely that what is being played is blues in the Bessie Smith/Ma Rainey vein. Moreover, while blues has its share of guitar and piano virtuosos, percussionists are hardly ever featured in an unaccompanied solo. In jazz, on the other hand, the swing era also saw the first drummers to play pivotal solo roles in their respective outfits, most notably Chick Webb and Gene Krupa. Similarly, Kimberly Drake's analysis of Lutie as a "blues singer" is not viable for much the same reason (91). As the following discussion of *The Street* will show, the songs Lutie sings, "Swing It, Sister," and "Darlin'," are decidedly not blues—even though, of course, both are to varying degrees blues-inflected—nor does the repertoire and personnel of Boots Smith's orchestra correspond to an orchestra playing strictly blues.

4. Significantly, (musical) quarrels on the bandstand have involved drummers and pianists more than any other combination of instrumentalists. As drummer Charli Persip explains the historic antagonism, "Many drummers play too loud, and this can really do damage to a delicate acoustic instrument like the piano. . . . There are many wars between pianists and drummers" (qtd. in Berliner 396). Kid Jones's homicidal fantasies cannot help but remind one of the deranged percussionist Herbert White, who knifed his boss, James Europe (a trained pianist), in the latter's dressing room (D. Lewis 33–34).

5. It is therefore perhaps no coincidence either that all but one of the twenty-nine subjects Ferdinand Jones interviewed for his positivistic analysis of the psychology of improvising were male (149).

6. This is a recurring allusion in Petry's fiction, the notion that consumer capitalism saps black music of its spiritual authenticity. Lutie Johnson's experience here parallels that of Kid Jones as he bows after his spectacular drum solo. In marked contrast, *The Narrows*'s Mamie Powther is the only one of Petry's singers or musicians who is not somehow marred psychologically. Mamie Powther, née Smith, is of course Petry's fictional reincarnation of blues Singer Mamie Smith, whose 1920 "Crazy Blues" sounded the start of the blues craze (Baraka, *Blues* 99–100; Garvey 138–39; Spottswood 88–89). Unlike Mamie Smith, Kid Jones, and Lutie Johnson, Mamie Powther-Smith does not perform professionally. She possesses "[a] big warm voice with a lilt in it, and something else, some extra, indefinable quality which made Abbie [her neighbor] listen, made her want to hear more, and more; as though the singer leaned over, close, to say, I'm talking to you, listen to me, I made up this song for you and I've got wonderful things to tell you and to show you, listen to me" (22). This, then, is the quality that is being lost when African American music becomes a commercial commodity. African-derived storytelling-time, both musical and verbal, is thus different from Western "mechanical" time (Wilson 573–74; Reichardt 476–81; Raussert 519–25). Because *The Narrows'* Mamie sings her songs outside the commercial realm regulated by the Juntos of American capitalism, the authenticity of her art remains uncorrupted. (See also Jacques Attali's concept of "living use-time" in chapter 3.)

7. "Being a woman, and being a black woman, and playing a trumpet—that's three things I consider against me. Now, if I played piano, I don't think sex or race would enter into it," says veteran jazz musician Clora Bryant (qtd. in Dahl 217). The "pattern of systematic erasure" of the so-called all-girl bands of the 1940s that Sherrie Tucker has found in jazz historiography is a pattern that continues to extend, only somewhat diminished, to recording and performance opportunities for female jazz instrumentalists today (Tucker, *Swing* 9; Gourse 8–9, 66–72; Handy 121–26).

8. The novel is set in November of 1944, the year after the AFM recording ban finally came to an end. Although recordings by vocalists were excepted from the ban, the wartime shortage of shellac caused a drop in record distribution. It was therefore not unusual for jukeboxes to be stocked with ten-year-old hits (Schuller, *Swing* 690–91; DeVaux, *Birth* 295–306). The Mills Brothers had started their career in 1930, when they became an instant success on CBS radio. Originally billed as "Four Boys and a Guitar," the brothers' vocal skills were so stunning that their early records were accompanied by a leaflet assuring listeners that the only instrument they were hearing was John Mills's guitar. In the 1930s and 40s, their popularity rivaled that of the likes of Louis Armstrong or Frank Sinatra, and the quartet continued to tour and record in various incarnations into the 1990s (Friedwald, *Jazz* 173–77).

9. In addition, A. Yemisi Jimoh argues that the figure of Junto and the power he exerts over the street and its inhabitants functions like a jazz riff, subtly yet firmly directing the foregrounded 'solos' of Boots, Mrs. Hedges, and of course Lutie (125–26). However, a much more viable candidate is the character of Min. As the near-homonym of her name already suggests (*Min/men*), Min has lived with a series of men—she calls them "husbands"—who, for a while at least, provide her with some semblance of "a secure, happy feeling" (116, 117). She continues to follow this pattern when she leaves Jones and, realizing that "a woman living alone really didn't stand much chance," eyes the man whom she hired to move her cherished table and other belongings: "This was a very strong man. His back muscles bulged as he pushed the cart. She moved closer to him. 'Say,' she said, and there was a soft insinuation in her voice, 'you know anywhere a single lady could get a room?' Then she added hastily, 'But not on this street'" (371). Min is certainly no strong improviser like Lutie, and so, rather than breaking the pattern, she continues with the riff of cohabitation. A riff is a recurrent phrase of two or four bars, whose repetitive melody is constructed in such a way that it requires but minimal adjustment to harmonic changes ("Riff"). Min's minimal adjustment from Jones to the moving man, like the adjustments between any of her previous "husbands," is just such a riff. And just as a riff is designed to heighten the tension and intensify the swing, so does Min's departure effect yet another heightening of the dramatic tension: in the next chapter, Jones points investigators from the Postal Service in the direction of Bub, whose arrest directly leads to Lutie's murder of Boots. I thank La Vinia Jennings for this suggestion.

10. Millinder's trumpet section especially was considered to be "boss at that time," remembers Dizzy Gillespie in his memoirs (60). Gillespie also offers some entertaining if probably not completely accurate insights into Millinder's leadership qualities, especially his "fire complex" (60–62, 109, 163–64). High praise also comes from Count Basie, who had to concede defeat to Millinder in a battle of the bands: "Lucky and those guys turned it on! Boy, did they turn it on. Whew! It was a rough

night. Lucky had a lot of top-notch musicians in that band. . . . Lucky himself didn't play any instruments. He just fronted the band, but he was one of the best front men in the business, right up there giving Cab Calloway and Willie Bryant some real competition" (211).

11. Millinder's orchestra became quite an influential musical force in the latter half of the 1940s. Along with Louis Jordan, Millinder pioneered and perfected the jump blues genre, an important antecedent of rock 'n' roll. Unlike Jordan, Millinder left the music business in 1952 and fell into obscurity, trying to eke out a living in a variety of occupations, most notably perhaps that of fortune-teller, until his death in 1966 (McCarthy 289–91).

12. The inside cover of *The Street* announces that two lines of the song are being used by permission of the Duo Publishing Corporation. However, Lutie's lines "There's no sun, Darlin.' [/] There's no fun, Darlin'" are not part of the recorded version she is listening to, nor did Decca market different versions of "Darlin'," if alternate takes were ever issued at all. Incidentally, A. Yemisi Jimoh errs when she gives the release date of "Darlin'" as 1945; Decca's records indicate that the song was recorded and released in 1944 (Jimoh 220; Schenker, booklet). However, like Jimoh, I have been unable to locate any recording with the title "Rock, Raleigh, Rock," the song Lutie hears in chapter thirteen as she ascends the stairs to her apartment (Jimoh 220, 243; Petry, *The Street* 312).

13. See Clark (501–2), N. McKay (133–35), Lattin (69–70), Pryse (118), and Wurst (3–22).

14. Mrs. Hedges and Boots can only participate in the American Dream by acknowledging the dominant status of the white man who controls all and who is named after Benjamin Franklin's secret society, Junto. Consequently, Boots must die in the end because his rape of Lutie would have threatened the power of Junto. Min is the only black character on 116th Street who is not destroyed, physically or mentally, by the economic system Junto oversees. Unlike Boots, Mrs. Hedges, and Lutie, Min does not subscribe to the ideology of upward social mobility, and, as critics have mentioned, Min's involvement with the root doctor David the Prophet suggests an alternative value system (Clark 499–501; Drake 68–80; C. Henderson 854–59; Pryse 123–27). Accordingly, the cross David gives her becomes a tool for her liberation from Jones. Lutie, too, is confronted with a cross, but for her it symbolizes oppression rather than liberation. The lecherous advances of Mr. Crosse, proprietor of the Crosse School for Singers, furthers Lutie's entrapment even more: "Yes, she thought, if you were born black and not too ugly, this is what you get, this is what you find. It is a pity he [Mr. Crosse] hadn't lived back in the days of slavery, so he could have raided the slave quarters for a likely wench any hour of the day or night" (321–22). *The Street* here echoes the essential contention of Harriet Jacobs's *Incidents in the Life of a Slave Girl,* that "the condition of a slave confuses all principles of morality, and, in fact, renders the practice of them impossible," especially for the female slave (55). The socio-economic system that regulates life on the street and is governed by the all-powerful Junto is hence a system of neo-slavery really, making Petry's novel a grim neo-slave narrative (Park and Wald 618–20). Perhaps not quite coincidentally, musicologist Stephan Richter alludes to a related issue in his analysis of Thelonius Monk's "Blue Monk": "Monk's village of festivities is indeed a more democratic concept than Winthrop's city upon a hill," as exemplified perhaps most effectively in the 1958 live version ("Beauty" 263).

15. The motif of the circle is prefigured in the scene in chapter six when Lutie goes to the Junto Bar and Grill. Trying "to recapture the feeling of self-confidence she had had earlier in the evening," she cannot erase "the thought of day after day of work and night after night caged in that apartment" (147). As she is pondering the bleakness of her situation and her lack of options, "[s]he moved the beer glass on the bar. It left a wet ring and she moved it again in an effort to superimpose the rings on each other" (147). Fittingly, this is immediately followed by Lutie's rendition of "Darlin'" that tells the story all the other patrons "knew by heart and had always known because they had learned it soon after they were born and would go on adding to it until they died" (148).

16. The connection between the trope of the circle and literacy (in its most general sense) is a recurrent motif in African American literature. For instance, this connection informs all of Frederick Douglass's autobiographies, beginning with the famous description of the slave songs in the 1845 narrative where Douglass avers that "I was, myself, within the circle; so that I could then neither hear nor see as those without might see and hear" (57). The motif of the circle reappears in Jean Toomer's *Cane,* in which the arcs prefacing the three sections symbolize the modernistic fragmentation of what the author elsewhere had called "the spiritual truth of the South" (qtd. in Kerman and Eldridge 95; Toomer 1, 39, 81). More recently, the motif of the circle also occurs in Toni Morrison's *Beloved,* in the scene where Sethe is unable to put into words the killing of her baby daughter: "Sethe knew that the circle she was making around the room, him [Paul D], the subject, would remain one. That she could never close it, pin it down for anybody who had to ask. If they didn't get it right off, she could never explain" (163). It is perhaps not all too farfetched to discern in these literary examples an echo of the West African ritual of the ring, which survived in various transformations in the New World and which, according to Samuel Floyd's research, has had a decisive influence on black American musics (*Power* 26–33). (See also note 15.)

17. I am referencing here the take that Columbia originally chose to release, the second take of the session, rather than the equally famous, but not readily available, take three that was not issued because, at three minutes and fifty-eight seconds, it exceeded the limitations of the 78 rpm records (Nicholson 90–91; Schaap 265).

18. By way of contrast, compare Holiday's version of "All of Me" with that of Dee Dee Bridgewater, recorded almost half a century later. Taken at a faster clip than the Billie Holiday recording, bassist Hein Van de Gein's rather conservative arrangement does not reharmonize or otherwise alter the original score either. Bridgewater's snappy on-the-beat phrasing, though, assisted primarily by André Ceccarelli's crisp snare drum accentuating her requests, changes the emotional content of the song, especially in the second chorus. There, with a nod to Ella Fitzgerald, Bridgewater practices a sort of inverted vocalese; that is, she retains the lyrics of the song but completely improvises the melody and rhythm. Her playful melodic and rhythmic recasting of the lyrics, followed by a prolonged scat solo, create a persona not lonely, pleading, and melancholy as Holiday's, but rather teasing and flirtatious. Note that both Holiday's and Bridgewater's versions, like Lutie's reinvention of "Darlin'," change the emotional essence of the song not so much by altering the lyrics, but primarily by manipulating the rhythm; they are different not because of *what* they sing, but because of *how* they sing it.

19. Consider, for instance, Sidney Bechet's solo on the old New Orleans staple

"High Society," recorded on February 5, 1940. Bechet, on soprano saxophone, duplicates almost exactly one of the most famous of all 'set' jazz solos, the clarinet obbligato adapted decades earlier by Crescent City legend George Baquet from the original piccolo part. The inclusion of Baquet's solo was—and still is—virtually mandatory in any performance of "High Society" (Chilton 122; Schuller, *Early* 183). In modern jazz, even a John Coltrane would practice set solos in advance. For his solo on "Giant Steps," still considered to be the *pièce de résistance* for any aspiring jazz improviser, Coltrane lifted entire chunks from Nicolas Slonimsky's *Thesaurus of Scales and Melodic Patterns,* then part of his extensive practice routine, and his solo on the last movement of *A Love Supreme,* "Psalm," is a recitation of sorts of the poem in the album's liner notes—Coltrane himself called it "a musical narration"—a recitation where each note corresponds exactly to the syllabic structure of the poem's words, and a recitation that therefore suggests at least an unusual amount of pre-planning (Coltrane 5; L. Porter 148–51, 244–49).

Notes to Chapter Three

1. It is interesting to observe, and merits further study, that the exact same charges leveled against jazz in its early years—it's not music, it corrupts our youth, it glorifies violence and debauchery, it's primitive, and so on and so forth—have been leveled against hip-hop.

2. The connection between violence and music is nothing new in Western thought. In the twentieth century alone, Oswald Spengler and Theodor Adorno, to mention just two figures, theorized at some length about sound as a weapon (Jameson ix–x). For an in-depth analysis of violence in African American blues culture and how it differs from the jazz idiom, see Adam Gussow's *Seems Like Murder in Here* (2–8).

3. While I largely concur with Alan J. Rice's assessment of the significance of jazz in *Home to Harlem,* I disagree with his larger contention that many Harlem Renaissance prose writers availed themselves of a jazz aesthetic. Deploying a structuralist approach, Rice argues that "[t]he conscious use of alliteration, antiphony, non-standard punctuation, signifying, and repetition to build up passages that resemble jazz interactions in their construction is a process that began in the twenties soon after the arrival of jazz in the North and mirrors the development of the music itself" ("Finger Snapping" 105–6). I believe that "a jazz feel" or "an onomatopaeic reaction to the sensual sounds" of jazz alone does not suffice to constitute a jazz text (108, 110). (See also chapter 4 for a detailed discussion of the shortcomings of structuralism for a literary jazz criticism.)

4. Hughes himself had no formal or informal musical training. With characteristic understatement, he writes in *The Big Sea* of the poetry he penned during his Washington years:

> The blues poems I would often make up in my head and sing on the way to work. (Except that I could never carry a tune. But when I sing to myself, I think I am singing.) One evening, I was crossing Rock Creek Bridge, singing a blues I was trying to get right before I put it down on paper. A man passing on the opposite side of the bridge

> stopped, looked at me, then turned around and cut across the roadway.
>
> He said: "Son, what's the matter? Are you ill?"
>
> "No," I said, "Just singing."
>
> "I thought you were groaning," he commented. "Sorry!" And went his way.
>
> So after that, I never sang my verses aloud in the street any more. (217)

5. *Not without Laughter* is set in Kansas, and it is interesting to note that this account, without a doubt autobiographical, of the fictional Rattle Benbow's Famous Kansas City Band—a so-called territory band—describes the exact same kind of black music, weaving fluidly and daringly between different styles and genres, yet always grounded in the blues, that left an indelible impression on young Oklahoman Ralph Ellison. See Gunther Schuller's two-volume history of jazz for an in-depth discussion of these territory bands (*Early* 279–317, *Swing* 770–805).

6. The basic premise, as well as much of the text itself, of the original column and the revised short story is identical. The single major difference is that the 1949 column opens with Simple sitting at the bar scatting by himself, whereas "Bop" has Simple sitting on his stoop, scatting along with a recording of Dizzy Gillespie's "Ool-ya-koo" blaring out of an upstairs window (Hughes, "Simple" 6).

7. "Ool-ya-koo" is a simple yet infectious blues, spiced up with a quote from Thelonius Monk's "Well, You Needn't," whose hallmark is the humorous bop-scatting of Gillespie and Kenny Hagood. Recorded by Gillespie's big band in 1947 (also the year of the copyright of Monk's composition), "Ool-ya-koo" was one in a string of recordings bearing similar titles—"Oop-bop-sh'bam," "Jump Di-le-ba," or "Oo-pop-a-da," for instance—which helped bring bebop to a broader audience. With composer credits usually attributed to Gillespie and arranger Gil Fuller, "Ool-ya-koo" is actually based on a riff by Joe Wilder (Shipton 222).

8. The reference to the death of bebop is one of the very few amendments Hughes made for the revised 1953 "Bop." Most jazz histories in fact place the end of the bebop era in that same year, 1953, with the famous Massey Hall concert of Dizzy Gillespie, Charlie Parker, Bud Powell, Charles Mingus, and Max Roach in Toronto, commonly considered the swansong of bop—or in 1955 with Parker's death. Even so, Gillespie himself dates the end of the era in early 1950, with the demise of his big band (355–57). Of course, the transition from bebop to hard-bop (or cool jazz) was a very fluid one, without any definitive breaks. Bebop was certainly not "finished." It has established itself as the source and reference point for the entire postwar jazz tradition. As Scott DeVaux puts it succinctly, "[t]o understand jazz, one must understand bebop," because "jazz as we know it today is shaped in bebop's image" ("Advent" 292; *Birth* 3).

9. Consider saxophonist Budd Johnson's eye- and earwitness account of the tireless efforts of Dizzy Gillespie, "the theoretician to this music," to spread the gospel of bop to other jazz musicians and how the music got its name accordingly:

> Dizzy tried to hum everything; he had to hum everything to everybody to get them to see what he was still talkin' about. It would be hard to explain it. It could be notated, but it was very hard to read, because cats weren't used to reading. . . . So he would sing [imitates

> Diz], and actually, that's how I think it got its name, bebop. Because he would be humming this music, and he'd say, "Ooop bop ta oop a la doo bop doo ba." So people said, "Play some more of that bebop" because he would be saying, "Bebop." And the cats would say, "Sing some more of that bebop," and actually, I think that's how it got its name, because that's the way he would have to sing it to make you get the feeling that he wanted you to play with. (qtd. in Gitler, *Swing to Bop* 119)

10. This can be plainly heard on, for instance, an air-check of "Dizzy Atmosphere" from the Los Angeles "Jubilee" radio show of December 29, 1945, where emcee Ernie "Bubbles" Whitman announces Gillespie as "Professor Rebop."

11. It is to be emphasized here that Attali's theories are only partially applicable to jazz, as they are based on Western European history and art. Although Attali does reference African American musics, he betrays a rather rudimentary understanding of jazz. For instance, when he claims that "[t]he absence of noise (of blemish, error) in the stockpiled objects [i.e., recordings] has become a criterion of enjoyment," he seems unaware that in jazz—as in other African and African diaspora musics—the exact opposite is often true (124). Both musicians and listeners value a highly individualized sound rather than an abstract sound ideal that performers must approximate, as is the case in classical European concert music. For example, Miles Davis's trumpet sound would not only be considered 'blemished' by classical standards, but his 'clams' or wrong notes—on studio recordings, too—were so frequent that they became an integral part of his personal style, a style imitated by scores of younger trumpeters (Walser 158–63). Davis himself remained typically unconcerned about his clams: "Sometimes you run out of notes. The notes just disappear and you have to play a sound" (qtd. in Burns, liner notes).

12. Simple here refers to Dizzy Gillespie, Thelonius Monk, and Mary Lou Williams.

13. Interestingly, R. Baxter Miller comes to a very similar conclusion in his analysis of Hughes's *Ask Your Mama:* the long poem, Miller writes, moves toward "a design of Pan-African and human struggle within the evolution of modern consciousness—Be" ("Framing" 12). Also, the more strictly musicological implications of Simple's differentiation between bebop and rebop prefigure the scholarship of Charley Gerard and Jon Panish in this field (Gerard 97–115; Panish 141–44). How strongly the issue of race still resonates within the jazz community was exemplified by a special issue of *Jazz Times* in the fall of 2000 devoted almost exclusively to this subject matter (see also chapter 4). Hughes himself did certainly not subscribe to Simple's view of jazz. After all, he tapped British musicologist and pianist Leonard Feather, who also wrote the liner notes, to score the first half of his album of poetry and jazz, *Weary Blues.* Interestingly, the music for the rest of the album was composed and arranged by Charles Mingus.

14. Accordingly, Simple moves from the relatively private confines of the bar in Hughes's original column to the very public, secular pulpit of the stoop, with "Ool-ya-koo" resounding from high up above. For more in-depth analyses of the influence of bebop and jazz on Hughes's poetry, especially in *Montage* as well as his later *Ask Your Mama: 12 Moods for Jazz,* see Hokanson (66–80), Miller ("Framing" 9–11), Lowney (368–79), and Brooker ("Modernism" 244–47). Michael Borshuk makes a

convincing case that even Hughes's blues poems are the product of a jazz aesthetic at work: "Hughes is not a bluesman standing at a mythical site of black expressive origins—an anonymous folk voice singing at the crossroads of Africa and America—but rather, a jazzman who signifies on that tradition with an all-encompassing inter-textual/intermusical approach" (19). Unlike some detractors of bebop (including Ralph Ellison), Hughes did definitely not see bop as a dilution of jazz's roots in the blues, on the contrary: *Montage,* for instance, is informed to a lesser degree also by the recurrent, riff-like motif of boogie-woogie, a largely blues-based form of solo jazz piano (Tracy 224–36).

15. As if in an ironic counterpoint to Simple's take on bebop, Hughes became a witness to jazz's potential to turn symbolic violence into physical action: On July 2, 1960, a riot erupted in the genteel town of Newport, Rhode Island. The town had been the site of the annual Newport Jazz Festival since 1954—Langston Hughes, in fact, sat on the board of directors—which had turned into a great success despite the suspicions and objections of the city fathers. Early that afternoon, a throng of about three thousand, mostly young whites, found itself shut out from the concerts in Freebody Park, where a capacity audience occupied every last seat. Fueled by alcohol, the crowd outside became more and more restless and vocal and eventually stormed the premises, creating havoc all around. The ensuing riot subsequently spilled over into the streets of Newport, with local law enforcement battling youths throwing bottles and rocks with tear gas and water hoses. The situation spun out of control so dramatically that the governor sent in three companies of the Rhode Island National Guard, effectively shutting down the entire city, and order was not restored until around 2:00 AM (Berry 323; Rampersad, *Life II* 314–15). To be sure, the motivations of the predominantly white mob were hardly political, and yet, as Hughes's biographer Arnold Rampersad relates perceptively,

> The Newport riot, though modest as American riots went, seemed to him [Hughes] portentous. In the vented rage of these young whites he saw what a later leader, Malcolm X, would describe as chickens coming home to roost, the whirligig of American history bringing, at long last, a token of its nearing final revenge. The rioters had been like dry tinder, to which black jazz had been a lighted match. In a city of wealth and elegance built on the stinking cargoes of slave ships, and where Langston in the early days of the festival had more than once endured racist snubs, Africa had returned to haunt Europe. The descendants of masters now danced to the music of the descendants of slaves; American "civilization" had begun, in however modest a degree, a fateful slide toward revolution. (315–16)

Witnessing the growing unrest earlier that afternoon, Hughes had written the caustic "Goodbye Newport Blues" on the back of a telegram form and passed it on to the Muddy Waters band performing on stage, where it was sung by Waters's pianist, Otis Spann (C. Murray 10). (Waters was only semiliterate, hence he delegated the vocals to his half-brother.) This anecdote, Dexter Gordon's reminiscences, and, if to a lesser degree, "Bop" all appear to underscore another of Attali's stipulations, namely that music is inherently premonitory (11).

16. One is reminded here of the more or less farfetched explanations the title of

the Charlie Parker composition "Klact-oveeseds-tene" engendered, which worshipping hipsters took to be everything from pidgin German to musical aesthetics in code (Harrison 223; Komara 148). No one has yet offered a plausible 'translation' of *klact-oveeseds-tene*—with the possible exception of Dean Benedetti, the supreme Bird acolyte, who told Ross Russell, producer of the Dial recording sessions and victim of many of the altoist's notorious pranks, "Why, man, it's just a sound!" (qtd. in Russell, *Bird* 252). The introduction of the 1947 recording of the song is identical with the one of "The Chase" penned by Dexter Gordon and recorded just a few months earlier, also for Russell's Dial label (see chapter 4).

17. "How High the Moon" was one of the anthems of bebop, especially as the Barry Harris arrangement retitled "Ornithology."

18. Although Ellison and Hughes had had a close, warm friendship initially—Ellison's career as a writer began when Hughes introduced him to Richard Wright—the two grew apart more and more after the publication of *Invisible Man.* Hughes was partly jealous of his protégé's success, but irritated mostly at the younger writer's increasing reclusiveness. On his part, Ellison came to believe that his mentor was squandering his talent and blamed him for a lack of intellectual rigor (Rampersad, *Life II* 200–202; Berry 252–53).

19. Callahan excised all but one paragraph of the "Cadillac Flambé" episode from *Juneteenth.* In the context of the novel, the Ellisonian ironies of "Cadillac Flambé" deepen even more: Senator Sunraider is possibly part black. Before he decided to pass for white, Sunraider, then known as Bliss, was the child-protégé of Reverend Hickman, a jazz trombonist turned itinerant preacher. The climax of their spiritual revival routine included little Bliss dressed in a white suit rising from a white coffin—just as Lee Willie wears a white suit and drives a white Cadillac convertible. Ellison's original manuscript also identifies the reporter-narrator of the "Cadillac Flambé" episode as McIntyre, a white liberal journalist who keeps a mistress in Harlem, a relationship about which he feels rather ambivalent. At lectures, Ellison would frequently read "Cadillac Flambé" in conjunction with other excerpts from the manuscript that identified these contexts (O'Meally ed. 212–13; H. Porter 95–106).

20. I wonder if Ellison got the idea for "Cadillac Flambé" from Dizzy Gillespie's parody of the popular spiritual which the trumpeter retitled "Swing Low, Sweet Cadillac." Gillespie had recorded the original spiritual in 1950, where the ironic juxtaposition of Johnny Richardson's saccharine string arrangement with Carlos Vidal's Cuban bongos already foreshadows the later parody. A year later, Gillespie recorded the first of several versions of "Swing Low, Sweet Cadillac," and the tune quickly became a crowd-pleaser at concerts: "I look over Jordan and what did I see / *Comin' for to carry me home* / Oh, an Eldorado comin' after me / *Comin' for to carry me home*" (Gillespie 370–71). Unlike Charlie Parker but like Louis Armstrong, Gillespie never shied away from the role of entertainer. At the same time, though, the bebop pioneer Gillespie played the kind of jazz Ellison saw as a corruption of 'real' jazz.

21. The narrator in this respect displays a complete lack of what Alan Perlman and Daniel Greenblatt have termed "improvisational competence" that divides a small "inside audience" from the much larger "outside audience" at a jazz concert:

> The rest of the listeners—the outside audience—really do not hear or understand improvised solos. For the outside audience, jazz impro-

> visation does not have structural or historical meaning. Once the written melody of the song is over and improvisation begins, the members of this audience stop attending minutely and notice only gross features. . . . They cannot follow the repetitions of the basic harmonic pattern of the song; in fact, they have no sense at all of what to *expect* from a solo. These people have no improvisational competence, and, although a jazz performance as a whole may have some significance for them . . . they do not understand the intent of the improvisational section. (181)

McIntyre's improvisational ignorance is corroborated by Hickman, the former jazz trombonist, in *Juneteenth: "That reporter—McIntyre?—yes, waiting out there in the hall. He would've just thought that I was crazy the same as he does anyway. He wouldn't know how to add up the figures; couldn't get with the beat, even if I gave it to him"* (274).

22. As Ellison's hero Duke Ellington said of the extended composition *Black, Brown and Beige,* his "tone parallel to the history of the American Negro": "Coming more up to date, we found the Negroes struggling for solidarity and in the confusion of it all, just as we were beginning to get our teeth into the issue, we discovered that our country was in big trouble again. So, just as always before, the Black, Brown, and Beige were soon in there for the Red, White, and Blue" (181, 182).

23. *Oklahoma!* was the result of the first of many collaborations between composer Richard Rodgers and lyricist Oscar Hammerstein. One song from the musical, "The Surrey with the Fringe on Top," has become a jazz standard reworked by the likes of Miles Davis, Wes Montgomery, Stan Getz, Ahmad Jamal, Sonny Rollins, and many others.

24. This utopian impulse is neither new nor unique to jazz. What Paul Gilroy has called "Black music's obstinate and consistent commitment to the idea of a better future" is, of course, the driving force in the slave spirituals, extending to the Soul music of the 1960s and, more recently, the so-called neo-soul movement (*Black Atlantic* 36). As Baraka himself pointed out correctly, "Black people's songs have carried the fire and struggle of their lives since they first opened their mouths in this part of the world. They have always wanted a better day" (*Black* 207). Naturally, the same utopian impulse also propels, to varying degrees, the slave narratives. Sometimes, the slave's glimpse of (utopian) freedom was even occasioned by an act of violence, as was the case for Frederick Douglass: to him, his fight with Covey was "a glorious resurrection, from the tomb of slavery, to the heaven of freedom" (113). Also interesting in this context is Baraka's futuristic play *Primitive World: An Anti-Nuclear Jazz Musical.* In its post-apocalyptic setting, two unnamed black jazz musicians, a male tenor saxophonist and a female pianist (bringing to mind John and Alice Coltrane), combat and eventually vanquish the evil Money Gods Sado and Maso with *"a solo, like the horn is talking! It's trying to identify the* MONEY GODS *and attack them murderously"* and, respectively, with *"an explosive piano run, like machine-gunning colonialists from the high ground, on a very clear day!"* (442). Baraka's reference here is to the Lane-Lerner standard "On a Clear Day."

25. According to Jerry Watts, Baraka's jazz criticism displays "his ignorance of the formal musical qualities of jazz" (497). Consider, for instance, Baraka's attempt to describe the harmonic innovations of bebop: "Bebop proved that so-called 'changes,' i.e. the melodic and harmonic structure of a tune, are almost arbitrary.

That is, that they need not be *stated,* and that since certain chords infer certain improvisatory uses of them, why not improvise on what the chords infer rather than playing the inference itself" (*Black* 77). First of all, while bebop amends the scalar and harmonic range—with extended chords that include the ninth, eleventh, and thirteenth interval; the notorious flatted fifth; or the popular tri-tone substitution (where a bII7 chord replaces the V7)—those extensions are anything *but* arbitrary, as are the changes themselves. Also, one may recall that, ironically, it was precisely the increased formal complexity of the bebop idiom which to Ralph Ellison signaled a deplorable turn away from jazz's origins in black vernacular blues culture. Secondly, Baraka's gloss is a simplified summary of Charlie Parker's alleged epiphany:

> I remember one night before Monroe's I was jamming [with guitarist Bill "Biddy" Fleet] in a chili house on Seventh Avenue between 139th and 140th. It was December, 1939. Now I'd been getting bored with the stereotyped changes hat were being used all the time at the time, and I kept thinking there's bound to be something else. I could hear it sometimes but I couldn't play it. Well, that night, I was working over [the Ray Noble composition] Cherokee, and, as I did, I found that by using the higher intervals of a chord as a melody line and backing them with appropriately related changes, I could play the thing I'd been hearing. I came alive. (Shapiro and Hentoff 354).

This passage, among the most famous in all of jazz lore, is still taken to be bebop gospel when, in fact, only the two telling sentences "I kept thinking there's bound to be something else. I could hear it sometimes but I couldn't play it" can be attributed to Parker directly. The rest is a very creative paraphrase of a 1949 *Down Beat* article, which critics Nat Shapiro and Nat Hentoff gave a dramatic makeover for their purported oral history of jazz, *Hear Me Talkin' to Ya* (DeVeaux, *Birth* 189). Be that as it may, even if Watts is correct, it probably would not disturb Baraka greatly, for whom, at least in the sixties, formal musical training equaled "doctrinaire whitening" (Baraka, *Black* 202). My hunch is that the finer points of music theory probably elude Baraka, even though he dabbled in piano, drums, and trumpet respectively when he was in high school—which in and of itself does not necessarily disqualify his jazz writings by any means (Baraka, *Autobiography* 63, 84–85). For proof that a writer's ignorance of harmony theory does not result automatically in pretentious mediocrity, one need look no further than to Langston Hughes—who may not have been able to carry a tune, but he certainly had what jazz musicians admiringly call "big ears"—or indeed to any of Baraka's own recorded collaborations with Archie Shepp, as for instance the Hughes-influenced "We Are the Blues: Funklore."

26. It is therefore perhaps also not quite coincidental that Baraka's conversion to Marxist-Leninism occurred in the 1970s, when the revolutionary music of free jazz had all but run its course (John Coltrane, Baraka's hero, had passed away in 1967 at the age of forty) and was quickly succeeded by the commercialized excesses of fusion. Interestingly, starting in the mid-1970s shortly after his conversion, Baraka began an off-and-on collaboration with Swiss composer, bandleader, and pianist George Gruntz. Baraka agreed to furnish the libretto for the latter's pet project, the "World Jazz Opera." The opera was never performed in its entirety, and Baraka's

libretto was eventually dropped in 1988 at the insistence of Rolf Liebermann, then the head of the Hamburgische Staatsoper. This rather surprising collaboration that lasted for the better part of fifteen years would have been simply unthinkable during Baraka's nationalist phase (Gruntz 108, 128–41, 165–66). Baraka was even sufficiently interested in the project that he apparently recycled a few of the ideas for Gruntz's opera for his own play *Primitive World.*

27. To be sure, Baraka was very much aware, too, of the intense spirituality of Coltrane's music. In his interpretation, though—and true to the jazz aesthetic's constant realigning of ostensible polar opposites—violence and spirituality are not necessarily mutually exclusive. On the contrary, for black spirituality to express itself authentically, it had to combat and kill white culture: for Baraka, "*TRANE* [Coltrane] is now a scope of feeling. A more fixed traveler, whose wildest onslaughts are now gorgeous artifacts not even deaf people should miss" (*Black* 173).

28. Ellison never thought highly of Baraka's work, and his famous negative review of *Blues People* argued that its ill-advised emphasis on sociology was "enough to give even the blues the blues" (*Shadow* 279; Watts 201–7). Hughes had initially liked Baraka's early work, especially *Dutchman,* but the increasing militancy expressed by the graphic verbal assaults in the former's later writings disturbed him as he believed them to be counterproductive to the Civil Rights movement (Rampersad, *Life I* 383–84). "That Boy LeRoi," the title of Hughes's review of *The Toilet* in the *New York Post,* is clearly a direct jab at Baraka. (On the other hand, Baraka must have been pleased that Hughes also mentioned that "[a]t one point in the proceedings, [black actor Al Freeman, Jr.] pointed his pistol dead at [white jazz critic] Nat Hentoff in the first row of the auditorium" [22].) Both Ellison and Hughes were board members of the Newport Jazz Festival, which was not welcoming at all to the younger generation of black free jazzers, and this to Baraka most certainly indicated that the two older writers had 'sold out' to the establishment.

29. In "The Screamers," the participants of the initially minor uprising "screamed and screamed at the clear image of ourselves as we should always be. Ecstatic, completed, involved in a secret communal expression. It would be the form of the sweetest revolution, to huckle-buck into the fallen capital, and let the oppressors lindy hop out" (79). This "sweetest revolution" eventually fizzles out, though, and the story ends with the narrator's plaintive admission that "for a while, before the war had reached its peak, Lynn and his musicians, a few other fools, and I, still marched, screaming thru the maddened crowd. Onto the sidewalk, into the lobby, halfway up the stairs, then we all broke our different ways, to save whatever it was each of us thought we loved" (80). The character of Lynn Hope is not, as some critics have erroneously assumed, fictional. Philadelphia-based tenor saxophonist Lynn Hope was a so-called "honker": honkers were, as Baraka's story describes accurately, tenorists whose jazz-inflected rhythm-and-blues combined hypnotic riffing, often in the altissimo register, with antics like what was known as "walking the bar." Hope, who had converted to Islam, and his band often performed wearing turbans, and Hope's playing exerted a certain influence on John Coltrane, Baraka's hero (L. Porter 96). The other honkers named in the story are also historical figures: Jean Baptiste "Illinois" Jacquet, Willis "Gator" Jackson, Cecil "Big Jay" McNeely, and Gene "Jug" Ammons (76).

30. "Answers in Progress" also makes mention of Smokey Robinson, the Motown Records star, whose music is blaring from loudspeakers along Newark

streets and is part of the soundtrack of the uprising (130). Although his primary allegiance lay with the young generation of free jazzers, Baraka also championed Robinson, James Brown, Martha and the Vandellas, and other soul acts. In them, he saw just another expression of what he called the blues continuum, but it was also partly due to his desire to ground his revolutionary aesthetics on a populist base (Baraka, *Blues* 173; Coleman 94–95). One of the characters in the narrator's posse is named Omar, which is probably purely coincidental, since Baraka seems to have named at least some of the black revolutionaries in the story after people he knew in his youth, most notably Pinball, like Baraka an aspiring bebop trumpeter, "who I thought was one of the hippest dudes in the world," as he would later recall (*Tales* 127; *Autobiography* 84).

31. Noteworthy in this context is that during his Black Nationalist phase, Baraka published some of his works by his own publishing house, which he named Jihad Press (Baraka, *Autobiography* 346; Watts 216–17).

32. In his youth, Baraka had been an avid reader of science fiction and was later also influenced, in part, by surrealist art (W. Harris 51).

33. It must be noted here that Blakey himself always rejected a direct correlation between jazz and African musics. Although he had introduced certain African techniques into his drumming fairly early on—for instance, changing the pitch of the tom-tom through elbow-pressure applied to the skin—Blakey insisted that jazz was a music invented and perfected by black *Americans* (Gerard 63–64).

34. The outspoken Baraka has always had to confront charges of racism, sexism, homophobia, or anti-semitism, some of them justified, some of them not. Jerry Gafio Watts, in his intellectual biography of Baraka, comes to the damning conclusion that "Baraka owes many black Americans a debt that he cannot pay. Because of his public actions, many political opportunities were either lost or distorted beyond viability. Yes, he was committed to black freedom. And yes, he was seemingly inexhaustible in his commitment to the struggle. But yes, he advanced a political line that was socially retarded even for the times. . . . *It is not enough to say that Baraka meant well*" (477; Watts's emphasis). On the other hand, Komozi Woodard paints a much more positive picture of Baraka's nationalist politics, in which "there are many examples of the community's generating alternative rituals and progressive standards of both manhood and womanhood in the postindustrial society . . . The overarching strategy was to provide an alternative value system that bound oppressed peoples together with new identity, purpose, and direction" (265–66). My aim here, however, is not to pass judgment on either Baraka himself or on his varying ideologies, but to investigate how he makes use of a literary jazz aesthetic in prose fiction. But since, as we have already seen, the jazz aesthetic deliberately denies any clear separation of art from politics, fact from fiction, or author from character, it does demand that one look not only at the text, but its context, too.

35. In his revised 1995 autobiography, Baraka confessed about this tumultuous episode that "[i]t was a very low point in my life. The Smokey Robinson hit 'The Tracks of My Tears' was popular at the time, and for me that summed up what was going on in my life. . . . Fuckin' Smokey, the poet of the age" (334). In the discrepant escapism of "Answers in Progress," this particular recording is conspicuously absent: "Smokey Robinson was on now. But straight up fast and winging. No more unrequited love. Damn Smokey got his thing together too. No more tracks or mirages. Just the beauty of the whole" (130). For detailed discussions of Sun Ra's

music and ideology as discrepant *engagement,* see Graham Lock's *Blutopia* (13–74) or John Szwed's biography *Space is the Place* (310–16)

36. On the other hand, hip-hop's rituals and images can easily be interpreted as just the latest reincarnations of the traditional trickster figure of African American folklore. Like many rappers, the trickster is wily, boastful, often endowed with irresistible sexual prowess, and profits from the manipulation of the dominant power structure. Especially considering that hip-hop is quite often an explicit expression of racial pride but its primary audience in terms of record sales are young, white, upper middle-class suburban males, rappers flaunting the status symbols of white America—Bentley limousines, Rolex watches, diamond jewelry—seem decidedly trickster-like. (Paul Gilroy has made a related argument in *Against Race* [201–6].) Nor is this to say that there is no good jazz in the twenty-first century. Artists like Joshua Redman or Branford Marsalis keep the language of jazz alive and vibrant, while others like Matthew Shipp, John Zorn, or Don Byron derive their own, new dialects from the tradition.

Notes to Chapter Four

1. Feather, however, had his own agenda, too. Using Eldridge's blindfold test, he goes on to criticize the widespread acceptance by European critics of what had come to be known as "Crow Jim," that is, the idea that whites are incapable of fully appropriating the jazz idiom, as jazz was the intrinsic property of the black American. Writing in 1965, Feather—who, in 1958, had served as composer, arranger, and pianist for much of Langston Hughes's poetry-and-jazz album, *Weary Blues*—was reacting against what he perceived as a lamentable rise in nationalism and separatism among African Americans in general (*Book* 53). As the doyen of jazz criticism, he was instrumental in orchestrating the jazz establishment's branding of the free jazz avant garde as "anti- jazz" and insisted that music should be evaluated separately from the social conditions of those who performed it (Kofsky 120–30; Evans 1–10). Interestingly, in his analysis of the various authenticating strategies in Japanese jazz—or "yellow jazz"—E. Taylor Atkins reports a similar claim as Eldridge's made by many Japanese jazz aficionados (40). And Joel Rudinow's insightful essay on the blackness of blues attempts to find the answer to a similar question, namely, "Do the notes sound different when played by black fingers?" (128).

2. Janowitz's only black character is Bibi, a dancer, who is relatively ancillary to the plot. And even though Janowitz is not interested in the sociology of jazz—to him, jazz was the ultimate expression of his utopian political dream, a pan-European democracy (Hentz 66; Riess 129–30)—it is nevertheless interesting to note that his *Jazz* in this respect echoes the larger European tradition of "negrophilia," where, as Petrine Archer-Straw observes,

> The Negrophiles who fraternized with blacks cultivated a shadowy world of nightclubs and bohemianism; their interests were in conflict with mainstream, 'traditional' values. 'Blackness' was a sign of their modernity, reflected in African sculptures that scattered their rooms, in the look of natural furs that fringed their coats, and in the frenzy of

> their dancing that mimicked the black bottom. Only rarely are black people depicted in this world. They and their mystique are the invisible presence in a multitude of negrophiliac images and texts from the era. . . . (19)

In Germany, as elsewhere, blackness (and jazz) signaled both sexual liberation and exotic-primitivistic rejuvenation on the one hand, as well as Dionysian chaos, moral decadence, and a threat to the national identity on the other. This ideological dialectic is also mirrored in the handful of novels from the period that portray jazz. Unlike Janowitz's novella, however, these books by Vicki Baum, René Schickele, Bruno Frank, Hermann Hesse, and others "indicate a greater preoccupation with extramusical notions of cultural despair and with the recent memory of French-African occupational forces in Germany than with jazz," as Marc Weiner points out (482).

3. All translations of Janowitz's *Jazz* are my own.

4. For a detailed discussion of the jazz aesthetic in Morrison's other novels, see Anthony J. Berret's "Toni Morrison's Literary Jazz" and the essays by Robin Small-McCarthy and Alan J. Rice. Morrison has tapped classical European concert music as well: her only published short story to date, "Recitatif," draws its title from a musical term in classical opera, the recitative (*recitatif* is but one of several spelling variants), which is a musical declamation in between formal numbers where the singer is accompanied only by harpsichord and follows the rhythmic patterns of ordinary speech rather than song ("recitative"). Also, in 1991 Morrison collaborated with singer Kathleen Battle and composer André Previn, providing the lyrics to *Honey & Rue,* which the liner notes define as a cycle of "contemporary art songs" that could also be classified as Third Stream music (Gurewitsch 6). And in 2003, the Michigan Opera Theatre commissioned Morrison together with classical composer Richard Danielpour to write an opera entitled *Margaret Garner,* based on her novel *Beloved* (Stryker C1; L. Johnson E3). Curiously, Morrison herself has questioned how appropriate the title of *Jazz* really is, and several critics argue along the same lines, observing that jazz functions merely as metaphor or image rather than a crucial catalyst of the narrative (Bigsby 28; Brooker, *New York* 200–9, Peach 114–15; Tally 4–5; Townsend 121–23). As I hope my argument shows, though, the novel and the music, at least in some aspects, enact the same aesthetic gesture, Morrison's doubts notwithstanding.

5. See also C. Brown (629–31), Dubey (303–4), Grewal (135–36), Paquet-Deyris (221–23), H. Rice (129–31), Rubinstein (152–55), Ryan (157), Small-McCarthy (293–94), and Walcott (320–22). Although Eckard offers only scant and tenuous textual evidence for her contention that the novel's narrative voice is indeed jazz itself, it is not as far-fetched as it may appear at first. Roger T. Dean argues that musical improvisation in the group "involves the merging of the self with another, so that it may be impossible to tell who has done what" (35). This merging of selves and their voices is, of course, precisely what happens to Morrison's narrator in the course of improvising new voices who sometimes take over narrative control.

6. This is another one of those murky contentions that is incessantly regurgitated by critics of literary jazz, and even Morrison herself has stated that jazz is open-ended and lacks closure (Morrison, "Toni Morrison" 42). In terms of form, this is correct, as in mainstream jazz the length of any tune or improvisation is theoretically open-ended as long as it consists of multiples of thirty-two measures, the length of

traditional AABA standards, or the twelve measures of the blues (or multiples of four respectively in an introduction or a coda). In modal jazz, the length of a chorus is not determined by the number of measures, for example in John Coltrane's 1960 version of "My Favorite Things." However, most jazz—modal jazz too—is diatonic music; that is, within the structure of the chord progression, there is almost always a return to the tonic, even in the chromaticism of bebop (Kofsky 262–64, 280, 317; Heble 32–33). The move towards a truly open-ended form and harmony happens only in free jazz, as for instance in the music of Ornette Coleman. But even there, a theme more often than not frames the solos: to pick just one obvious example, Coleman's "Story Writing" even includes the proverbial stranger (in the guise of Coleman's violin) coming to town. However, my aim here is not primarily to critique the criticism but to arrive at more feasible jazz criticism of literature. For an insightful if occasionally flawed discussion of some of the mistakes and errors committed by Morrison's jazz critics, see Alan Munton's essay "Misreading Morrison, Mishearing Jazz" as well as Stephan Richter's much more balanced analysis in "Magic Books and a Jam Session."

7. That the narrator is not Janowitz himself, becomes clear when Henry is being interviewed by an American journalist: "If you want to know more, Mr. Hennings, how Lord Punch's Jazz Band got together and so on, then read that story in Hans Janowitz's jazz novel, Mr. Hennings, in chapter five, if I'm not mistaken" (33). This quasi-postmodernist moment is echoed in numerous passages in which the narrative voice identifies itself as presently engaged in composing the story of *Jazz.*

8. See also Berret, "*Jazz*" (115), Eckard (16–18), Pici (382–89), and Walcott (320–21).

9. Friedrich Hollaender, one of Germany's jazz pioneers in the 1920s, reminds us that Germans used to pronounce the word *jazz* as *ja:s:* "Jass! Jass! rufen alle, als ob jemand vergessen hätte, den Hahn abzudrehen. 'Jazz' meinen sie, und jeder will's haben" (qtd. in Rotthaler 135).

10. Like John Coltrane, Eric Dolphy, Charlie Parker, Clifford Brown, or Charlie Christian, Wardell Gray died at a young age and is one of those tantalizing 'what-ifs' of jazz history. Gray's body was found in the middle of the desert outside of Las Vegas in 1955 just ten weeks after Parker's passing. The circumstances of Gray's death were rather suspicious—he had sustained severe head trauma and a broken neck—and have never been fully explained. Gordon later claimed that Gray had overdosed on heroin in his hotel room, after which two panicked band mates dumped his body in the Nevada desert (Britt 19–20; Morgan, liner notes). Although it is usually Gordon who is credited with being the first to translate Parker's innovations to the tenor saxophone, a very solid case can be made for Gray having at least paralleled Gordon in that regard. His homage to Lester Young, "One for Prez," based on the chord changes of "How High the Moon" and recorded in the fall of 1946 for the Sunset label, displays Gray's matured bebop style and indicates that at that time, he had already fused the previously pervasive Young influence with the new idiom seamlessly. Gray was "one of the first to put it all together," seconds fellow Central Avenue graduate Hawes (Hawes and Asher 80). Due to the recording ban, there is unfortunately no recorded evidence of Gray's career beginnings, but it is likely that he developed his bebop chops in the Earl Hines band, where he played alto saxophone initially, replacing the departed Charlie Parker (Britt 53; Morgan, liner notes; Gitler, *Jazz* 216–17).

11. A variant of "I Got Rhythm," "The Hunt" is also known as "Rocks 'n' Shoals." (Joop Visser posits that "The Hunt" derives from "Stompin' at the Savoy," which of course betrays a close affinity with "I Got Rhythm" [26].) The recorded track lacks the head; since the jam session was recorded on two portable disc cutters, it is likely that the recording was started late in order to conserve as much disc space as possible for the solos. "Rocks 'n' Shoals" probably acquired its new title only when the appropriately named if short-lived Bop record label issued it commercially on four 78s in an attempt to capitalize on the success of "The Chase" (Visser 26; Tarrant 177). Incidentally, this is the very recording purchased by the narrator of Jack Kerouac's *On the Road:* "They ate voraciously as Dean, sandwich in hand, stood bowed and jumping before the big phonograph, listening to a wild bop record I had just bought called 'The Hunt,' with Dexter Gordon and Wardell Gray blowing their tops before a screaming audience that gave the record fantastic frenzied volume" (113). In fact, "The Hunt" became so popular that musicians began to get wary of bootleg recordings. Sonny Criss, the altoist on that jam session, complained that Ralph Bass, the jazz enthusiast who recorded the battle, had hidden his two portable disc cutters underneath the bandstand, "[a]nd this is what really started the musicians to frown on people bringing recorders around, because prior to that, if somebody wanted to bring a recorder and record us, fine. But after that everybody really became very, very conscious of that kind of thing. 'Cause nobody got paid for that" (qtd. in Gitler, *Swing* 170).

12. Here, the numbers in parentheses denote minutes and seconds elapsed.

13. Gray deploys the exact same lick in another encounter with Gordon three years later at a jam session at the Hula Club in Los Angeles. Although not a cutting contest, "Move" is nevertheless textbook call and response, with all the soloists feeding off of each other's musical ideas and challenges. Gray's signature lick occurs in measures nine through twelve of his fifth solo chorus. (Note that the Prestige CD-reissue misidentifies "Move" as "Scrapple from the Apple.")

14. In terms of the novel's narrative aesthetics, Morrison is not interested in a synchronic historicity of the period jazz of the 1920s, as her numerous interviews make clear, even though Nicholas Pici argues that the novel "remains faithful to jazz history by referring only to . . . particular instruments and by never mentioning instruments that had not yet come on the jazz scene" (379). Pici's argument is flawed, however, since it misses the allusion to Charlie Parker, and generally fails to explain why a novel whose narrative structure moves across time and space would strive for mimetic historicity of aesthetic referents to begin with. Even more inconsistent is Pici's use of a diachronic critical approach when he adduces "Jig-A-Jug," a tune composed and recorded in 1995 by tenor saxophonist Joshua Redman, son of the free jazz iconoclast Dewey Redman. Even if *Jazz* were employing a literary aesthetic derived exclusively from 1920s jazz music, Pici undermines his own argument by citing a composition perhaps best classified as a post-bop tune (even though its title, of course, is a nod to Gene "Jug" Ammons) instead of any 1920s recording by, say, Sidney Bechet, Louis Armstrong, or of analyzing the Washingtonians' "Trombone Blues."

15. Coincidentally, Hunters Hunter's double name echoes another track by Gordon, recorded in 1945 and entitled "Dexter's Deck." The session that produced "Dexter's Deck" yielded several other sides, whose titles all include Gordon's first

name in some fashion. However, the record label, Savoy Records, was responsible for the titles, not Gordon himself (Gitler, *Jazz* 209).

16. "Double-time" denotes the seeming acceleration of the rhythm where a soloist, for example, halves the predominant note value from, say, eighth notes to sixteenth notes, thereby 'doubling' the speed. In pre-bebop jazz, this technique was also referred to as "double-tongue," deriving from the tongue-technique used by wind players in fast staccato passages ("Double-time"; Smith 214). Again, the 'chase' sections of Morrison's text interface with this term as well, as there are two 'tongues' or voices soloing over the same theme.

17. In this context, it is worth pointing out again that many jazz musicians use the metaphor of a conversation to describe their art (Berliner 348–86; Monson, *Saying* 73–96). For example, drummer Ralph Peterson's observation of musical interaction on the bandstand is remarkable for its similarity to Morrison's narrative strategy: "But you see what happens is, a lot of times when you get into a musical conversation one person in the group will state an idea or the beginning of an idea and another person will *complete* the idea or their interpretation of the same idea, how they hear it. So the conversation happens in fragments and comes from different parts, different voices" (qtd. in Monson, *Saying* 78). Critical to this conversational interaction is what Paul Berliner calls "the third ear," that is, the individual musician's ability to assess and adjust, in the practice room as well as on stage, not just his or her own ideas, but how they fit in with and contribute to those of others (243–44). Towards the end of the novel, it seems that the narrative voice begins to develop just such a third ear.

18. Where Mark Tucker counts twenty-five breaks out of a total of 139 measures, I can count—generously—only eighteen, thus bringing down the average from roughly one break every five-and-a-half to one every seven-and-a-half measures; still, I must concur with his assessment of the performance. Tucker speculates that the overly prominent novelty effects of the arrangements—presumably penned by Ellington—might have been Ellington's or the record company's effort to increase further the Washingtonians' appeal as a popular (commercial) dance band (153–55). Ellington's is the only known recording, even though the song was in Fletcher Henderson's band book. It, like "I'm Gonna Hang around My Sugar," was composed by Spencer Williams, who had scored a hit earlier that same year with "I've Found a New Baby"—which, it so happens, applies both to Violet's kidnapping of the baby boy at the beginning of the novel and the Traces' adoption of Felice at the end (M. Tucker 149–50).

19. Robinson (reeds), Hardwick (reeds), and Davis (trumpet, filling in for an absent Bubber Miley) were among the musicians recording "Trombone Blues" and "I'm Gonna Hang around My Sugar." My point here is not to judge the musicianship of these men, but to extend Tucker's point to Morrison's novel. Although the comparison of Otto "Toby" Hardwick with Gordon and Gray is admittedly somewhat unfair if not to say pointless (as comparisons of this kind are wont to be in jazz), the latter two also played in big bands at the beginning of their careers. What is more, it stands to reason that the arranger, at least as much as the musicians themselves, is to blame for the shortcomings of "Trombone Blues."

20. For another fist-hand account of the Weimar Republic's lively jazz scene, see Michael Danzi's engrossing memoir, *American Musician in Germany, 1924–1939.*

Danzi's recollections bear out Janowitz's take on jazz in Europe: like Henry, Danzi performed in ensembles whose personnel was multinational and whose music often straddled the fence between jazz and cabaret. "Berlin," Danzi avers, "was jumping" (17). Although he does not mention Janowitz, it is possible that the latter heard one of several Berlin-based bands with whom Danzi was crisscrossing Europe in the 1920s, especially since Danzi also worked for the silent movie industry (11–35). In Berlin, jazz had by the middle of the decade become what Cornelius Partsch calls a "metropolitan *Gebrauchsmusik*," reaching its apex with the premiere of Bertolt Brecht and Kurt Weill's *Die Dreigroschenoper,* that influential fusion of European art song and African American jazz (Partsch 107; Tischler 190–92).

21. Golson here concisely (and, probably, inadvertently) echoes what has become the accepted analytical model in the field of so-called ethnomusicology. As John Blacking summarizes it, "Because in music the code is the message and unwritten music can only be produced by social interaction, in the analysis of oral traditions the *musical product* cannot be isolated as a *niveau neutre* from the performance meanings it has to those who are making it and perceiving it" (189). The analytical approaches of Berliner's *Thinking in Jazz* and Monson's *Saying Something,* for instance, both heed this kind of integrative analysis.

22. See Christian (489–91), Hardack (453–54), Kubitschek (139, 157–61), and Nowlin (160–66). Also, Dorcas's name harks back to a character in Nathaniel Hawthorne's short story "Roger Malvin's Burial," in which Dorcas's husband shoots and kills their son in a hunting accident. Furthermore, Morrison's Dorcas is in many ways the foil to a minor character by the same name in *Uncle Tom's Cabin:* the injured Tom Loker is taken to "Grandmam Stephens there,—Dorcas, they call her,—she's most an amazin' nurse" (Stowe 200). Stowe's Aunt Dorcas is "a tall, dignified, spiritual [Quaker] woman, whose clean muslin cap shades waves of silver hair, parted on a broad, clear forehead, which overarches thoughtful gray eyes. A snowy handkerchief of lisse crape is folded neatly across her bosom; her glossy brown silk dress rustles peacefully, as she glides up and down the chamber" (380). And finally, in the Old Testament, Acts 9 tells the story of "a certain disciple named Tabitha, which *by interpretation* is called Dorcas: this woman was full of good works and almsdeeds which she did" and is eventually resurrected from her deathbed by Peter (Acts 9.36–42; emphasis added).

23. Lutie's nightmare recalls the opening paragraph of the vignette "Rhobert" in Jean Toomer's *Cane:*

> Rhobert wears a house, like a monstrous diver's helmet, on his head. . . . He is way down. Rods of the house like antennae of a dead thing, stuffed, prop up in the air. He is way down. He is sinking. His house is a dead thing that weights him down. He is sinking as a diver would sink in mud should the water be drawn off. Life is a murky, wiggling, microscopic water that compresses him. Compresses his helmet and would crush it the minute that he pulled his head out. He has to keep it in. Life is water that is being drawn off. (42)

24. In another intertextual linkage between the two novels, Bub, who is arrested for mail theft, is reincarnated in *Jazz*'s Sweetness, guilty of the same crime. Furthermore, both *The Street* and *Jazz* revisit the traditional trope of literacy and free-

dom in their final paragraphs, and in both texts, jazz offers not only opportunity, but also harbors danger.

25. In addition to Wild, *Jazz* has yet another "Omar," this time even a documented one: Morrison has said that the initial inspiration for the novel came from a photograph in James Van Der Zee's *The Harlem Book of the Dead* depicting the body of a young black woman who had been killed by her lover (Gates, Rev. 53).

Notes to Coda

1. To indicate modernism's fluctuating boundaries, Craig Werner for instance uses the term "(post)modernist" (4). Similarly, I feel the distinction between modernism and the avant-garde is not really a useful one when it comes to jazz. For example, Scott DeVaux's and Gary Giddins's studies of bebop both echo Andreas Huyssen's classification: at least in Europe, "the historical avant-garde aimed at developing an alternative relationship between high art and mass culture and thus should be distinguished from modernism, which for the most part insisted on the inherent hostility between high and low" (DeVeaux, *Birth* 22–24; Giddins, *Rhythm* xiii; Huyssen viii). But the modernists around Charlie Parker *were* after all the avant-garde in the 1940s, while the avant-gardist John Coltrane of the 1960s was decidedly modernistic in his esoteric forays and his explicit and repeated insistence that his art was not directly related to any socio-political concerns. And, as Alfred Appel reminds us, the modernisms of preceding jazz movements were the avant-garde in their day, too: "To call Armstrong, Waller, et al., 'modernists' is to appreciate their procedures as alchemists of the vernacular who have 'jazzed' the ordinary and given it new life" (13).

2. The narratives referenced here are thus also, interestingly, in the tradition of American modernism because, as Hugh Kenner notes at the outset of *A Homemade World,* "it is characteristic of American genius that the casual eye does not easily distinguish it from charlatanry" (12).

3. Edward Pavliç correctly points out that Ellison's literary modernism is actually more closely related to Bird's bebop than to the modernism of Ellington or Armstrong (44–50).

4. For other examples of how literary criticism in the wake of Baraka and Gates has canonized Coltrane as a representative of authentic blackness, see Berret (280–81); A. Rice ("Jazzing" 424–25); Small-McCarthy (298); or Snead (71–73). In general, Gatesian Signifyin(g) frequently betrays an unfamiliarity with jazz and its history in its tenuous connections and erroneous interpretations, as Stephan Richter has shown in his detailed analysis of the jazz references in Gates's books ("Magic" 28–36). At the opposite end of the critical spectrum is Alan Munton's polemic "Misreading Morrison, Mishearing Jazz," which accurately exposes many of the distortions to which Morrison's jazz critics subject Coltrane's music, but is flawed in other aspects: his categorical pronouncement that jazz and literature have nothing in common is simply not tenable in light alone of the poetry of Langston Hughes. Munton pontificates that "Coltrane's achievement is to have united European forms with rhythmic and improvisatory devices which originated in Africa" and then goes on to argue that "[t]he image of a black diaspora is the only generic concept that is true both to Morrison's fiction and to jazz; but if we accept this as truth, we must

refuse the Africanization of jazz and any 'Africanization' of Morrison's fiction based upon it" (243, 251). And when Munton concludes that therefore "[a]ny search for authenticity will be in vain," one must wonder why his own rhetoric implies an ideology of cultural authenticity throughout, as for example in the quotation above that situates the origins of certain musical forms in Europe, the origins of certain rhythmic patterns in Africa (251). Apparently, then, Europe and Africa are each loci of cultural authenticity, but black America cannot make the same claim. And lastly, Munton states that the term "cut" is unknown in jazz lingo (245). While he is correct in pointing out how other critics have misused the term, he is apparently unaware of the cutting contest.

5. It must be mentioned here that, at least according to his drummer Elvin Jones, Coltrane and his bandmates did not view Indian and African musics as unrelated: "even Indian music has its origins in the African art form. You can see the influences. Whatever we do, it can be traced to some of the African art forms" (qtd. in Kofsky 231). Coltrane's admiration for Shankar was such that, some years later, he would name one of his children after him. In recent years, Ravi Coltrane has become an accomplished saxophonist in his own right who has recorded several critically acclaimed albums with major record labels.

Selected Discography

Armstrong, Louis. "Hotter Than That." Rec. 13 Dec. 1927. *Early Satch: 1923–1929.* Jazz Legends, 2003.

Baraka, Amiri. "We Are the Blues: Funklore." Rec. 23 or 24 Sept. 2000. *Live in New York.* By Archie Shepp and Roswell Rudd. Verve, 2001.

Bechet, Sidney. "High Society." Rec. 14 Sep. 1939. *The Sidney Bechet Story.* 4 vols. Proper, 2001.

_____. "Summertime." Rec. 8 June 1939. *The Best of Sidney Bechet.* Blue Note, 1994.

Blakey, Art, and the Jazz Messengers. "Moanin.'" *Moanin'.* Rec. 30 Oct. 1958. Blue Note, 1999.

Bridgewater, Dee Dee. "All of Me." *In Montreux.* Rec. 18 July 1990. Polydor, 1991.

Coleman, Ornette, and Joachim Kühn. "Story Writing." *Colors.* Rec. 31 Aug. 1996. Verve, 1997.

Coltrane, John. "Giant Steps." Rec. 4 May 1959. *Giant Steps.* Atlantic, n.d.

_____. "My Favorite Things." Rec. 21 Oct. 1960. *My Favorite Things.* Atlantic, n.d.

_____. "Psalm." *A Love Supreme.* Rec. 9 Dec. 1964. Impulse, 1995.

_____. "Summertime." Rec. 24 Oct. 1960. *My Favorite Things.* Atlantic, n.d.

Davis, Miles. *Kind of Blue.* Rec. March–April 1959. Columbia, n.d.

____, and Gil Evans. "Summertime." Rec. 4 Aug. 1958. *Porgy and Bess.* LP. CBS, n.d.

Ellington, Duke. "Jack the Bear." Rec. 6 March 1940. *Never No Lament: The Blanton Webster Band.* 3 vols. RCA, 2003.

_____. "Trombone Blues." Rec. Sept. 1925. *Duke Ellington and His Orchestra: 1924–1927.* Jazz Chronological Classics, 1996.

Fitzgerald, Ella, and Louis Armstrong. "Summertime." Rec. 18 Aug. 1957. *Porgy and Bess.* LP. GEMA/BIEM, n.d.

Gillespie, Dizzy. "Dizzy Atmosphere." Rec. 29 Dec. 1945. *The Dizzy Gillespie Story: 1939–1950.*

_____. *The Dizzy Gillespie Story: 1939–1950.* 4 vols. Proper, 2001.

_____. "Ool-ya-koo." Rec. 30 Dec. 1947. *The Dizzy Gillespie Story: 1939–1950.*

_____. "Swing Low, Sweet Cadillac." Rec. 25 or 26 May 1967. *Swing Low, Sweet Cadillac.* Impulse, 1996.

_____. "Swing Low, Sweet Chariot." Rec. 31 Oct. 1950. *The Dizzy Gillespie Story: 1939–1950.*

Gordon, Dexter. "The Chase." Rec. 12 June 1947. *Dexter Gordon with Wardell Gray.* Giants of Jazz, 1998.

_____. "Dexter's Deck." Rec. 30 Oct. 1945. *Dexter Rides Again.* Savoy, 1992.

_____. "The Duel." Rec. 4 Dec. 1947. *Dexter Gordon with Wardell Gray.* Giants of Jazz, 1998.

_____. "The Hunt." Rec. 6 July 1947. *Settin' the Pace.* 4 vols. Proper, 2001.

Gray, Wardell. "Move." Rec. 27 Aug. 1950. *Wardell Gray Memorial, Volume 2.* Prestige, 1992.

_____. "One for Prez." *One for Prez.* Rec. Nov. 1946. 1201 Music, 1989.

Hancock, Herbie. "Watermelon Man." *Takin' Off.* Rec. 28 May 1962. Blue Note, 1996.

Holiday, Billie. "All of Me." Rec. 21 March 1941. *Billie Holiday: The Golden Years.* 3 vols. LP. Columbia, n.d.

Hughes, Langston. *Weary Blues.* Rec. 1958. Polygram, 1990.

Millinder, Lucky. "Darlin'." Rec. 26 May 1944. *Lucky Millinder and His Orchestra: 1943–1947.* Classics, 1998.

The Mills Brothers. "Swing It, Sister." Rec. 24 Feb. 1934. *The Essential Mills Brothers: Four Brothers and a Guitar.* Legacy/Columbia, 1995.

Monk, Thelonius. "Blue Monk." Rec. Aug. 1958. *Thelonius in Action.* Riverside, 1988.

Morrison, Toni. *Honey and Rue.* By Kathleen Battle. Rec. July 1992. Deutsche Grammophon, 1995.

Parker, Charlie. "Klact-oveeseds-tene." Rec. 4 Nov. 1947. *Charlie Parker.* LP. 3 vols. Joker, 1980.

Ra, Sun. "Space Is the Place." *Space Is the Place.* Rec. 19 or 20 Dec. 1972. Impulse, 1998.

Redman, Joshua. "Jig-A-Jug." *Spirit of the Moment: Live at the Village Vanguard.* Rec. March 1995. Warner Bros., 1995.

The Washingtonians. "Trombone Blues." Rec. Sept. 1925. *Duke Ellington and His Orchestra: 1924–1927.* Jazz Chronological Classics, 1996.

Works Cited

Aguiar, Sarah Appleton. "'Everywhere and Nowhere': Beloved's 'Wild' Legacy in Toni Morrison's *Jazz*." *Notes on Contemporary Literature* 25.4 (1995): 11–12.

Anderson, Paul Allen. *Deep River: Music and Memory in Harlem Renaissance Thought.* Durham: Duke University Press, 2001.

Andrews, William L. *To Tell a Free Story: The First Century of Afro-American Autobiography, 1760–1865.* Urbana: Illinois University Press, 1986.

Ansermet, Ernst-Alexandre. "Bechet and Jazz Visit Europe, 1919." Trans. Walter Schaap. In *Frontiers of Jazz.* Ed. Ralph de Toledano. 3rd rev. ed., 111–18. Gretna: Pelican, 1994.

Appel, Alfred, Jr. *Jazz Modernism: From Armstrong to Matisse and Joyce.* New York: Knopf, 2002.

Archer-Straw, Petrine. *Negrophilia: Avant-Garde Paris and Black Culture in the 1920s.* New York: Thames and Hudson, 2000.

Atkins, E. Taylor. *Blue Nippon: Authenticating Jazz in Japan.* Durham: Duke University Press, 2001.

Attali, Jacques. *Noise: The Political Economy of Music.* 1977. Trans. Brian Massumi. Minneapolis: University of Minnesota Press, 1985.

Baker, Houston A., Jr. *Blues, Ideology, and Afro-American Literature: A Vernacular Theory.* Chicago: University of Chicago Press, 1984.

Baldwin, James. *Notes of a Native Son.* 1955. Boston: Beacon, 1984.

_____. "Of the Sorrow Songs: The Cross of Redemption." 1979. In *The Picador Book of Blues and Jazz.* Ed. James Campbell, 324–31. London: Picador, 1996.

_____. "Sonny's Blues." In *Call and Response: The Riverside Anthology of African American Literary Tradition.* Eds. Patricia Liggins Hill et al., 1298–1316. Boston: Houghton Mifflin, 1998.

Balliet, Whitney. *Jelly Roll, Jabbo, and Fats: 19 Portraits in Jazz.* New York: Oxford University Press, 1983.

Baraka, Amiri. *The Autobiography of LeRoi Jones.* 1984. Chicago: Lawrence Hill, 1997.

_____. *Black Music.* 1967. New York: Da Capo, 1998.

_____. *Blues People: The Negro Experience in White America and the Music That Developed from It.* New York: Morrow, 1963.

_____. *Daggers and Javelins: Essays, 1974–1979.* New York: Morrow, 1984.

_____. *Dutchman.* 1964. In *The LeRoi Jones/Amiri Baraka Reader.* Ed. William J. Harris, 76–99. New York: Thunder's Mouth, 1991.

_____. *Primitive World: An Anti-Nuclear Jazz Musical.* 1984. In *The LeRoi Jones / Amiri Baraka Reader.* Ed. William J. Harris, 400–49. New York: Thunder's Mouth, 1991.

_____. *Tales.* 1967. New York: Grove, 1968.

Baraka, Amiri, and Amina Baraka. *The Music.* New York: Morrow, 1987.

Barthes, Roland. "Le grain de la voix." In *L'obvie et l'obtus: essais critiques III,* 236–45. Paris: Seuil, 1982.

Basie, Count. *Good Morning Blues: The Autobiography of Count Basie, as Told to Albert Murray.* New York: Random House, 1985.

Bechet, Sidney. *Treat It Gentle: An Autobiography.* 1960. New York: Da Capo, 1978.

Bercovitch, Sacvan. *The Rites of Assent: Transformations in the Symbolic Construction of America.* New York: Routledge, 1993.

Berendt, Joachim E. *Das grosse Jazzbuch: Von New Orleans bis Jazz Rock.* 5th rev. ed. Frankfurt am Main: Fischer, 1985.

Berliner, Paul F. *Thinking in Jazz: The Infinite Art of Improvisation.* Chicago: University of Chicago Press, 1994.

Berret, Anthony J. "*Jazz:* From Music to Literature." In *Approaches to Teaching the Novels of Toni Morrison.* Eds. Nellie Y. McKay and Kathryn Earle, 113–17. New York: MLA, 1997.

_____. "Toni Morrison's Literary Jazz." *CLA Journal* 32.3 (1989): 267–83.

Berry, Faith. *Before and Beyond Harlem: A Biography of Langston Hughes.* Avenel: Wings, 1992.

Bigsby, Christopher. "Jazz Queen." *Independent,* 26 April 1992, 28–29.

Blacking, John. "The Problem of 'Ethnic' Perceptions in the Semiotics of Music." In *The Sign in Music and Literature.* Ed. Wendy Steiner, 184–94. Austin: University of Texas Press, 1981.

Blesh, Rudi. *Combo: USA–Eight Lives in Jazz.* Philadelphia: Chilton, 1971.

"Bop." In *The New Grove Dictionary of Jazz.*

Borshuk, Michael. "'Noisy Modernism': The Cultural Politics of Langston Hughes's Early Jazz Poetry." *Langston Hughes Review* 17 (2002): 4–21.

Brady, Philip. "'Saxophon–guter Ton!' On Hans Janowitz's Jazz-Novel of 1927." In *Expeditionen nach der Wahrheit: Poems, Essays, and Papers in Honour of Theo Stammler.* Eds. Stefan Horlacher and Marion Islinger, 461–70. Heidelberg: Carl Winter, 1996.

Britt, Stan. *Dexter Gordon: A Musical Biography.* New York: Da Capo, 1989.

Brooker, Peter. "Modernism Deferred: Langston Hughes, Harlem and Jazz Montage." In *Locations of Literary Modernism: Region and Nation in British and American Modernist Poetry.* Eds. Alex Davis and Lee M. Jenkins, 231–88. Cambridge: Cambridge University Press, 2000.

_____. *New York Fictions: Modernity, Post-Modernism, the New Modernism.* London: Longman, 1996.

Brown, Caroline. "Golden Gray and the Talking Book: Identity as a Site of Artful Construction in *Jazz.*" *African American Review* 36.4 (2002): 629–42.

Brown, Lee B. "Postmodernist Jazz Theory: Afrocentrism, Old and New." *Journal of Aesthetics and Art Criticism* 57.2 (1999): 235–46.

Brown, Lloyd W. *Amiri Baraka.* Boston: Twayne, 1980.

Brown, Sterling A. "Spirituals, Blues, and Jazz." 1945. In *Jam Session: A Jazz Anthology.* Ed. Ralph J. Gleason, 17–24. London: Peter Davis, 1961.

Bunnett, Rexton S., Michael Patrick Kennedy, and John Muir. *Collins Guide to Musicals.* Rev. ed. Glasgow: Harper Collins, 2001.

Burns, Kephra. Liner Notes. *Aura.* By Miles Davis. Sony, 2000.

Cable, George Washington. *The Grandissimes: A Story of Creole Life.* New York: Charles Scribner's, 1880.

_____. "The Story of Bras-Coupé." In *Creoles and Cajuns: Stories of Old Louisiana.* Ed. Arlin Turner, 20–46. Gloucester: P. Smith, 1965.

Callahan, John F., ed. *The Collected Essays of Ralph Ellison.* New York: Modern Library, 1995.

Carmichael, Thomas. "*Beneath the Underdog:* Charles Mingus, Representation, and Jazz Autobiography." *Canadian Review of American Studies* 25.3 (1995): 29–40.

Cataliotti, Robert H. *The Music in African American Fiction.* New York: Garland, 1995.

"Chase." In *The New Grove Dictionary of Jazz.*

Chilton, John. *Sidney Bechet: Wizard of Jazz.* 1987. New York: Da Capo, 1996.

Christian, Barbara T. "Layered Rhythms: Virginia Woolf and Toni Morrison." *Modern Fiction Studies* 39.3 & 4 (1993): 483–500.

Ciardi, John. "Writing *Treat It Gentle:* A Letter to Vince Clemente, September 22, 1985." In *John Ciardi: Measure of the Man.* Ed. Vince Clemente, 82–83. Fayetteville: University of Arkansas Press, 1987.

Cifelli, Edward M. *John Ciardi: A Biography.* Fayetteville: University of Arkansas Press, 1997.

Clark, Keith. "A Distaff Dream Deferred? Ann Petry and the Art of Subversion." *African American Review* 26.3 (1992): 495–505.

Clausewitz, Carl Philipp Gottfried von. *Vom Kriege.* 1832. 19th rev. ed. Ed. Werner Hahlweg. Bonn: Ferd. Dümmlers, 1990.

Coleman, Larry G. "LeRoi Jones' *Tales:* Sketches of the Artist as a Young Man Moving toward a Blacker Art." In *Imamu Amiri Baraka (LeRoi Jones): A Collection of Critical Essays.* Ed. Kimberly W. Benston, 84–95. Englewood Cliffs: Prentice-Hall, 1978.

Collier, James Lincoln. *Jazz: The American Theme Song.* New York: Oxford University Press, 1993.

Coltrane, John. Liner Notes. *A Love Supreme.* Impulse, 1995.

Crow, Bill. "The Bass in Jazz." In *The Oxford Companion to Jazz,* 668–80.

"Cutting contest." In *The New Grove Dictionary of Jazz.*

Dahl, Linda. *Stormy Weather: The Music and Lives of a Century of Jazz Women.* New York: Pantheon, 1984.

Danzi, Michael, and Rainer E. Lotz. *American Musician in Germany, 1924–1939: Memoirs of the Jazz, Entertainment, and Movie World of Berlin during the Weimar Republic and the Nazi Era, and in the United States.* Schmitten: Ruecker, 1986.

Davis, Angela Y. "I Used to Be Your Sweet Mama: Ideology, Sexuality, and Domesticity." *Write Me a Few of Your Lines: A Blues Reader.* Ed. Steven C. Tracy, 470–501. Amherst: University of Massachusetts Press, 1999.

Davis, Francis. "In the Macho World of Jazz, Don't Ask, Don't Tell." *New York Times,* 1 Sept. 2002, sec. 2, p. 19.

Dean, Roger T. *New Structures in Jazz and Improvisational Music since 1960.* Philadelphia: Open University Press, 1992.

Demsey, David. "Jazz Improvisation and Concepts of Virtuosity." In *The Oxford Companion to Jazz,* 788–98.

DeVeaux, Scott. "The Advent of Bebop." In *The Oxford Companion to Jazz,* 292–304.

_____. *The Birth of Bebop: A Social and Musical History.* Berkeley: University of California Press, 1997.

"Double-time." In *The New Grove Dictionary of Jazz.*

Douglass, Frederick. *Narrative of the Life of Frederick Douglass, an American Slave, Written by Himself.* 1845. Ed. Houston A. Baker, Jr. New York: Penguin, 1982.

Drake, Kimberly. "Women on the Go: Blues, Conjure, and Other Alternatives to Domesticity in Ann Petry's *The Street* and *The Narrows.*" *Arizona Quarterly* 54.1 (1998): 65–95.

Du Bois, W. E. B. *The Souls of Black Folk.* 1903. New York: Dover, 1994.

Dubey, Madhu. "Narration and Migration: *Jazz* and Vernacular Theories of Black Women's Fiction." *American Literary History* 10.2 (1998): 291–316.

Eckard, Paula Gallant. "The Interplay of Music, Language, and Narrative in Toni Morrison's *Jazz.*" *CLA Journal* 38.1 (1994): 11–19.

Ehrlich, Blake. "Old Man with a Horn: Sidney Bechet, at Sixty-one, Is America's Most Renowned Expatriate Musician." *Esquire* July (1958): 95–98.

Ellington, Duke. *Music Is My Mistress.* Garden City: Doubleday, 1973.

Ellison, Ralph. "Cadillac Flambé." 1973. In O'Meally, *Living with Music,* 214–33.

_____. "A Coupla Scalped Indians." 1956. In O'Meally, *Living with Music,* 179–95.

_____. *Going to the Territory.* 1986. In Callahan, *The Collected Essays,* 487–781.

_____. *Invisible Man.* 1952. New York: Vintage, 1972.

_____. *Juneteenth.* Ed. John F. Callahan. New York: Random House, 1999.

_____. Letter to Albert Murray, 28 Sept. 1958. In O'Meally, *Living with Music,* 244–50.

_____. *Shadow and Act.* 1964. In Callahan, *Collected Essays,* 47–340.

Elman, Richard. "John Ciardi and *Treat It Gentle.*" In *John Ciardi: Measure of the Man.* Ed. Vince Clemente, 79–81. Fayetteville: University of Arkansas, 1987.

Ervin, Hazel Arnett, ed. *Ann Petry: A Bio-Bibliography.* New York: G. K. Hall, 1993.

Evans, Nicholas M. *Writing Jazz: Race, Nationalism, and Modern Culture in the 1920s.* New York: Garland, 2000.

Feather, Leonard. *The Book of Jazz: From Then till Now.* New York: Horizon, 1965.

_____. "Little Jazz Goes Color Blind." *Down Beat* 13 July 1951: 12.

Floyd, Samuel A., Jr. "African Roots of Jazz." In *The Oxford Companion to Jazz,* 7–16.

_____. *The Power of Black Music: Interpreting Its History from Africa to the United States.* New York: Oxford University Press, 1995.

Friedwald, Will. Booklet. *The Essential Mills Brothers: Four Brothers and a Guitar.* By The Mills Brothers. Legacy/Columbia, 1995.

_____. *Jazz Singing: America's Great Voices from Bessie Smith to Bebop and Beyond.* New York: Collier, 1992.

Garvey, Johanna X. K. "That Old Black Magic? Gender and Music in Ann Petry's Fiction." In *Black Orpheus: Music in African American Fiction from the Harlem Renaissance to Toni Morrison.* Ed. Saadi A. Simawe, 119–51. New York: Garland, 2000.

Gates, Henry Louis, Jr. *Figures in Black: Words, Signs, and the "Racial" Self.* New York: Oxford University Press, 1987.

_____. Rev. of *Beloved,* by Toni Morrison. In *Toni Morrison: Critical Perspectives Past and Present.* Eds. Gates and Kwameh Antony Appiah, 52–55. New York: Amistad, 1993.

_____. *The Signifying Monkey: A Theory of African-American Literary Criticism.* New York: Oxford University Press, 1988.

Gebhardt, Nicholas. *Going for Jazz: Musical Practices and American Ideology.* Chicago: University of Chicago Press, 2001.

Gennari, John. "Jazz Criticism: Its Development and Ideologies." *Black American Literature Forum* 25.3 (1991): 449–523.

Gerard, Charley. *Jazz in Black and White: Race, Culture, and Identity in the Jazz Community.* Westport: Praeger, 1998.

Giddins, Gary. *Celebrating Bird: The Triumph of Charlie Parker.* New York: William Morrow, 1987.

_____. *Rhythm-a-ning: Jazz Tradition and Innovation in the '80s.* New York: Oxford University Press, 1985.

Gildea, Robert. *France Since 1945.* New York: Oxford University Press, 1996.

Gillespie, Dizzy, with Al Fraser. *To BE, or Not . . . To BOP.* New York: Da Capo, 1979.

Gilroy, Paul. *Against Race: Imagining Political Culture beyond the Color Line.* Cambridge: Belknap, 2000.

_____. *The Black Atlantic: Modernity and Double Consciousness.* Cambridge, Harvard University Press, 1993.

Gioia, Ted. *West Coast Jazz: Modern Jazz in California 1945–1960.* New York: Oxford University Press, 1992.

Gitler, Ira. *Jazz Masters of the '40s.* 1966. New York: Da Capo, 1983.

_____. Liner Notes. *Wardell Gray Memorial, Volume One.* By Wardell Gray. Original Jazz Classics, 1992.

_____. *Swing to Bop: An Oral History of the Transition in Jazz in the 1940s.* New York: Oxford University Press, 1985.

Göbel, Walter. "Musik im postmodernen afrikanisch-amerikanischen Roman: Ellison, Reed, Cartier." *Amerikastudien/American Studies* 40.1 (1995): 69–81.

Golson, Benny. "Forward Motion: An Interview with Benny Golson." *Boundary 2* 22.2 (1995): 53–93.

Gourse, Leslie. *Madame Jazz: Contemporary Women Instrumentalists.* New York: Oxford, 1995.

Grewal, Gurleen. *Circles of Sorrow, Lines of Struggle: The Novels of Toni Morrison.* Baton Rouge: Louisiana State University Press, 1998.

Gruntz, George. *Als weisser Neger geboren: Ein Leben für den Jazz.* Ed. Gerd Haffmans. Berneck: Corvus, 2002.

Gurewitsch, Matthew. "Toni Morrison on 'Honey & Rue.'" Booklet. *Honey & Rue.* By Kathleen Battle. Deutsche Grammophon, 1995.

Gussow, Adam. *Seems Like Murder in Here: Southern Violence and the Blues Tradition.* Chicago: University of Chicago Press, 2002.

Gysin, Fritz. "From 'Liberating Voices' to 'Metathetic Ventriloquism': Boundaries in Recent African-American Jazz Fiction." *Callaloo* 25.1 (2002): 274–87.

Handy, D. Antoinette. *Black Women in American Bands and Orchestras.* Metuchen: Scarecrow, 1981.

Hardack, Richard. "'A Music Seeking Its Words': Double-Timing and Double- Consciousness in Toni Morrison's *Jazz.*" *Callaloo* 18.2 (1995): 451–71.

Harding, James M. "Adorno, Ellison, and the Critique of Jazz." *Cultural Critique* 31.3 (1995): 129–58.

Harper, Donna Akiba Sullivan. *Not So Simple: The "Simple" Stories by Langston Hughes.* Columbia: University of Missouri Press, 1995.

Harris, Trudier. *Fiction and Folklore: The Novels of Toni Morrison.* Knoxville: University of Tennessee Press, 1991.

Harris, William J. *The Poetry and Poetics of Amiri Baraka: The Jazz Aesthetic.* Columbia: University of Missouri Press, 1985.

Harrison, Max. "A Rare Bird." In *The Charlie Parker Companion: Six Decades of Commentary.* Ed. Carl Woideck, 204–25. New York: Schirmer, 1998.

Hawes, Hampton, and Don Asher. *Raise Up Off Me: A Portrait of Hampton Hawes.* 1972. New York: Da Capo, 1979.

Hawthorne, Nathaniel. "Roger Malvin's Burial." 1832. In *The Complete Short Stories of Nathaniel Hawthorne,* 328–61. Garden City: Hanover House, 1959.

Hebdige, Dick. "Even Unto Death: Improvisation, Edging, and Enframement." *Critical Inquiry* 27.2 (2001): 333–53.

Heble, Ajay. *Landing on the Wrong Note: Jazz, Dissonance, and Critical Practice.* New York: Routledge, 2000.

Henderson, Carol E. "The 'Walking Wounded': Rethinking Black Women's Identity in Ann Petry's *The Street.*" *Modern Fiction Studies* 46.4 (2000): 849–67.

Henderson, Stephen. *Understanding the New Black Poetry: Black Speech and Black Music as Poetic References.* New York: William Morrow, 1973.

Hentz, Stephan. "Jazz ist, wenn die Hoffnung klingt." Rev. of *Jazz,* by Hans Janowitz. *Neue Zürcher Zeitung* 16 March 2000, 66.

Heyward, Du Bose, and Ira Gershwin. "Summertime." In *Porgy and Bess,* 15–17. New York: Chappell, 1935.

Hokanson, Robert O'Brien. "Jazzing It Up: The Be-bop Modernism of Langston Hughes." *Mosaic* 31.4 (1998): 61–82.

The Holy Bible: King James Version. New York: Ivy, 1991.

Huggins, Nathan Irvin. *Harlem Renaissance.* New York: Oxford University Press, 1971.

Hughes, Langston. *The Best of Simple.* New York: Hill & Wang, 1961.

_____. *The Big Sea.* 1940. New York: Hill & Wang, 1993.

_____. *The Collected Poems of Langston Hughes.* Eds. Arnold Rampersad and David Roessel. New York: Knopf, 1994.

_____. *The Early Simple Stories. The Collected Works of Langston Hughes.* Vol. 7. Ed. Donna Akiba Sullivan Harper. Columbia: University of Missouri Press, 2002.

_____. *The First Book of Jazz.* 1955. Hopewell: Ecco, 1982.

_____. *I Wonder as I Wander.* 1956. New York: Hill & Wang, 1997.

_____. *Not without Laughter.* 1930. In *The Novels. The Collected Works of Langston Hughes.* Vol. 4. Ed. Dolan Hubbard, 13–209. Columbia: University of Missouri Press, 2001.

_____. "Simple Declares Be-Bop Music Comes from Bop! Bop! Bop! Mop!" *Chicago Defender* 19 Nov. 1949, 6.

_____. "That Boy LeRoi." Rev. of *The Toilet,* by Amiri Baraka. In *Imamu Amiri Baraka (LeRoi Jones): A Collection of Critical Essays.* Ed. Kimberly W. Benston, 21–22. Englewood Cliffs: Prentice-Hall, 1978.

_____. "Trumpet Player." In *Selected Poems of Langston Hughes,* 114–15. 1959. New York: Vintage, 1990.

Huyssen, Andreas. *After the Great Divide: Modernism, Mass Culture, Postmodernism.*

Bloomington: University of Indiana Press, 1986.

Ivy, James W. "Ann Petry Talks about First Novel." In *Sturdy Black Bridges: Visions of Black Women in Literature.* Eds. Roseann P. Bell, Bettye J. Parker, and Beverly Guy-Sheftall, 197–200. Garden City: Anchor, 1979.

Jacobs, Harriet A. *Incidents in the Life of a Slave Girl, Written by Herself.* 1861. Ed. Jean Fagan Yellin. Cambridge: Harvard University Press, 1996.

Jameson, Frederic. Foreword. In *Noise: The Political Economy of Music.* By Jacques Attali, vii–xiv. Minneapolis: University of Minnesota Press, 1985.

Janowitz, Hans. *Jazz.* 1927. Ed. Rolf Riess. Bonn: Weidle, 1999.

Jarrett, Michael. *Drifting on a Read: Jazz as a Model for Writing.* Albany: SUNY Press, 1999. "Jazz and Race: Black, White, and Beyond." *Jazz Times,* 10 Sept. 2001 <http:// www.jazz-times.com/ race_jazz1. cfm (15 Sept. 2001).

Jimoh, A. Yemisi. *Spirituals, Blues, and Jazz People in African American Fiction: Living in Paradox.* Knoxville: University of Tennessee Press, 2002.

Johnson, Lawrence B. "MOT Backs Morrison, Danielpour Collaboration." *Detroit News* 20 Feb. 2003, E3.

Jones, Ferdinand. "Jazz and the Resilience of African Americans." In *The Triumph of the Soul: Cultural and Psychological Aspects of African American Music.* Eds. Ferdinand Jones and Arthur C. Jones, 127–51. Westport: Praeger, 2001.

Jones, Gayl. *Liberating Voices: Oral Tradition in African American Literature.* New York: Penguin, 1992.

Kenner, Hugh. *A Homemade World: The American Modernist Writers.* Baltimore: Johns Hopkins University Press, 1975.

Kenney, William Howland, III. "'Going to Meet the Man': Louis Armstrong's Autobiographies." *MELUS* 15.2 (1988): 27–46.

Kerman, Cynthia Earl, and Richard Eldridge. *The Lives of Jean Toomer: A Hunger for Wholeness.* Baton Rouge: Louisiana State University Press, 1987.

Kerouac, Jack. *On The Road.* 1957. New York: Penguin, 1976.

Kirchner, Bill. Introduction. In *The Oxford Companion to Jazz,* 3–6.

Knauer, Wolfram. "Musikergespräch mit Michael Naura: Es war ein lustiges Völkchen." In *Jazz in Deutschland.* Ed. Wolfram Knauer, 159–73. Darmstädter Beiträge zur Jazzforschung 4. Hofheim: Wolke, 1996.

Kofsky, Frank. *John Coltrane and the Jazz Revolution of the 1960s.* New York: Pathfinder, 1998.

Komara, Edward M. *The Dial Recordings of Charlie Parker: A Discography.* Westport: Greenwood, 1998.

Kracauer, Siegfried. *From Caligari to Hitler: A Psychological History of German Film.* Cambridge: Princeton University Press, 1970.

Kramer, Lawrence. *Musical Meaning: Towards a Critical History.* Berkeley: University of California Press, 2002.

Kubitschek, Missy Dehn. *Toni Morrison: A Critical Companion.* Westport: Greenwood, 1998.

Lattin, Vernon E. "Ann Petry and the American Dream." *Black American Literature Forum* 12.2 (1978): 69–72.

Lawrence, A. H. *Duke Ellington and His World: A Biography.* New York: Routledge, 2001.

Lees, Gene. *Cats of Any Color: Jazz Black and White.* New York: Oxford University Press, 1994.

Lewis, David Levering. *When Harlem Was in Vogue*. New York: Oxford University Press, 1979.

Lewis, George E. "Improvised Music after 1950: Afrological and Eurological Perspectives." *Black Music Research Journal* 16 (1996): 91–122.

Lock, Graham. *Blutopia: Visions of the Future and Revisions of the Past in the Works of Sun Ra, Duke Ellington, and Anthony Braxton*. Durham: Duke University Press, 1999.

Lott, Eric. "Double V, Double-Time: Bebop's Politics of Style." *Callaloo* 11.3 (1988): 597–605.

Lowney, John. "Langston Hughes and the 'Nonsense' of Bebop." *American Literature* 72.2 (2000): 357–85.

Mackey, Nathaniel. *Atet A. D.* From a Broken Bottle Traces of Perfume Still Emanate, vol. 3. San Francisco: City Lights, 2001.

_____. *Bedouin Hornbook*. From a Broken Bottle Traces of Perfume Still Emanate, vol. 1. Charlottesville: University of Virginia Press, 1986.

_____. *Discrepant Engagement: Dissonance, Cross-Culturality, and Experimental Writing*. New York: Cambridge University Press, 1993.

"Made in the Shade." *Times-Picayune* [New Orleans] 4 May 1997, A-1.

Marvin, Thomas F. "Children of Legba: Musicians at the Crossroads in Ralph Ellison's *Invisible Man*." *American Literature* 68.3 (1996): 587–608.

McCarthy, Albert. *Big Band Jazz*. London: Putnam's, 1974.

McFarlane, Al. "*The Black Scholar* Interviews: McCoy Tyner." *Black Scholar* 2.2 (1970): 40–46.

McKay, Claude. *Home to Harlem*. 1928. New York: Chatham, 1973.

McKay, Nellie Y. "Ann Petry's *The Street* and *The Narrows:* A Study of the Influence of Class, Race, and Gender on Afro-American Women's Lives." In *Women and War: The Changing Status of American Women from the 1930s to the 1950s*. Eds. Maria Diedrich and Dorothea Fischer-Hornung, 127–40. New York: Berg, 1990.

Merod, Jim. "Jazz as Cultural Archive." *Boundary 2* 22.2 (1995): 7–18.

Miller, R. Baxter. *The Art and Imagination of Langston Hughes*. Lexington: University of Kentucky Press, 1989.

_____. "Framing and Framed Languages in Hughes's *Ask Your Mama: 12 Moods for Jazz*." *MELUS* 17.4 (1991–1992): 3–13.

_____. "Race, Globalization, and New Ethnic Studies." Signifyin' across Literary Boundaries: Modernism, Quest for Identity, and Multiculturalism. CLA Convention. Washington Marriott Hotel, Washington, D.C., 26 April 2003.

Monson, Ingrid. "Doubleness and Jazz Improvisation: Irony, Parody, and Ethnomusicology." *Critical Inquiry* 20 (1994): 283–313.

_____. *Saying Something: Jazz Improvisation and Interaction*. Chicago: Chicago University Press, 1996.

Morgan, Alun. Liner Notes. *One for Prez*. By Wardell Gray. 1201 Music, 1989.

Morgenstern, Dan. Liner Notes. *The Best of Sidney Bechet*. By Sidney Bechet. Blue Note, 1994, 3–7.

Morrison, Toni. *Beloved*. 1987. New York: Plume, 1988.

_____. "An Interview with Toni Morrison." In *Conversations with Toni Morrison*. Ed. Danille Taylor-Guthrie, 138–55. Jackson: University of Mississippi Press, 1994.

_____. *Jazz*. New York: Knopf, 1992.

_____. *Playing in the Dark: Whiteness and the Literary Imagination.* Cambridge: Harvard University Press, 1992.

_____. "Recitatif." In *Confirmation: An Anthology of African American Women.* Eds. Amiri Baraka and Amina Baraka, 243–61. New York: Quill, 1983.

_____. "Toni Morrison." *Belles Lettres* 10.2 (1995): 40–43.

Mouly, Raymond. *Sidney Bechet, notre ami.* Paris: Alain Pierson, 1959.

Mullener, Elisabeth. "French Envoy Saw Bechet Take Paris." *Times-Picayune* [New Orleans] 7 May 1997, B-1–B-2.

Munton, Alan. "Misreading Morrison, Mishearing Jazz: A Response to Toni Morrison's Jazz Critics." *Journal of American Studies* 31.2 (1997): 235–51.

Murray, Albert. *Stomping the Blues.* 1976. New York: Da Capo, 2000.

Murray, Charles Shaar. *Boogie Man: The Adventures of John Lee Hooker in the American Twentieth Century.* New York: St. Martin's, 2000.

The New Grove Dictionary of Jazz. Ed. Barry Kernfeld. New York: St. Martin's Press, 1994.

Nicholson, Stuart. *Billie Holiday.* Boston: Northeastern University Press, 1995.

Nisenson, Eric. *Ascension: John Coltrane and His Quest.* New York: St. Martin's, 1993.

_____. *Open Sky: Sonny Rollins and His World of Improvisation.* New York: St. Martin's Press, 2000.

Nowlin, Michael. "Toni Morrison's *Jazz* and the Racial Dreams of the American Writer." *American Literature* 71.1 (1999): 151–74.

Ogren, Kathy. "Controversial Sounds: Jazz Performance as Theme and Language in the Harlem Renaissance." In *The Harlem Renaissance: Revolutions.* Eds. Amritjit Singh, William S. Shiver, and Stanley Brodwin, 159–93. New York: Garland, 1989.

_____. "'Jazz isn't just me': Jazz Autobiographies as Performance Personas." In *Jazz in Mind: Essays on the History and Meanings of Jazz.* Eds. Reginald T. Buckner and Steven Weiland, 112–27. Detroit: Wayne State University Press, 1991.

_____. *The Jazz Revolution: Twenties America and the Meaning of Jazz.* New York: Oxford University Press, 1989.

Oliver, Paul. *Blues Fell this Morning: The Meaning of the Blues.* New York: Collier, 1960.

O'Meally, Robert G. *The Craft of Ralph Ellison.* Cambridge: Harvard University Press, 1980.

_____. "Introduction: Jazz Shapes." In O'Meally, *Living with Music,* ix–xxxv.

_____, ed. *Living with Music: Ralph Ellison's Jazz Writings.* New York: Modern Library, 2001.

Ostendorf, Berndt. "Ralph Waldo Ellison: Anthropology, Modernism, and Jazz." In *New Essays on Invisible Man.* Ed. Robert G. O'Meally, 95–121. Cambridge: Cambridge University Press, 1988.

The Oxford Companion to Jazz. Ed. Bill Kirchner. New York: Oxford University Press, 2000.

Panish, Jon. *The Color of Jazz: Race and Representation in Postwar American Culture.* Jackson: University of Mississippi Press, 1997.

Paquet-Deyris, Anne-Marie. "Toni Morrison's *Jazz* and the City." *African American Review* 35.2 (2001): 219–31.

Park, You-me, and Gayle Wald. "Native Daughters in the Promised Land: Gender, Race, and the Question of Separate Spheres." *American Literature* 70.3 (1998): 607–33.

Partsch, Cornelius. "Hannibal ante Portas: Jazz in Weimar." In *Dancing on the Volcano: Essays on the Culture of the Weimar Republic.* Eds. Thomas W. Kniersche and Stephen Brockmann, 105–16. Columbia: Camden House, 1994.

Pavliç, Edward M. *Crossroads Modernism: Descent and Emergence in African-American Literary Culture.* Minneapolis: University of Minnesota Press, 2002.

Peach, Linden. *Toni Morrison.* London: Macmillan, 1995.

Perlman, Alan M., and Daniel Greenblatt. "Miles Davis Meets Noam Chomsky: Some Observations on Jazz Improvisation and Language Structure." In *The Sign in Music and Literature.* Ed. Wendy Steiner, 169–83. Austin: University of Texas Press, 1981.

Persica, Dennis. "Hometown Acclaim Comes Late to Legend." *Times-Picayune* [New Orleans], 4 May 1997, A-1+.

Petry, Ann. "From *Interviews with Black Writers.*" In Ervin, *Ann Petry,* 72–77.

_____. "Just a Few Questions More, Mrs. Petry." In Ervin, *Ann Petry,* 101–3.

_____, a.k.a. Arnold Petri. "Marie of the Cabin Club." *Afro-American* [Baltimore], 19 Aug. 1939, 14.

_____. *The Narrows.* 1953. Boston: Mariner, 1999.

_____. "Solo on the Drums." In *Miss Muriel and Other Stories,* 235–42. Boston: Houghton Mifflin,1971.

_____. *The Street.* 1946. Boston: Houghton Mifflin, 1991.

_____. "A Visit with Ann Petry, May 16, 1984: College of Pharmacy, University of Illinois at Chicago." In Ervin, *Ann Petry,* 77–88.

Pici, Nicholas F. "Trading Meanings: The Breath of Music in Toni Morrison's *Jazz.*" *Connotations* 7.3 (1997/98): 372–98.

Polillo, Arrigo. *Jazz: Geschichte und Persönlichkeiten.* Trans. Egino Biagioni. Munich: Goldmann Schott, 1981.

Porter, Horace A. *Jazz Country: Ralph Ellison in America.* Iowa City: University of Iowa Press, 2001.

Porter, Lewis. *John Coltrane: His Life and Music.* Ann Arbor: University of Michigan Press, 1998.

, and Michael Ullman. "Sidney Bechet and His Long Song." *The Black Perspective in Music* 16.2 (1988): 135–50.

Pryse, Marjorie. "'Pattern against the Sky': Deism and Motherhood in *The Street.*" In *Conjuring: Black Women, Fiction, and Literary Tradition.* Eds. Marjorie Pryse and Hortense J. Spillers, 116–31. Bloomington: University of Indiana Press, 1985.

Rampersad, Arnold. *The Life of Langston Hughes, Volume 1: 1902–1941. I, Too, Sing America.* New York: Oxford University Press, 1986.

_____. *The Life of Langston Hughes, Volume 2: 1941–1967. I Dream a World.* New York: Oxford University Press, 1988.

Rasula, Jed. "Jazz as Decal for the European Avant-Garde." In *Blackening Europe: The African American Presence.* Ed. Heike Raphael-Hernandez, 13–34. New York: Routledge, 2004.

Raussert, Wilfried. "Jazz, Time, and Narrativity." *Amerikastudien/American Studies* 45.4 (2000): 519–34.

"Rebop." In *Reclams Jazzführer.* Eds. Carlo Bohländer, Karl Heinz Holler, and Christian Pfarr. Stuttgart: Reclam, 1989.

"Recitative." In *Baker's Dictionary of Opera.* Ed. Laura Kuhn. New York: Schirmer, 2000.

Redman, Joshua. Liner Notes. *Moodswing*. Warner Brothers, 1994.

Reed, Ishmael. *Mumbo Jumbo*. 1972. New York: Atheneum, 1989.

Reichardt, Ulfried. "Time and the African-American Experience: The Problem of Chronocentrism." *Amerikastudien/American Studies* 45.4 (2000): 465–84.

Reisner, Robert, ed. *Bird: The Legend of Charlie Parker*. 1962. New York: Da Capo, 1987.

Rice, Alan J. "Finger-Snapping to Train-Dancing and Back Again: The Development of Jazz Style in African American Prose." *Yearbook of English Studies* 24 (1994): 105–16.

_____. "Jazzing It Up A Storm: The Execution and Meaning of Toni Morrison's Jazzy Prose Style." *Journal of American Studies* 28.3 (1994): 423–32.

Rice, Herbert William. *Toni Morrison and the American Tradition: A Rhetorical Reading*. New York: Peter Lang, 1996.

Richter, Stephan. "The Beauty of Building, Dwelling, and Monk: Aesthetics, Religion, and the Architectural Qualities of Jazz." *African American Review* 29.2 (1995): 259–69.

_____. "Magic Books and a Jam Session: Das Spannungsfeld von Literatur, Literaturtheorie und Jazz." In *Jazz und Sprache, Sprache und Jazz*. Ed. Wolfram Knauer, 21–36. Darmstädter Beiträge zur Jazzforschung 5. Hofheim: Wolke, 1998.

Riess, Rolf. Nachwort. In *Jazz*. By Hans Janowitz, 124–34. Bonn: Weidle, 1999.

"Riff." In *The New Grove Dictionary of Jazz*.

Rodrigues, Eusebio L. "Experiencing *Jazz*." *Modern Fiction Studies* 39.3&4 (1993): 733–54.

Rotthaler, Viktor. "'Es kommt auf das Ohr an': Marginalien zu 23 Liedern." In *Jazz*. By Hans Janowitz. Ed. Rolf Riess, 135–43.Weidle, 1999.

Rubenstein, Roberta. "Singing the Blues / Reclaiming Jazz: Toni Morrison and Cultural Mourning." *Mosaic* 31.2 (1998): 147–63.

Rudinow, Joel. "Race, Ethnicity, Expressive Authenticity: Can White People Sing the Blues?" *Journal of Aesthetics and Art Criticism* 52.1 (1994): 127–37.

Russell, Ross. *Bird Lives! The High Life and Hard Times of Charlie (Yardbird) Parker*. 1972. New York: Da Capo, 1996.

_____. Liner Notes. *The Hunt*. By Dexter Gordon and Wardell Gray. LP. Savoy, 1977.

Ryan, Judylyn S. "Morrison's *Jazz*: 'A Knowing So Deep.'" In *Approaches to Teaching the Novels of Toni Morrison*. Eds. Nellie Y. McKay and Kathryn Earle, 154–60. New York: MLA, 1997.

Sanders Mobley, Marilyn. "Ann Petry." In *African American Writers*. Eds. Lea Baechler and A. Walton Litz, 347–59. New York: Scribners, 1991.

Saxon, Lyle, Robert Tallant, and Edward Dreyer, eds. *Gumbo Ya-Ya: A Collection of Louisiana Folk Tales*. Cambridge: Riverside, 1945.

Schaap, Phil. Discography. In *Billie Holiday*. By Stuart Nicholson, 254–83. Boston: Northeastern University Press, 1995.

Schenker, Anatol. Booklet. *Lucky Millinder and His Orchestra: 1943–1947*. By Lucky Millinder. Classics, 1998.

Schuller, Gunther. *Early Jazz: Its Roots and Historical Development*. New York: Oxford University Press, 1968.

_____. *The Swing Era: The Development of Jazz, 1930–1944*. New York: Oxford University Press, 1989.

Shapiro, Nat, and Nat Hentoff, eds. *Hear Me Talkin' to Ya: The Story of Jazz as Told by the Men Who Made It*. 1955. New York: Dover, 1966.

Shipton, Alyn. *Groovin' High: The Life of Dizzy Gillespie.* New York: Oxford University Press, 1999.

Sidran, Ben. *Black Talk.* New York: Holt, Rinehart and Winston, 1971.

Small-McCarthy, Robin. "The Jazz Aesthetic in the Novels of Toni Morrison." *Cultural*

Studies 9.2 (1995): 293–300.

Smith, Buster. Interview. In *Bird: The Legend of Charlie Parker.* 1962. Ed. Robert Reisner, 213–15. New York: Da Capo, 1987.

Snead, James. "Repetition as a Figure of Black Culture." In *The Jazz Cadence of American Culture.* Ed. Robert G. O'Meally, 63–81. New York: Columbia University Press, 1998.

Sollors, Werner. *Amiri Baraka / LeRoi Jones: The Quest for a "Populist Modernism."* New York: Columbia University Press, 1978.

Spottswood, Richard K. "Country Girls, Classic Blues, and Vaudeville Voices: Women and the Blues." In *Nothing But the Blues: The Music and the Musicians.* Ed. Lawrence Cohn, 87–105. New York: Abbeville, 1993.

Stokes, W. Royal, ed. *Living the Jazz Life: Conversations with Forty Musicians about Their Careers in Jazz.* New York: Oxford University Press, 2000.

Stowe, Harriet Beecher. *Uncle Tom's Cabin.* 1852. New York: Bantam, 1981.

Stryker, Mark. "Nobel-Winning Author to Turn a Slave's Tale into Opera for MOT." *Detroit Free Press* 20 Feb. 2003, C1.

Such, David G. *Avant-Garde Jazz Musicians: Performing 'Out There.'* Iowa City: University of Iowa Press, 1993.

Sudhalter, Richard M. "Hot Music in the 1920s: The 'Jazz Age,' Appearances and Realities." In *The Oxford Companion to Jazz,* 148–62.

_____. *Lost Chords: White Musicians and Their Contributions to Jazz, 1915–1945.* New York: Oxford University Press, 1999.

Szwed, John F. *Space Is the Place: The Life and Times of Sun Ra.* New York: Pantheon, 1997.

Tally, Justine. *The Story of Jazz: Toni Morrison's Dialogic Imagination.* Hamburg: Lit, 2001.

Tarrant, Don. Discography. In *Dexter Gordon: A Musical Biography.* By Stan Britt, 171–207. New York: Da Capo, 1989.

Taylor, Art, ed. *Notes and Tones: Musician-to-Musician Interviews.* New York: Pedigree, 1977.

Tischler, Barbara L. "Europa Jazz in the 1920s and the Musical Discovery of Harlem." In *The Harlem Renaissance: Revaulations.* Ed. Amritjit Singh et al., 185–93. New York: Garland, 1989.

Toomer, Jean. *Cane.* 1923. Ed. Darwin T. Turner. New York: Norton, 1988.

Townsend, Peter. *Jazz in American Culture.* Edinburgh: University of Edinburgh Press, 2000.

Tracy, Steven C. *Langston Hughes and the Blues.* Urbana: University of Illinois Press, 1988.

Tucker, Mark. *Ellington: The Early Years.* Urbana: University of Illinois Press, 1991.

Tucker, Sherrie. *Swing Shift: "All-Girl" Bands of the 1940s.* Durham: Duke University Press, 2000.

_____. "'Where the Blues and the Truth Lay Hiding': Rememory of Jazz in Black Women's Fiction." *Frontiers* 13.2 (1993): 26–44.

Visser, Joop. "Dexter Gordon: Settin' the Pace." Booklet. *Settin' the Pace.* By Dexter Gordon. Proper, 2001.

Walcott, Rinaldo. "'Out of the Kumbla': Toni Morrison's *Jazz* and Pedagogical Answerability." *Cultural Studies* 9.2 (1995): 318–37.

Walser, Robert. "'Out of Notes': Signification, Interpretation, and the Problem of Miles Davis." In *Keeping Score: Music, Disciplinarity, Culture.* Eds. David Schwarz, Anahid Kassabian, and Lawrence Siegel, 147–68. Charlottesville: University of Virginia Press, 1997.

Watts, Jerry Gafio. *Amiri Baraka: The Politics and Art of a Black Intellectual.* New York: New York University Press, 2001.

Weiner, Marc A. "*Urwaldmusik* and the Borders of German Identity: Jazz in Literature of the Weimar Republic." *German Quarterly* 64.4 (1991): 475–87

Wells, Dicky. *The Night People: The Jazz Life of Dicky Wells.* Ed. Stanley Dance. Washington: Smithsonian, 1991.

Werner, Craig Hansen. *Playing the Changes: From Afro-Modernism to the Jazz Impulse.* Urbana: University of Illinois Press, 1994.

Wiggins, Gerald. Interview. In *Central Avenue Sounds: Jazz in Los Angeles.* Eds. Clora Bryant et al., 311–23. Berkeley: University of California Press, 1998.

Wilber, Bob. *Music Was Not Enough.* Ed. Derek Webster. New York: Oxford University Press, 1988.

Wilder, Joe. "Tell a Story: An Interview with Joe Wilder." *Boundary 2* 22.2 (1995): 117–49.

Wilk, Max. *OK! The Story of* Oklahoma! *A Celebration of America's Most Loved Musical.* New York: Applause, 2002.

Williams, Martin. *Jazz Masters of New Orleans.* New York: MacMillan, 1967.

Wills, David. "Jasz Annotations: Negotiating a Discursive Limit." *Paragraph* 21.2 (1998): 131–49.

Wilson, Peter Niklas. "Living Time: Ancient to the Future, Concepts and Fantasies of Micro- and Macro-Time in Contemporary Jazz." *Amerikastudien/American Studies* 45.4 (2000): 567–75.

Woodard, Komozi. *A Nation within a Nation: Amiri Baraka (LeRoi Jones) and Black Power Politics.* Chapel Hill: University of North Carolina Press, 1999.

Wurst, Gayle. "Ben Franklin in Harlem: The Drama of Deferral in Ann Petry's *The Street.*" In *Deferring a Dream: Literary Sub-Versions of the American Columbiad.* Eds. Gert Buelens and Ernst Rudin, 1–23. Basel: Birkhäuser, 1994.

Yansané, Aguibou Y. *Decolonization in West African States, with French Colonial Legacy, Comparison and Contrast: Development in Guinea, the Ivory Coast, and Senegal (1945–1980).* Cambridge: Schenkman, 1984.

Youngren, William H. "European Roots of Jazz." In *The Oxford Companion to Jazz,* 17–28.

Index